# Britain
# 1850–1979

*...veloping democracy*

*...e, Wood*

Oliver and Boyd
Addison Wesley Longman Limited
Edinburgh Gate
Harlow
Essex CM20 2JE
An imprint of Longman Group UK Ltd

First published 1992
Fourth impression 1998

British Library Cataloguing in Publication Data

Wood, Sydney
  Britain, 1850–1979: Developing Democracy. –
  (Higher Grade History Series)
  I. Title   II. Series
  941.08

  ISBN 0–05–004602–0

Set in 10/12 Bembo Linotron
Printed in Singapore through Addison Wesley Longman China Limited

The publisher's policy is to use paper manufactured from sustainable
forests.

# Acknowledgements

We are grateful to the following for permission to reproduce photo-
graphs; Aberdeen Journals, page 125; Aberdeen University Library,
George Washington Wilson Collection, pages 7, 12 and 17; *Daily Express*/
Solo Syndication, pages 132 and 171 below (cartoons Vivky); ET Archive,
page 171 below; Mary Evans Picture Library, pages 69 above and below
and 80; Gernsheim Collection, Harry Ransom Humanities Research
Center, University of Texas at Austin, page 51 (photo J. Birtles); Greater
London Record Office and History Library, pages 79, 85 and 98; Hastings
Museum and Art Gallery, page 64; Hulton Picture Company, pages 16,
65 left and right, 71, 128, 135, 137, 140, 145, 164 above right, 167 and
171 above; Illustrated London News Picture Library, page 169; Labour
Party Library, pages 164 above left and 166; Mansell Collection, pages 47
and 68; Museum of London, pages 24 and 45; National Railway Museum,
pages 8 and 13; Popperfoto, pages 115, 116, 127, 130, 131 and 164 below;
Punch Publications, pages 33, 50, 104 and 108; Salvation Army International Heritage Centre, pages 10, 21, 83 and 87; St. Bride Printing
Library, Corporation of London, page 19; Topham Picture Library,
pages 43, 129 above, 133, 150, 162 above and below, 170, and 172 above
and below; TUC Library, page 123.

The cover photograph on the left shows the unemployed marching on
London (the Scottish contingent) in 1932 and of Winston Churchill in
1951; both are from the Hulton Picture Company.
Illustrated by Hardlines.

# Contents

# Introduction

In Britain in the 1850s few men and no women had the right to vote to choose members of parliament. For those few who were able to participate in elections, voting took place openly, not in secret, and bribery was far from uncommon. Elected MPs attended a parliament that met infrequently; and those who were ministers belonged to governments that did not like to interfere in the daily lives of ordinary people.

By the 1970s all adults were able to vote – in secret – and highly organised political parties fought for their support, using all the weaponry of the mass media. Modern governments control life in the most detailed way, using taxes on a scale that would have horrified Victorians, and backed by many thousands of civil servants, whose existence would once have been unthinkable.

How and why did these changes take place? How did governments think it proper to use their power?

This book deals with such themes by separating the period into two parts, clearly divided by the start of the Great War in 1914. In each part there is material on the changes in society; on the widening of the franchise; on the development of the political parties; on the use of power by those parties which were successful in capturing office; and finally on the question of how far the United Kingdom was a single political entity, and how far people in a formerly independent country like Scotland found this acceptable. The use of the same structure in each part allows an issue to be pursued through the whole period if desired.

The material is organised so that students can explore it by considering issues, gathering and organising evidence, and presenting arguments. In this way a number of the key features of Higher History will be fulfilled:

1. Ideas identified as central to this theme of British history will be studied, that is

- *Ideology* – through the ideas and beliefs of politicians and political groups and parties.
- *Identity* – through the kinds of people who gathered to form and shape political movements, and through the study of whether the United Kingdom was a single political unit acceptable to the people living in different parts of it.
- *Authority* – through the way that politicians in office used power, and through the way that political parties and government developed in order to have more effective means of exercising power.

2. Activities appropriate to the assessment of this course are suggested. Candidates must develop essay-writing skills that will

show both their knowledge and understanding, and their ability to evaluate through

- selecting material suitable to an issue that is being explored
- organising the selected material clearly and logically
- showing that the ideas in the material have been properly understood
- presenting the material clearly and in an interesting fashion using suitable, accurate language
- referring, where appropriate, to the views of people at the time and to assessments by historians writing since that time. To help students with this, quotations are provided throughout the book.

The activities are of two types. The Task at the beginning of each chapter is intended to provide students with a subject for them to focus on while they are studying the chapter. The Essay at the end of each chapter gives students a chance to use the knowledge which they have gained by studying the chapter.

The Essay gives practice for Paper I. It is vital to build up experience in essay-writing, given the source-handling nature of Standard Grade and of Paper II. But essays may also benefit from the use of quotations from people of the time and from historians, so sources here serve a somewhat different function from their role in Paper II.

# *Key events*

| | |
|---|---|
| 1867 | The Second Reform Act |
| | The Conservative National Union is set up |
| 1872 | The secret ballot is introduced |
| 1877 | The National Liberal Federation is set up |
| 1881 | The Social Democratic Federation is established |
| 1883 | The Corrupt Practices Act |
| 1884 | The Third Reform Act |
| | The Fabian Society is established |
| 1886 | Liberal Unionists split away |
| 1893 | The Independent Labour Party is founded |
| 1900 | The Labour Representation Committee is established |
| 1901 | Taff Vale decision |
| 1903 | Liberal–Labour electoral pact |
| 1906 | Liberal victory |
| 1909 | The Lloyd George budget |
| | The Osborne judgement |
| 1911 | The Parliament Act |
| 1914 | Outbreak of the Great War |
| 1915 | Asquith's coalition government |
| 1916 | Lloyd George replaces Asquith and leads new coalition |
| 1918 | The Fourth Reform Act – some women get the vote |
| | Labour Party Constitution |
| | 'Coupon' election won by Lloyd George |
| 1922 | Fall of Lloyd George's coalition |
| 1923 | Liberals reunited |
| 1924 | First Labour Government under Ramsay MacDonald |
| 1926 | The General Strike |
| 1928 | Universal suffrage – women get the vote on terms equal to men |
| 1931 | Formation of the National Government led by Ramsay MacDonald |
| 1935 | Baldwin becomes Prime Minister |
| 1937 | Chamberlain becomes Prime Minister |
| 1939 | Outbreak of the Second World War |
| 1940 | Churchill forms coalition |
| 1942 | The Beveridge Report |
| 1945 | Labour electoral victory |
| 1949 | Representation of the People Act |
| 1955 | Gaitskell becomes Labour leader |
| 1957 | Macmillan defeats Butler for Conservative leadership |
| 1960 | Gaitskell defeated at Labour conference on defence issue |
| 1965 | Heath becomes first elected leader of the Conservatives |
| 1975 | Thatcher becomes Conservative leader |
| 1975 | EEC referendum |
| 1979 | March, devolution referendum |
| | May, Conservative election victory |
| | June, European elections |

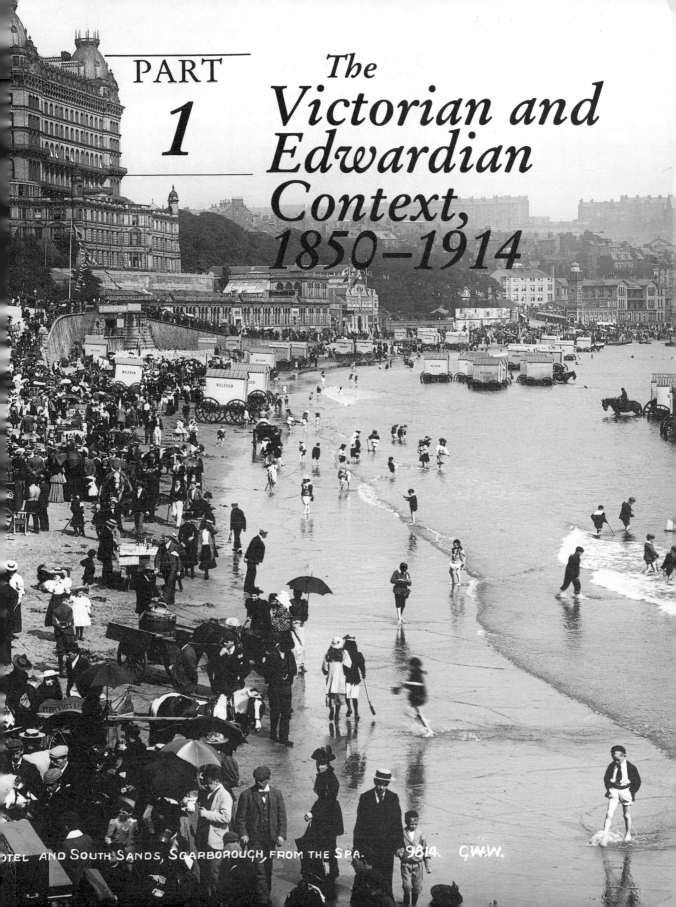

PART

# 1

# *The*
# *Victorian and*
# *Edwardian*
# *Context,*
# *1850–1914*

OTEL AND SOUTH SANDS, SCARBOROUGH, FROM THE SPA. 9814. G.W.W.

# How and why did British society change between 1850 and 1914?

In 1832, after a lengthy struggle, the right to vote in elections in Britain was reformed. The numbers voting probably at least doubled to reach a figure of 653,000, but this still left the vast majority of men, and all women, without the vote. Voting was seen as the right of a small number of well-to-do people. The historian F. M. L. Thompson suggests:

> 'The First Reform Act was an attempt to adapt political institutions to the alteration in the balance of social forces brought about by this transformation [of the British economy]'.
> (*The Rise of Respectable Society*, 1988)

He maintains that Britain's political system was shaped by the country's changing *identity*. This view can be found not only in the works of historians, but in the comments of politicians too. In 1906 the Liberal minister David Lloyd George told a crowded meeting:

> 'If, at the end of an average term of office, it was found that the Liberal Party had done nothing to cope seriously with the social condition of people, to remove the national degradation of slums and widespread poverty in a land glittering with wealth and that they had shrunk from attacking boldly the main causes of this wretchedness, then would a real cry arise in this land for a new party and many of us here in this room would join in that cry.'
> (Quoted in S. H. Wood, *The British Welfare State*, 1982)

These comments show the importance to the speaker of belonging to a party whose *ideology* he could support, a party which, once in power, would use its *authority* to reshape society. The material in this section examines changing society and the changing economy in order to consider the possible political results of these changes.

## TASK

How might the changing nature of British society, from 1850 to 1900 affect the policies of the period?

List any relevant points from this chapter. Consider
- who might expect to get the vote
- whether conditions made large-scale national parties possible

- whether people would know about and understand the political affairs of the time
- what sorts of policies different groups in society might expect politicians to promise them.

Compare your conclusions with those reached by others.

# The 1850s

Around half the twenty-one million people in mid-nineteenth-century Britain lived in the countryside. Agriculture prospered, employing large numbers, and turning out a rich variety of products. Wealthy aristocratic landowners watched over enormous estates from the comfort of their elaborate country houses. In parliament such men wielded great power in the House of Lords; over their tenants and villagers they exercised enormous influence, providing employment and even insisting upon attendance at church. According to one historian:

> 'The average man of the mid-nineteenth century was much more likely to accept without question his inherited social rank and to defer to his "betters" than his descendant would be a century later. A deeply rooted respect for rank and strong feeling of the obligations of authority were the basis for much of the social behaviour of the mid-nineteenth century.'
> (J. Roebuck, *The Making of Modern English Society*, 1973)

Agricultural production was expanding and there seemed little to fear from foreign competition. Prosperous tenants and owner-occupier farmers were able to rebuild their homes, providing their families with sizeable properties in which to live in comfort. But prosperity had yet to reach the farm labourer. Whether housed in the farm buildings or in a cramped and squalid cottage, the labourer endured endless toil, low wages, and a diet monotonous in its dependence on bread, porridge, potatoes, cabbage, milk, and occasionally pieces of bacon.

The wealth of the landed aristocracy was often swelled by factors other than farming production. Britain had experienced a century of economic change and population growth. Some land-owners found their land contained coal or iron; others sold or rented land to shipyards and railway companies. Yet further profit might be derived from land required by house-building. By 1850 the population of urban Britain equalled that of rural Britain. This represented a revolution marked by the coming of steam power and factories. Mines and quarries transformed the appearance of the country. Towns and cities like Manchester, Leeds and Glasgow expanded rapidly, giving far more emphasis to the north of Britain than it had ever had in an earlier rural age. The new industrial age brought a crowding together of people in cramped town dwellings. It brought dirt and smoke that meant that dark drab clothes were the only sensible forms of clothing for ordinary people. Dreadful diseases like cholera and typhus flourished in the filth of middens and in polluted water. In 1858 the Thames stank so foully that parliament had to abandon its sitting.

Yet the achievements of textile factories, engineering works and other developing centres of activity were such that Britain could truly claim to be the workshop of the world. No other land could rival Britain's industrial output. In 1851 these achievements were celebrated in a Great Exhibition held in a glass construction so vast that mature trees were enclosed by its walls and roof. It is a sign of the times that the well-to-do went to the exhibition on Tuesdays when admission was a guinea. It is also a sign of the times that six million other people were able to go to the exhibition on the ordinary shilling days: the dawning age of the railway made possible travel unheard of twenty years earlier.

Ordinary people lived very vulnerable lives. The dangers of disease and the weariness of long working days (including

*The struggle to survive: a whole family at work making wire brushes.*

Saturdays) troubled their existence; and sudden trade slumps, illness or accident, could plunge them into poverty. Around fifteen or sixteen babies out of every hundred born never reached the age of one. Those that did survive were not required to attend school, and, if they did, they experienced a very limited and repetitive education. Skilled workers and an expanding middle class struggled to establish for themselves a life of comfort and respectability. Church congregations were larger than those of modern times. But this was also an age when prostitution flourished, for many women were desperate to survive without being compelled to enter a workhouse or a poorhouse. No state welfare system existed to support those in distress. Bleak institutions awaited the desperately poor, where they were housed in dormitories, controlled by strict rules, and deprived of freedom.

The dawning age of the machine and the factory threatened the livelihoods of those who had sustained their existence by skilled hand-work. In 1850 there were still 50,000 handloom cotton weavers. Half those involved in producing woollen cloth worked at home or in small workshops. Tailoring and shoemaking too were still largely small-scale operations. Such people viewed the spread of the steam-powered factory with alarm.

And whatever the kind of employment involved, women were likely to be more poorly paid than men. Married women had no control of their possessions or their children – these were the property of their husbands. Divorce required an Act of Parliament. Many women found a kind of security by joining the vast numbers who earned their living as domestic servants. By the 1850s not having to work had become a badge of female respectability. As one wealthy lady wrote:

'A lady, to be such, must be a mere lady and nothing else. One must not work for profit or engage in any occupation that money can command . . . ladies, dismissed from the dairy, the store room, the poultry yard, the kitchen garden, have hardly yet found themselves a sphere equally useful and important in the pursuits of trade and art to which to apply their too abundant leisure . . . Life is too often divested of any real and important purpose.'

> (Diary of Margaret Grey, 1853, in T. May,
> *An Economic and Social History of Britain*, 1987)

British society in the 1850s was in a state of rapid change and development. Its unsettled condition can be seen in political affairs too, for the efforts of the Chartists to spread the vote so widely as to create a democratic state were only a year or two in the past (see p. 27).

# The changing economy
## Towns and travel

Between mid-Victorian and Edwardian times the population of the United Kingdom not only grew, but also became a population of town and city dwellers. 31.8 million inhabitants lived in the United Kingdom in 1871; 45.3 million in 1911. By 1911 about 80 per cent of them dwelt in towns and cities – a dramatic change from the mid-nineteenth century when half the population lived in the countryside. Manchester swelled in size from 182,000 in 1831 to 544,000 in 1901; and Birmingham over the same period grew from 144,000 to half a million. Numerous other places experienced a similar expansion.

Not only was the kingdom's population larger and more urbanised, it was also more inter-connected. The mere 7360 kilometres of railway track in 1848 had become 28,800 kilometres by the time of the Great War. Few country towns and large villages were far from a railway station, whilst cities were the focus of the numerous lines of competing private companies. Better signalling, more comfortable coaches (the standard coach with corridor and lavatories appeared in 1882), lower fares, and improved locomotives all added up to a network that tied together the different parts of Britain as never before.

*The massive Forth Bridge north of Edinburgh under construction in 1887. Over fifty workers died in the creation of this rail link to northern Scotland.*

The combination of railways and urban growth had all sorts of consequences. New towns grew up, large areas of older cities were torn down to make way for track, stations and sidings. Railways allowed the wealthier to move further away from city centres, and to travel into work from suburbs. House builders exploited stations near cities, putting up properties and advertising them as offering country life close to city amenities. The Great Eastern Railway led other companies into providing cut-price travel for working people. By 1900 thousands of commuters spilled out of trains daily into London. Moreover the Underground system had grown from its small beginnings in 1863, when it only linked Paddington to Farringdon Street. The transformation of an area by a railway, and the implementation of the 1883 Cheap Trains Act (requiring the running of workmen's

*One of the Great Eastern Railway's workmen's trains, 1884. This train operated from Liverpool Street to Enfield Town.*

trains), were personally felt by the Great Eastern Railway's manager. In 1884 he grumbled that Stamford Hill had been altered beyond recognition:

'That used to be a very nice district indeed, occupied by good families, with houses of from £150 to £250 a year, with coach houses and stables, a garden and a few acres of land. But very soon after this obligation was put upon the Great Eastern to run workmen's trains, . . . speculative builders were down into the neighbourhood and, as a consequence, each good house was one after another pulled down and the district is given up entirely to the working man. I lived down there myself and I waited until most of my neighbours had gone: and then at last, I was obliged to go.'

(*Royal Commission on the Housing of the Working Class*, 1884)

The railways moved goods as well as people. In 1860, 90 million tonnes travelled by rail; by 1900 the figure had risen to 425 million. Fresh fruit and vegetables, milk and newspapers, all helped to alter daily lives by arriving regularly in urban areas. Even clocks and watches told exactly the same time, from Wick to Plymouth: local variations could not be accepted by railway timetables. In 1889 an Act of Parliament standardised time throughout Britain.

## Industry

Coal, textiles, iron and steel, and engineering, continued to provide employment for much of the population. The numbers working in textiles remained steady at around 1.3 million, but the labour force in coal mining increased from 200,000 to a million by 1911. Together these occupations provided about half the economy's output in 1907, and furnished employment for a quarter of the working population. Moreover the size of the typical industrial unit grew during the nineteenth century; the typical worker of the 1900s worked in larger premises for a more remote employer. Many working in small-scale workshops and at home could not compete. Hand-made textiles declined and, by the 1900s, small-scale tailoring and shoemaking were on the retreat before factory-made goods produced with the help of adaptations of the Singer sewing machine of 1851. The late nineteenth and early twentieth centuries were a time of increasing mechanisation. Skilled craftsmen watched with alarm as enterprising manufacturers copied American products, installing machines capable of giving products fine finishes, such as automatic, high-speed cutting tools, or turret lathes that could handle complex shaping operations. Such machinery allowed employers to use semi-skilled rather than skilled labour, and to pay lower wages as a result.

Britain's traditional industries provided the backbone of her export drive. In 1870 Britain still contributed almost a third of the world's manufacturing output. But by 1913 dangerous rivals – notably the USA and Germany – had emerged, and Britain's share of world manufacturing had sunk to 14 per cent.

Britain's rivals seemed readier to invest in new equipment and to deploy a more skilled labour force. Their enterprise showed in their ability to develop new industries for making motor vehicles, chemical products and electrical goods. By the 1900s worried observers in Britain noted not only that Britain lagged behind in these 'new' industries, but also that the older industries were looking increasingly dated. But, for the moment, with British coal and cotton and Clydeside shipping all in great demand across the world, such anxieties were voiced by the few and not generally felt.

# Agriculture

In 1850 around 20 per cent of Britain's labour force worked in farming; by Edwardian times under 9 per cent were similarly employed. Behind these figures lay a dramatic downturn for the farming industry which saw a 63 per cent shrinkage of the area devoted to wheat-growing; land falling into disuse; and farmers ruined. Foreign competition lay behind this disaster. Railways opened up continents, whilst steamships and clippers moved vast quantities of food across the oceans. Wheat from the American prairies and meat from Argentina and Australasia undercut the prices of home-produced foods. In 1867–71 the average price of wheat had been 56s. a quarter hundredweight; by 1894–98 it had fallen to 27s. 3d. In 1880 a British ship docked in London with forty tonnes of Australian beef and mutton on board. The development of refrigeration menaced the British meat producer, just as the vast area of the American prairies threatened the cereal grower. Oats and barley fell less sharply in price, and enterprising farmers turned increasingly to producing milk, eggs, fresh fruit and vegetables. The governments of the time resolutely resisted any calls for the taxing of foreign foods. Their commitment to free trade went beyond wishing to see cheap food reach the town dweller – it had become a matter of belief. All these changes, coupled with the increased mechanisation of farming and the low wages paid to farm workers, added up to a sharp shrinkage in the significance in British society of the 'landed interest'. Even aristocratic landowners became increasingly ready to see their sons and daughters marry the children of rich businessmen and American millionaires.

# Changing employment

About 1.3 million people were recorded by the 1901 census as members of professional and public services. Postmen and policemen, civil servants and teachers were but some in this expanding area of employment. From 1870 entry to the civil service was to be by examination instead of by influence as previously. The whole area of clean respectable 'white collar' work grew: it included clerks, typists, draughtsmen, accountants and shop workers. Such work provided jobs for an increasing number of women and was often marked by a strong desire for a decent law–abiding existence that helped make society in 1900 seem more settled than it had been in 1850. Riots and machine-breaking as ways of protesting about a changing economy were rare now, as machines and factories had become part of an accepted way of life. Instead workers began to get organised in trade unions, and professional people in societies (such as the Institute of Chartered Accountants of 1880).

# A better life?

The lifestyles of the wealthy in Edwardian times offer abundant evidence of the riches created by the economic changes of earlier years. Vast country houses and spacious town houses provided

*A well-to-do Edwardian family meal: the events of the outside world intruded through letters and newspapers.*

the setting for balls and banquets. A calendar of social events like Ascot and Henley, shooting, and visiting fashionable foreign resorts like Cannes and Biarritz completed a lifestyle amazing in its opulence. Vast armies of butlers, footmen, grooms, gardeners, cooks and housemaids toiled endlessly to ensure that their employers endured as little inconvenience as possible. In 1896 Lord Rosebery's income was such that he thought nothing of spending enough money to feed an ordinary family of four for a year on out-of-season strawberries for one course of one meal. Behind the very rich came growing numbers of well-to-do middle class families living in large properties and employing many servants – indeed the ability to pay for a servant was one of the signs of social success. A family with an income of £800 a year would commonly expect to afford a cook and housemaid, and even on £200 a year a family could hire a servant girl.

Skilled and white collar workers enjoyed a standard of living that probably rose in the late nineteenth century. One estimate suggests that real wages went up 10 per cent at least between 1889 and 1900, though they may then have started to fall back. Such workers were more likely to have a little leisure. Half-day working on Saturdays became widespread. Bank holidays arrived in

*Evidence of a more leisured society with access to travel: holidaymakers enjoy the seafront amenities of late Victorian Scarborough.*

1871. Working hours were slightly reduced, sometimes helped by legislation, as in the case of shop workers. This leisure-growth can be seen in the expansion of day trips and holidays and the consequent growth of seaside centres. In 1873 850,000 people visited Blackpool; in 1913 the figure was four million. Spectator sports flourished as people had time and money to attend them. The rules of association football were set out in 1863, and the first cup final in England took place in 1872. The 1883 victory in this event of the working men of Bolton Olympic over an Old Etonian side was a further sign of changing times.

The population's health was improving. A death rate of 22.9 for males and 21.2 for females per 1000 people in 1838–42 had fallen to 15 and 13.1 per 1000 by 1914. In the 1830s only 60 per cent of children survived to the age of 5; in the 1890s the figure was 80 per cent. In part this may have been because of improved cleanliness: water supplies were provided in urban areas and the soap industry expanded after the abolition of a tax on soap in 1853. Certainly many people ate far better in the 1900s than in the 1850s. In his survey of York, which was published in 1901, Seebohm Rowntree found that 12 per cent of workers had beef or mutton or pork on most days of the week. Tea consumption increased fourfold from the 1850s to the 1900s, and the average consumption of potatoes, eggs and meat went up. After 1870 ordinary people began to eat fruit, initially as jam. By the 1900s fish and chip shops had spread from their humble beginnings in 1870 in John Rouse's mobile cooking range in Oldham; cheap foreign food helped the town dweller by lowering food bills; and railways brought in fresh produce to the towns. By 1900 large-scale producers of food like Cadbury and Huntley & Palmer were turning out great quantities of mass-produced items and convenience foods in cans (machine-made from 1868); even cornflakes from America were available. The family that could afford them had a greater range of food items to choose from than ever before, and a greater range of shops in which to buy them. Multiple branches of firms like Boots and Liptons spread across Britain, and large department stores opened, selling a great variety of items. The Co-operative Society was especially successful in Scotland and northern England, providing a 'dividend' (a payment to shoppers from the Co-op's profits) for the working people who shopped at its many branches. Medical science had improved, hospitals had expanded, and a properly trained nursing profession had been established. For those who fell ill – and could afford treatment – care had greatly improved. Mass-produced clothing helped lower the cost of being properly clad. The falling size of families may have helped people to live more comfortably, since there were fewer mouths to feed. In part this may have been because of the increasing age of women at the time of marriage (over 26 in 1902) and because of the numbers who remained unmarried. It may also have been due to the spread of methods of birth control, though the rubber condom, despite being available from the 1870s, was not widely purchased before the Great War.

Certainly the population of the 1900s was better educated and better informed than the population of the 1850s. Education from the age of five to the age of twelve was now a requirement and beyond twelve an increasing possibility. In 1855 *The Daily Telegraph* appeared, Britain's first national penny newspaper. In 1880 the publication of *Titbits* marked the opening of a campaign to provide mass-circulation papers and magazines. *Titbits* contained illustrations, undemanding stories, and scraps of information. In 1896 Alfred Harmsworth published *The Daily Mail*, and in three years was enjoying the profits of sales of well over half a million papers a day. With the repeal of the paper duty in 1861 and the development of high-speed presses, cheap book production be-

*David Payne's Wharfedale Press (c. 1850) was one of the first rotary printing presses that were to ease access to the printed word.*

came possible. The railways which took newspapers to every part of the kingdom were the focus of the sales of cheap books too. By the late nineteenth century station bookstalls of firms like W. H. Smith were stocked not only with fiction but also with works like *Cassel's Popular Education* that sold at a penny an issue and encouraged an interest in history and in languages.

By 1900 a lifestyle had emerged in many parts of urban Britain that, the historian E. J. Hobsbawm noted,

'came to be thought of as age-old and unchanging because it ceased in fact to change very much until . . . the affluent 1950s, . . . it was neither a very good life nor a very rich life but it was probably the first kind of life since the Industrial Revolution which provided a firm lodging for the British working class within industrial society.'

(E. J. Hobsbawm, *Industry and Empire*, 1968)

This life of factory work, watching football matches, visiting music halls, and a sense of loyalty to and community with fellow workers may have become a myth. At the time it impressed some observers as an enormous achievement. In 1898 one such commentator wrote:

'During the last 25 or 30 years the wealth of Great Britain has increased in an extraordinary degree. The increase in the amount of property assessable to the income tax from 1855 to 1885 [is] about 100%. 50 years ago one third of the working masses of the United Kingdom were agricultural labourers: at present less than one eighth of the whole number are so employed. Money wages of all classes of labour have advanced 100%; the purchasing power of the British people in respect of necessities and luxuries of life has therefore been progressively increasing.'

(D. A. Wells, *Recent Economic Change*, 1898)

# Social problems

In 1894 a Royal Commission investigating working conditions produced two reports. The majority of members reached an optimistic conclusion, stating:

'The general impression left by the information before us is that the level of wage rates has risen considerably during the last 50 years in respect of (and with the exception of house rents in large towns) their power of purchasing commodities. The daily hours of labour have, during the same period, been in most cases shortened and the sanitary conditions of work have improved.'

A minority of members produced their own report. Whilst not disagreeing with the evidence of greater prosperity, they pointed to the kind of lives endured by many people, maintaining:

'Notwithstanding the great increase in national wealth, whole sections of the population – at least 5 million – are unable to obtain a subsistence compatible with health or efficiency. Probably 2 million are, every year, driven to accept Poor Relief, and even in well-organised and skilled trades where the normal working day is often 9 hours, an excessive amount of overtime is systematically worked. Many thousands of workers still toil under circumstances which make disease and accident an inevitable accompaniment of their lives.'

In his careful investigations of his home town, York, Seebohm Rowntree, a member of the wealthy sweet and chocolate making family, identified the times when a working man was poorest:

'The life of a labourer is marked by 5 alternating periods of want and comparative plenty. During early childhood, unless his father is a skilled worker, he probably will be in poverty; this will last until he or she or some of his brothers or sisters begin to earn money and thus augment their father's wages sufficiently to raise the family above the poverty line. Then follows the period during which he is earning money and living under his parents' roof. This is his chance to save money . . . this period of comparative prosperity may continue after marriage until he has 2 or 3 children, when poverty will again overtake him. This will last until the first child is 14 years old and begins to earn wages. While the children are earning and before they leave home, the man enjoys another period of prosperity – possibly only to sink back again into poverty when his children have married and he himself is too old to work, for his income has never permitted his saving enough for him and his wife to live upon for more than a very short time.'

(B. S. Rowntree, *Poverty: A Study of Town Life*, 1901)

*An Edwardian family with a soup kitchen meal that has been provided in enamel bowls. The children seem reasonably well-fed, though their clothes are probably secondhand.*

The evidence gathered by Royal Commissions and by individuals horrified some politicians. Leo Chiozza Money served as a Liberal MP from 1906 to 1918, then joined the Labour Party. In 1909 he worked out the numbers of people in Britain with riches, those with comfortable lives, and those with little:

*'Riches*
Persons with income of £700 per annum, and upwards, and their families.                    1,250,000

*Comfort*
Persons with incomes between £160 and £700 per annum and their families.                    3,750,000

*Poverty*
Persons with incomes of less than £160 per annum and their families.                    38,000,000

We have won through the horror of the birth and establishment of the factory system at the cost of physical deterioration. We have purchased a great commerce at the price of crowding our population into the cities. We have given our children what we grimly call elementary education and robbed them of the elements of a natural life. All this has been done that a few of us may enjoy a superfluity of goods and services. Deprivation for the many and luxury for the few have degraded our national life at both ends of the scale. Blessed indeed are the Rich, for theirs is the governance of the realm, theirs is the Kingdom.'

(Leo Chiozza Money, *Riches and Poverty*, 1909)

The Boer War (1899–1902) brought forth fresh evidence of the poor health of part of the nation. Over a quarter of the men volunteering were unfit for service. Surveys showed that, had conscription been used and the whole male population examined, perhaps 60 per cent would have been rejected as unfit. Surveys at the end of the Victorian period showed that at least a third of the population lived in desperate poverty. In the 1870s investigations found boys in upper class public schools were, on average, thirteen centimetres taller than working class boys in industrial schools; upper class infants had twice the chance of surviving infancy compared to the infants of the nation as a whole. No proper welfare system existed in the Britain of Queen Victoria to cope with the crises of unemployment, injury, or illness. Nor, as Rowntree showed, could most workers save enough to cope with these crises. Moreover his researches demonstrated that for many poverty was simply due to the low level of wages. He wrote:

'Wages paid for unskilled labour in York are insufficient to provide food, shelter and clothing adequate to maintain a family in a state of bare physical efficiency. And let us be clear what mere physical efficiency means. A family must never spend a penny on railway fare or omnibus, they cannot save, nor can they join a sick club or Trade Union. The children must have no pocket money. Should a child fall ill it must be attended by the parish doctor. The wage earner must never be absent from his work for a single day.'

(B. S. Rowntree, *Poverty: A Study of Town Life*)

A growing number of people raged against evidence that could not be denied. The Liberal Charles Masterman wrote:

'Public penury, private ostentation – that perhaps is the heart of the complaint. A nation with the wealth of England can afford to spend, and spend royally. The spectacle of a huge urban poverty confronts all this waste energy. Expenditure multiplies its return to human happiness as it is scattered amongst widening areas of population. The only justification for the present unnatural heaping up of great possessions in the control of the very few would be some return in leisure and cultivation of the arts. We have called into existence quick travelling. We have converted half the Highlands into deer forests for our sport. We fling away in ugly white hotels and in elaborate banquets of which everyone is weary, the price of of many poor men's yearly income. Yet we cannot build a new Cathedral. We cannot even preserve the Cathedrals bequeathed to us. We grumble at halfpenny increases in the rates for books or libraries.'

(C. F. G. Masterman, *The Condition of England*, 1909)

Men like this expected action from their political leaders.

## ESSAY

Write an essay on the following title. Use the notes you have gathered so far and the discussions you have been involved in to plan your answer.

'A country in desperate need of reform'. Do you agree with this assessment of Britain in the 1900s?

# ISSUE 2

# *Towards democracy?*

The political system that governed the country was shaped by the kind of society that Britain was becoming. According to one historian:

'Parliamentary reform was largely a reflection of changes in the economic and social structure of the country.'

(D. G. Wright, *Democracy and Reform*, 1970)

As British society changed and developed, so the questions arose of who had the right to control that society and whether there should be changes in the political system. The material in this section deals with these questions, i.e. with the political *identity* of Britain. Central to this section, therefore, is the issue of who should have political rights.

## TASK

Who should have political rights?

How might a journalist in 1914 have looked back over the sixty-odd previous years to consider and write about the above issue? Work through the material in this chapter, making notes, in order to show your readers

- the political situation of the 1850s
- the main changes that took place
- the reasons for these changes
- why certain people still have no vote
- whether more could (and should) have been done and will need to be done.

Turn your notes into an article.

# The political situation in the 1850s

Mid-nineteenth-century politics operated according to a system created by a reform of parliament in 1832. Though this reform had increased the number of voters, it still left them few in number. Voting openly, rather than in secret, meant that voters might be offered bribes or be subject to bullying.

## *Who had the vote?*

1. There were two quite separate types of constituencies.

*Boroughs.* A number of places were designated parliamentary boroughs. The vote here belonged to
- men who owned property with a £10 annual value (when assessed for rates), who had paid their rates and taxes, and had lived in the property for at least a year.
- male lodgers and tenants of properties (where the landlord was not in residence) with a £10 annual value, who had paid their rates and taxes, and had lived there for at least a year.

*Counties.* The vote here belonged to
- owners of property worth at least £2 for the payment of rates (the 'forty shilling freeholders').
- people with various kinds of leases on property not their own, including 'copyholders' of land worth at least £10, holders of leases of at least twenty years on land worth £50, and holders of sixty-year leases on land worth £10.
- tenants of land worth £50 a year.

In addition, people who for different reasons had possessed the right to vote before 1832 usually retained this right.
2. All voters had to be male adults over twenty-one years of age. The 1832 Act clearly stated this. Up till then there had been a handful of female voters.
3. Men who were peers, or men who worked for the customs and excise or for the post office, policemen, paupers, lunatics and aliens were not allowed to vote. (It was thought that people in government jobs would not vote independently.)
4. It was not easy to become a voter, even if a man was technically qualified, for a complicated system of registration had to be followed.
5. Voting took place openly, not in secret.
6. Voting did not take place on one day throughout the country, but was spread over 2 or 3 weeks to allow the police to cope.

This system gave the vote to about one out of every seven adult males living in the United Kingdom. By the early 1860s around

1.43 million could vote out of a total population of 30 million.

This system did not give equal representation to the different parts of the United Kingdom. Poverty in Ireland meant that only around one in twenty adult males was able to vote whereas the average in England was one in five. There were grumbles from Scotland that an allocation of fifty-three seats in Parliament was insufficient.

The parliamentary system of the 1850s was not democratic. It was not meant to be. Democracies were regarded as being at the mercy of ignorant people unfit to possess power. It favoured the wealthy in a number of ways. Until 1868 there was a requirement that no man could become an MP for a county unless he had a landed estate worth at least £610. In boroughs the required property had to be worth at least £300. Fighting an election (especially in boroughs) often cost between £400 and £1000 in official expenses, and to this had to be added unofficial expenses. Since voting openly was defended as manly and the secret ballot scorned as furtive, candidates could observe how the relatively small number of voters exercised their franchise. All sorts of inducements could, and were, offered to the voters. Votes were sometimes openly sold, perhaps for as much as £15. In 1865 the 1408 voters of Beverley managed to have £14,000 spent on them. In 1870 a Royal Commission reported on the constituency of Bridgewater.

> 'It is always three fourths, at least, of the actual consituency who are said to be hopelessly addicted to the taking of bribes. Rank and station appear to make no difference . . . It is the chronic disease of the place.'

Buying drinks for voters could lead to uproarious election scenes. Marches and counter-marches, demonstrations and fights were features of borough elections. Non-voters happily joined in the excitement, which including pelting candidates with vegetables, refuse and dung. County elections were less likely to be so troubled with upheaval. The distribution of seats to boroughs still heavily favoured the south and west of England, and here affairs were dominated by the land-owning classes. Around half of the MPs of the 1850s were near relatives of peers, clear evidence of the justice of the claims of Lord Grey, Prime Minister in 1832:

> 'I am indeed convinced that the more the bill is considered the less it will be found to prejudice the real interests of the aristocracy.'

Since landowners provided work, help in times of hardship, and a focus for social life, it is not surprising that rural voters chose their nominees.

The system of the 1850s was designed to bind the middle classes to the upper classes. Britain's leaders were well aware of the violent revolutions that had occurred in France after 1789, and again in 1830. They were determined to avoid similar revolutions in their own country, and this was most clearly put by Thomas Babington Macaulay, MP and historian:

'The principle is ... to admit the middle classes to a large ... share of the representation without any violent shock to the institutions of our country. There are countries in which the condition of the labouring classes is such that they may safely be entrusted with the right of electing members of the legislature ... if employment were always plentiful, wages always high, food always cheap, if a large family were considered not as an incumbrance but as a blessing – the principal objections to universal suffrage would be removed. But, unhappily, the lower orders are occasionally in a state of great distress ... distress makes even wise men irritable, unreasonable, and credulous, eager for immediate relief, heedless of remote consequences, it blunts their judgement, it inflames their passions, it makes them prone to believe those who flatter them. I oppose universal suffrage because I think it would produce a destructive revolution. I support this measure because I am sure that it is our best security against a revolution ... we must admit those whom it may be safe to admit ... We say that is it not by mere numbers, but by property and intelligence that the nation ought to be governed.'
(Parliamentary debates)

Some upper working class voters existed in places like London and Bristol where high property values brought them into the system. In total they may have amounted to a quarter of all the voters, but they were to be found in a limited number of places, not evenly spread. There were bitter complaints from would-be democrats, such as this writer in the *Poor Man's Guardian* of 1832. He complained about the wealthy political leaders:

'They knew that the old system could not last, and desiring to establish another as like it as possible, and also to keep their places, they framed the BILL, in the hope of drawing to the feudal aristocrats and yeomanry of counties a large reinforcement of the middle class. The Bill was, in effect, an invitation to the *shopocrats* of the enfranchised towns to join the Whigocrats of the country, and make common cause with them in keeping down the people, and thereby to quell the rising spirit of democracy in England.'
(Quoted in D. G. Wright, *Democracy and Reform*)

Protest boiled up into a major campaign, with a Charter of six major reforms. The wealthy closed ranks against petitions requesting that the vote should be given to all men and should be exercised in secret, that MPs should be paid and freed from needing property, and that parliaments should be elected anew every year by electoral districts reformed to be equal in population. After the final big Charter effort of 1848, demand for reform faded and would-be reformers despaired. One of them, Richard Cobden, complained:

> 'We are a servile, aristocracy-loving lord-ridden people... we have the labour of Hercules in hand to abate the power of the aristocracy and their allies – the snobs of the towns.'

In vain the Whig Lord John Russell put forward new reform bills in 1852, 1854 and 1860. His leader, Lord Palmerston, was not interested, nor was there great popular pressure for change. Experience after 1832 helped to reduce fears of the consequences of slowly widening the franchise. Walter Bagehot, a leading contemporary expert on the constitution of these times, wrote:

> 'The mass of the £10 householders did not really form their own opinions... they were in fact guided in their judgement by the better educated classes, they preferred representatives from those classes... they were influenced by rank and wealth ... they liked to have one of their "betters" to represent them; if he was rich they respected him much, if he was a lord they liked him the better. The issue put before these elections was which of two rich people would you choose?
>
> ... There is much that may be said against the Reform Act of 1832, but on the whole it has been successful. It is commonplace to speak of the legislative improvement of the last 25 years... Scarcely less important is the improvement which the Reform Bill has introduced into the general tone of our administration. Nor is this all. So much of agreement on opinion we see around is... the more singular as the nation is now less homogeneous in its social structure than it once was. The growth of manufacturers and trade had created a new world in the north of England... It is impossible not to ascribe this agreement to the habit of national discussion which the Reform Act has fostered.
>
> Two defects may be discussed. Parliament certainly has an undue bias towards the views of the landed interest [and] too little weight is at present given to the growing parts of the country, too much to the stationary.'
>
> (*Essays on Parliamentary Reform*, 1896)

# Extending the franchise

Between 1867 and 1886 several major changes were made to Britain's political system, and as a result the vote was extended to embrace two thirds of the adult male population. In part this was a reflection of Britain's changing society: the importance of the vote to members of an industrialising country was put by a Wolverhampton businessman:

> '. . . 50 years ago we were not in that need of Representatives which we are at present as we then manufactured nearly exclusively for home consumption. But the face of affairs is now changed – we now manufacture for the whole world and if we have not members to promote and extend our commerce, the era of our commercial greatness is at an end.'
> (Quoted in F. M. L. Thompson, *The Rise of Respectable Society*)

The actual timing and the detail of the reforms were the results of the political situation in Westminster.

## *Reform of the franchise in 1867*

1. In boroughs all male householders satisfying a one-year residence qualification could vote.
2. In boroughs all male lodgers living in rooms with an annual value of at least £10 (for rating purposes) could vote, provided that they had lived there for at least one year.
3. In counties all men owning property with an annual value of £5 could vote.
4. In counties all men renting property with an annual value of £12 could vote. (In Scotland the property value had to be £14.)
5. Thirty-five boroughs with populations of under 10,000 lost one of their two MPs; seventeen boroughs lost their MPs altogether and were merged into their counties.
6. Counties gained twenty-five extra MPs.
7. London University gained an MP.
8. The large cities of Manchester, Liverpool, Leeds and Birmingham each gained a third MP. Voters here had two votes each.
9. Scottish constituencies were increased in number from fifty-three to sixty (despite demands for sixty-eight).
10. Thirteen seats were awarded to new boroughs.
11. Two boroughs, Salford and Merthyr Tydfil, received a second MP.

This reform increased the numbers of voters by about 1,120,000, the bulk of them (around three quarters) being in the boroughs. The electorate in Leeds, for example, rose from 7217 to 30,010, and in Glasgow from 18,000 to 47,000. Yet southern England (excluding London) was still over-represented. Wiltshire and Dorset, for instance, with a rural population of 450,000, returned twenty-five MPs, three more than the West Riding of Yorkshire where two million people lived.

## Why did reform occur?

By the mid-1860s pressure for further reforms was building up once more. The journalist Henry Mayhew noticed the keen interest in politics taken by skilled workers in London:

'In passing from the skilled operative of the west-end to the unskilled workmen of the eastern quarter of London, the moral and intellectual change is so great, that it seems as if we were in a new land, and among another race. The artisans are almost to a man red-hot politicians. They are sufficiently educated and thoughtful to have a sense of their importance in the State . . . The political character and sentiments of the working classes appear to me to be a distinctive feature of the age, and they are a necessary consequence of the dawning intelligence of the mass.

   The unskilled labourers are a different class of people. As yet they are as unpolitical as footmen, and instead of entertaining violent democratic opinions, they appear to have no political opinions whatever; or, if they do possess any, they rather lean towards the maintenance of "things as they are", rather than towards the ascendancy of the working people . . .'
   (Henry Mayhew, *London Labour and the Labour Poor*, 1861–62)

It may be that the American Civil War encouraged renewed discussion of political rights. Certainly Gladstone was impressed by the steady support given by Lancashire cotton workers to the anti-slavery North, even though they suffered from the way war interrupted raw cotton supplies from the South. In 1864 a Reform League was born out of a group who originally gathered to organise a welcome for the Italian republican democrat, Garibaldi. The same year saw the establishment (in the old Manchester headquarters of the Anti-Corn Law League) of the National Reform Union. It campaigned for the secret ballot, a more equal distribution of seats, votes for all ratepayers, and a general election at least every three years. The veteran campaigner John Bright emerged once more to rally large public meetings, especially in the north. Within the Liberal Party, radicals saw reform of parliament as the necessary prelude to further changes, such as reform of the army, the civil service and the church. Some party leaders were persuaded that it was necessary to bind the skilled working class to the ruling establishment lest, in frustration at exclusion, they should organise hostile activities (such as an increasingly effective trade union system). The generally peaceful behaviour of skilled workers, their interest in politics and their educational achievements were noted by Gladstone in 1866:

> 'There never was a period in which religious influences were more active.... It is hardly an exaggeration to say that... the civilising and training powers of education have for all practical purposes been... brought into existence as far as the mass of the people is concerned. As regards the press,... for the humble sum of a penny, or even less, newspapers are circulated by the million... carrying home to all classes of our fellow countrymen, accounts of public affairs, enabling them to feel a new interest in the transaction of those affairs... by measures relating to labour, to police and to sanitary arrangements, Parliament has been labouring... to raise the level of the working community... we instituted for them Post Office saving banks,... and what has been the result?... there are now 650,000 depositors in those savings banks.... Parliament has been striving to make the working class progressively fitter and fitter for the franchise; and can anything be more unwise, not to say more senseless, than to persevere from year to year in this plan, and then blindly refuse to recognise its logical upshot – namely, the increased fitness of the working class for political power.'
>
> (Quoted in D. G. Wright, *Democracy and Reform*)

The death of Palmerston in 1865 cleared the way for reformers to lead the Liberals. Lord John Russell became Prime Minister, and Gladstone became the Chancellor of the Exchequer.

Nor were the Conservatives necessarily opposed to reform. Their leaders, Lord Derby and Benjamin Disraeli, feared that total opposition to all reform might exclude their party from power for very many years. They also entertained hopes that working class voters might prove to be on their side rather than on that of the Liberals. In 1865 the constituencies where working class voters formed a majority returned nine Conservative and five Liberals. Nor could they ignore the way that the over-representation of southern England had become more of a glaring abuse than ever. By 1865 a fifth of the electorate in England and Wales was returning half the MPs in the House of Commons.

## Carrying out reform

Having decided to work towards reform, Russell (Prime Minister in 1865) was pushed into prompt action by his dependence on the votes of the radical wing of the party. The discussion as to who should now get the vote was conducted on the assumption that it should go to those sufficiently educated and with a large enough stake in society to act responsibly. Not even John Bright demanded the vote for all men. And few MPs were enthusiastic about John Stuart Mill's suggestion that women too should gain the vote.

Gladstone, who took over management of the measure, eventually settled upon £7 as the property valuation for rating purposes above which all male adult householders would gain the vote. Yet his bill to implement this was defeated, and the government forced to resign.

Gladstone pitched the franchise at this level believing the upper working class to be Liberal, and fearing that the lower working class might prove to be Tory. His radical supporters were not pleased. But far more serious was the attitude of the wealthy remnant of the old Whig party that still formed a wing of the party. In Robert Lowe they found an outstandingly gifted speaker who tore apart Gladstone's arguments. Lowe predicted the consequences of awarding the franchise to the working class:

> 'The first stage . . . will be an increase of corruption, intimidation, and disorder, of all the evils that happen usually in elections . . . The second will be that the working men of England, finding themselves in a . . . majority . . ., will awake to a full sense of their power. They will say, "We can do better for ourselves . . . Let us set up shop for ourselves." . . .
>
> . . . Where is the line that can be drawn? . . . those who flatter and fawn upon the people are generally very inferior to the people, the objects of their flattery . . . We see in America, where the people have undisputed power, that they do not send honest, hard-working men to represent them in Congress, but traffickers in office, bankrupts, men who have lost their character and been driven from every respectable way of life and who take up politics as a last resource . . . Now, Sir, democracy has yet another tendency . . . It is singularly prone to the concentration of power. Under it, individual men are small, and the Government is great . . . and . . . absolutely tramples down and equalises everything except itself. And democracy . . . looks with the utmost hostility on all institutions not of immediate popular origin, which intervene between the people and the sovereign power . . .
>
> . . . with our own rash and inconsiderate hands, we are about to pluck down upon our heads the venerable temple of our liberty and our glory. History may tell of other acts as signally disastrous, but of none more wanton, none more disgraceful.'
>
> (*Hansard*, 3rd ser., clxxxii, 1866)

With Russell increasingly unwell, Gladstone was unable to cope with the crisis. Lowe gathered around him a sizeable group of rebels nicknamed 'Adullamites' (from the Old Testament story about David being chased into the cave of Adullam). Disraeli pounced upon the opportunity, skilfully exploiting the split. Together Conservatives and 'Adullamites' brought down the government.

## THE DERBY, 1867. DIZZY WINS WITH "REFORM BILL."

MR. PUNCH. "DON'T BE TOO SURE; WAIT TILL HE'S *WEIGHED*."

*A cartoonist's view of Disraeli's gamble with electoral reform shows him romping home ahead of rivals and thus winning success for himself.*

Lord Derby led the Conservative government that now took office. He had already come to the conclusion that his party must attempt to introduce parliamentary reform. The scale and frequency of pro-reform demonstrations (including one in Hyde Park that erupted into violence) added urgency to his efforts. Once he had been persuaded that Derby was right, Disraeli displayed wit, tactical skill, and great mastery of detail in piloting Conservative proposals through the Commons. He cheerfully accepted a whole range of amendments that gave the vote to more people than he had originally intended – provided that those amendments did not come from Gladstone. Conservatives watched gleefully as Disraeli ridiculed and outmanoeuvred Gladstone – indeed Gladstone's furious opposition helped rally the doubtful to Disraeli's cause. Three Conservatives – Peel,

Cranborne and Carnarvon – did resign from the government, but they remained an isolated small faction. And Disraeli had the satisfaction of winning radical Liberal support since his bill was more democratic than Gladstone's. Radicals flatly refused to help Gladstone insert a £5 property clause into borough franchises.

The consequence of the amendments was to treble the number of people to whom it had been originally proposed to give the vote. The reforms left the counties little changed and set up a boundary commission (to sort out the constituencies) which was dominated by Conservatives. The extension of the vote to lodgers probably added, initially, only about 12,000 new voters. Derby called his party's reform 'a leap in the dark': it was nevertheless a cautious leap confined by the belief that the vote had to be earned – it was still not seen as the automatic right of all citizens.

## The question of corruption

Since voting continued to be conducted openly, bribery, corruption and intimidation remained common at elections. In 1872 Gladstone's Liberal government attacked the problem by bringing in the secret ballot (where each voter cast his vote in secret). Even so the proposal was attacked. One Conservative MP, Colonel Barttelot, argued:

> 'not a man would come forward to say that he personally was
> afraid to record his vote unless he was protected by the
> Ballot . . . Were the classes who had obtained the franchise
> under the recent Reform Bill less independent that the class
> immediately above them? This Bill indirectly cast a great slur
> upon the working class of the community by insinuating that
> they were unable to protect themselves in giving their votes,
> but he was prepared to contend that the working classes were as
> independent and able to protect themselves as any class of
> people in the country. The small shopkeepers were not nearly
> so able to protect themselves, but the Government during the
> time that this class had power never introduced any Ballot
> Bill . . .'
>
> (Quoted in M. Willis, *Gladstone and Disraeli*, 1989)

Even this reform was insufficient. In small boroughs and counties especially, agents of the wealthy were able to observe those going to vote and guess the result since ballot boxes were separately opened to count the votes. A Royal Commission reporting on the conduct of the 1880 election in Macclesfield noted:

> '. . . it seems doubtful whether a contested election has ever been
> fought in Macclesfield on really pure principles, the corruption
> of the late election was far more widespread, and far more open
> than had been the case at any previous Parliamentary election,

at all events, of recent years, though the bribes were, in most cases, trifling in amount . . . of those who were proved before them to have received bribes . . . a large number of them were persons who would not have accepted money from the opposite side, but who thought that if money was going amongst their friends they were as much entitled to have some as anyone else, and therefore accepted their day's wages, or a few shillings wherewith to treat themselves before or after polling.'

(Quoted in M. Willis, *Gladstone and Disraeli*)

Where voters were very numerous the secret ballot certainly made a difference. In London, the Chief Commissioner of Police reported:

'Since the passing of the Ballot Act we have never had the slightest trouble at any election that has taken place in London, and the places that used to be the worst are now the best . . . [In

# WARNING

## TO

# FARMERS & LABOURERS.

It having been rumoured that certain TORY FARMERS have been intimidating their Labourers by threatening a REDUCTION of WAGES if the LIBERALS GET IN,

**WARNING IS HEREBY GIVEN**

to such persons that they have transgressed "The Corrupt Practices Act," and are liable to

**IMPRISONMENT FOR TWELVE MONTHS**

WITH HARD LABOUR,

and will certainly be prosecuted.

 Every Labourer is FREE TO VOTE as he PLEASES, and any one INTERFERING with his RIGHT of Voting, WILL BE PUNISHED with the UTMOST RIGOUR OF THE LAW.

HART AND SON, PRINTERS, SAFFRON WALDEN.

*A poster reminding working class voters electoral reform had provided a genuinely secret ballot.*

1868] the Tower Hamlets election was carried on in a general state of riot; we had to have 400 or 500 police on the ground to keep the peace.'

(Quoted in M. Willis, *Gladstone and Disraeli*)

In 1883 the Corrupt and Illegal Practices Act introduced fines and prison sentences for those who exceeded a set list of election expenses and engaged in activities like hiring carriages (wealthy people began supplying these free to those who were going to the polling stations to vote for them). The increase in the numbers of voters made bribery more difficult, though influence lingered on in smaller towns which were dominated by one or two employers. (In Norwich, for example, J. J. Colman, the mustard manufacturer, was regularly backed by the local community.) However, elections certainly became more orderly.

Though property qualifications for MPs vanished in 1858, attempting to enter Parliament remained very expensive. Agents' salaries could run to £100 or more a year and permissible expenses might rise to more than £800. Spending between elections continued too. In 1895 the novelist Rider Haggard fought Norfolk East and wrote:

'From the moment a candidate appears in the field he is fair game and every man's hand is in his pocket. Demands for "your patronage and support" fall on him thick as leaves. I was even pestered to supply voters with wooden legs! Why should an election cost, as this one did, over £2000?'

(*The Days of My Life*, 1926)

## The Third Reform Act, 1884–85

By the 1880s it was widely agreed that voters in counties ought to have the same political rights as voters in boroughs. A Bill was introduced in 1884 by Gladstone, who declared:

'Is there any doubt that the peasantry of the country are capable citizens, qualified for enfranchisement, qualified to make good use of their power as voters?'

Lord Salisbury, the Conservative leader, agreed with the justice of the argument. Parliamentary reform, therefore, was not just the cause of radicals like Joseph Chamberlain, although in fact Chamberlain saw it as just one of a cluster of measures that included land reform and the provision of free elementary education.

# The Third Reform Act, 1884, and the Redistribution Act, 1885

1. The old county/borough division was abolished; very small boroughs of under 15,000 people lost their MPs; and those from 15,000 to 50,000 people kept one MP. A basic principle of trying to create constituencies of around 50,000 people was adopted.

2. The 1867 franchise applied in all places; so adult males who were house owners, or tenants who had lived in a house for at least a year, and lodgers who had lived at least a year in rooms valued at £10 a year for rating purposes, all had the vote.

3. Plural voting (i.e. voting for more than one person) was permitted. University graduates had a second vote for their university MPs; borough freeholders could also vote in the counties except in four places; and those who owned property in several different constituencies could vote in each of those constituencies. By 1911 plural voting counted for 7 per cent of the votes. One man had twenty-three votes. Even the radical Chamberlain had six.

4. A redistribution of 142 seats took place, cutting the old dominance of southern England and increasing Scottish representation to seventy-two.

5. Voting was still spread over three weeks, enabling men to stand in more than one place. For example, in 1900 Keir Hardie stood in both Preston and Merthyr.

The vote was still denied to women. Also excluded were sons living at home, people on poor relief, servants living with their employers, and servicemen living in barracks. Since working class people moved home frequently (one estimate reckoned that 30 per cent moved every year), it was often difficult for them to meet the residence qualification. In Glasgow just 52 per cent of males were entitled to vote in 1900.

Lodgers had to go through a complex system of registration, which required annual renewal in the presence of an appointed lawyer, and this of course involved time off work. So the reform was by no means complete.

The reform increased the tendency of voters of a particular social group to dominate constituencies. There were suburban seats that Conservatives controlled, and working class seats eyed hopefully by candidates from the emerging Socialist and Labour parties. Joseph Chamberlain pointed out the implications of a parliament:

'. . . elected by 5 millions of men, of whom three fifths belong to the labouring population. It is a revolution which has been peacefully and silently accomplished. The centre of power has been shifted.'

Pressure for the vote for all men was ineffective prior to the Great War, as those still denied the vote did not form a coherent group capable of effective organisation. The unskilled labouring man was still regarded with suspicion: many politicians felt that such a voter would be swayed by short-term emotional appeals, and was so dominated by the need to earn a living as to be incapable of informed political decisions. Bills attacking plural voting were rejected by the House of Lords.

In 1885 the UK electorate was 5.7 million; by 1911 it was 7.9 million, but it did not include a single woman, and by 1911 this had become a major issue.

# Women's rights
## The changing role of women in society

The struggle to win votes for women was just one of a number of battles that were fought to improve the place of women in society. When Victoria became queen, society officially took the view expressed in the late eighteenth century by the eminent lawyer William Blackstone:

> 'By marriage the very being or legal existence of women is suspended, or at least it is incorporated and consolidated into that of the husband under whose protection and cover she performs everything.'

A society that denied women legal status equal to that of men, offered them inferior education, and gave them wage rates well below those of their male counterparts was not likely to regard women as worthy of the franchise. In 1854 Barbara Leigh Smith Bodichon's book *A Brief Summary in Plain Language of the Most Important Laws Concerning Women* noted:

> 'A man and wife are one person in law: the wife loses all her rights as a single woman and her existence is entirely absorbed in that of her husband. A woman's body belongs to her husband and he can enforce his right. What was her personal property before marriage such as money, jewels, clothes etc. becomes absolutely her husband's. Money earned by a married woman belongs absolutely to her husband. The legal custody of the children belongs to the father . . . the father may take them from her and dispose of them as he thinks fit. A married woman cannot enter into contracts except as the agent of her husband, that is, her word alone is not binding in law.'
>
> (Quoted in J. H. Murray, *Strong Minded Women*, 1984)

In fact, in 1839 women did win rights to the custody of their children under the age of seven, provided that the Lord Chancellor agreed; and a husband did need his wife's consent to dispose of her freehold land. Nevertheless, this was a situation bitterly resented by a growing number of wealthy intelligent women who had plenty of time to focus on the injustices of their position. The Victorian age evolved an attitude to women which regarded their proper role – if material circumstances allowed – as one of near idleness. The period has left us the furious recollections of women like Florence Nightingale, who were frustrated by a life devoted to supervising servants, socialising, and practising hobbies like music and needlework. The philosopher John Stuart Mill took as his second wife Harriet Taylor. She helped to persuade him of the justice of votes for women, stating:

'When we ask why the existence of one half of the species should be merely ancillary to that of the other – why each woman should be a mere appendage to a man, allowed to have no interests of her own that there may be nothing to compete in her mind with his interests and his pleasure, the only reason which can be given is, that men like it. It is agreeable to them that men should live for their own sake, women for the sake of men.'

(Quoted in J. H. Murray, *Strong Minded Women*)

Education was an area of life where such women battled for change. The Education Act of 1870 (1872 in Scotland) created a system of elementary education for girls as well as for boys. But most leading campaigners for women's rights were equally concerned with the fee-paying and higher education sectors to which their family wealth gave them access.

The education issue was of special importance to women who had to earn their own living. In the 1860s nearly a quarter of all adult females were either spinsters or widows – indeed, since two thirds of this figure were spinsters, the importance of being qualified for (and having access to) a range of worthwhile careers was a matter of major importance to the women concerned. (In 1913 63 per cent of subscribing supporters of the suffragette Pankhursts were spinsters.) So there was pressure for an education similar to that provided for boys. In 1853 Cheltenham Ladies College was founded. It offered its pupils subjects like Latin, Greek and Mathematics as well as the traditional literary and artistic accomplishments. During the century the number of such schools increased. Emily Davies (who in 1869 founded what eventually became Girton College, Cambridge) wondered:

'Is the improved education which it is hoped is about to be brought within reach of women to be identical with that of men? Only women can understand the weight of discouragement produced by being perpetually told that as women nothing much is ever to be expected of them, that whatever they do they must not interest themselves, except in a secondhand and shallow way, in the pursuits of men. Every effort to improve the education of women which assumes that they may study the same subjects as their brothers does something towards lifting them out of the state of listless despair of themselves into which so many fall.'

(Quoted in J. H. Murray, *Strong Minded Women*)

At the same time, there were women who argued in just the opposite way. In 1868 Sarah Sewell, an opponent of women's rights declared:

'The education of girls need not be of the same extended classical and commercial character as that of boys: they want more an education of the heart and feelings and expecially of firm, fixed moral principles. The profoundly educated women rarely make good wives or mothers, women who have stored their minds with Latin and Greek seldom have much knowledge of pies and puddings nor do they enjoy the hard and interesting work of attending to the wants of little children.'

(Quoted in J. H. Murray, *Strong Minded Women*)

But slowly access to higher education was prised open. In 1878 London University abandoned a twelve-year experiment of offering women separate awards and opened up all its degrees equally to men and to women. Two years afterwards, Victoria University, the forerunner of Manchester and Liverpool University, did the same, and in 1895 Durham University followed suit. The work of Elizabeth Garrett Anderson and Sophia Jex Blake led to the establishment of the London School of Medicine where women could train as doctors. It is significant that Emily Davies and Elizabeth Garrett Anderson were also responsible in 1866 for taking to parliament the first petition for women's suffrage. Gradually more careers opened up to suitably trained women. In 1860 the Nightingale School of Nursing at St Thomas's Hospital began the work of making nursing a proper career. The extension of education opened up teaching as a career for women – as long as they remained unmarried. By 1910 Britain had its first woman banker and its first woman chartered accountant. Women found employment in the post office, the civil service, and in private businesses, yet still they could not elect or be elected as MPs.

It might be thought that the presence of a queen on the throne helped their cause. Not so. Victoria wrote:

'The Queen is most anxious to enlist everyone who can speak or write, to join in checking this mad wicked folly of "Women's Rights" with all its attendant horrors on which her poor feeble sex is bent, forgetting every sense of womanly feeling and propriety. It is a subject which makes the Queen so furious that she cannot contain herself.'

However, even royal hostility could not prevent legal reforms to improve women's circumstances.

# Changes in the law

1. 1857 Matrimonial Causes Act. Divorce could now be obtained through the law courts instead of by a private Act of Parliament. The Act's main purpose was to ease divorce for men. For them, the proof of a wife's adultery was sufficient, but women had to prove more than adultery – an offence such as bigamy, incest, cruelty or desertion was required too. Nevertheless it did give women increased control of their property, especially where judicial separation or desertion was involved.
2. 1869 Municipal Franchise Act. Single female ratepayers could vote in local elections. (Married women got the same right in 1894.)
3. 1870–94. Women obtained the right to vote for, and stand for election to, organisations like School Boards (1870–72), Poor Law Guardians (1875), County Councils (1888–89), Parish and District Councils (1894).
4. 1870 Married Women's Property Act. This Act was a rather ineffective attempt to increase women's rights over their property, income and legacies.
5. 1873. The age of children over whom women could claim custody was raised from seven to sixteen.
6. 1882 Second Married Women's Property Act. This gave married women the same rights over their own property as were already possessed by unmarried women.
7. 1886 Married Women's (maintenance in case of desertion) Act. Women could sue for desertion without first having to go to the workhouse.
8. 1886 Repeal of the Contagious Diseases Act. This had allowed the forcible examination and imprisonment of any woman in an army garrison town or naval port who was thought to be a prostitute.
9. 1886 The Guardianship of Infants Act. In deciding the custody of children, their welfare was now to be the most important factor.

# Pressure for women's suffrage

When parliamentary reform was being debated in 1867, John Stuart Mill proposed an amendment that would have given the vote to women on the same terms as men. It was rejected by 194 votes to 73. It marked the beginning of a long campaign that eventually became quite violent, but had still not met with success by 1914. Some men (and women) were opposed to it in principle, arguing that physically and intellectually women were not suited to the rough and tumble of politics. There were even female reformers like Octavia Hill and (for a while) Beatrice Webb who did not favour votes for women. And some male politicians feared the long-term implications of such a reform. William Randall Cremer, MP, said:

> 'He had always contended that if once they opened the door and enfranchised ever so small a number of females, they could not possibly close it and that it ultimately meant adult suffrage. The government of the country would therefore be handed over to a majority who would not be men, but women. Women are creatures of impulse and emotion and did not decide questions on the ground of reason as men did.'
>
> (*House of Commons Debates*, Vol 155)

Some politicians supported the women's cause. In the Labour Party there were several, especially Keir Hardie. There were a number in the Liberal Party, notably Sir Edward Grey. The Conservative Party was by no means wholly hostile: A. J. Balfour, for example, privately expressed his sympathy. Yet the cause of women's suffrage was enmeshed in other considerations that always seemed to prevent action. The Liberals feared that giving women the vote on the property qualification basis would create Conservative voters. The Conservatives wished to see a more general reform which would cut the number of Irish MPs upon whom the Liberals depended in the last few years before the Great War. The Labour Party buried the issue in a general demand for adult suffrage. Some MPs pointed to reforms already carried out and argued that the existing system was well able to respond to women's interests; and many argued there were more urgent issues that had to receive priority. Nor was there an overwhelming and united pressure for reform from women. Some opposed it; some concentrated on other issues (like housing and health reforms, or working conditions); and most ordinary women were so overwhelmed by the daily battle for existence that they had no time and energy left for the cause. Moreover those who did support the cause were divided, and argued about tactics at a crucial period in the campaign.

During the nineteenth century, women's protests remained peaceful. Meetings, petitions and proposals in parliament were organised by different groups. Millicent Fawcett pulled together these groups to form the National Union of Women's Suffrage Societies (NUWSS). By the 1900s women who qualified were voting in local elections and some were actively involved as members of boards and councils. Mrs Emmeline Pankhurst commented:

> 'Our leaders in the Liberal Party had advised the women to prove their fitness for the Parliamentary franchise by serving in

*Suffragettes on the march in 1910.*

municipal office . . . A large number of women had availed themselves of this advice and were serving on Boards of Guardians, on School Boards and in other capacities.

When I came into office I found that the laws in our district were being very harshly administered. The old board had been made up of the kind of men who are known as rate savers. They were guardians not of the poor but of the rates. Old folks I found sitting on benches. They had no privacy, no possessions, not even a locker . . . It does gratify me when I look back and remember what we were able to do for the children.

The trouble is the law cannot do all the work, even for children. We shall have to have new laws and it soon became apparent to me that we can never hope to get them until women have the vote . . . I thought I had been a suffragist before I became a Poor Law Guardian, but now I began to think about the vote in women's hands not only as a right but as a desperate necessity.'

(*My Own Story*, 1914)

Mrs Pankhurst was to return repeatedly to this view – that the issue of 'votes for women' was not only right in itself, but the necessary means to other urgently needed reforms. In an appearance in a law court she argued:

> 'We believe that if we get the vote it will mean better conditions for our unfortunate sisters. We know what the condition of the woman worker is. Her condition is very bad. Many women pass through this court who I believe would not come before you if they were able to live morally and honestly. The average earnings of the women who earn their living are only 7s. 7d a week... We have been driven to the conclusion that only through legislation can any improvement be effected and that the legislation can never be effected until we have the same power as men have to bring pressure to bear upon our representatives and upon Governments to give us the necessary legislation.'

It was the failure of other approaches that led Mrs Pankhurst to action, as she explained in her memoirs:

> 'It was on October 10th 1903 that I invited a number of women to my house for purposes of organisation. We voted to call our society the Women's Social and Political Union [WSPU]. We resolved to limit our membership exclusively to women, to keep ourselves absolutely free from any party affiliation and to be satisfied with nothing but action...
>
> The old suffragist... clung to a hope that a private member's bill would sometime obtain consideration. Every year the association sents [sic] deputations to meet so-called friendly members. The ladies made their speeches and the members made theirs and renewed their assurances that they believed in women's suffrage and would vote for it when they had an opportunity to do so. Then the deputation, a trifle sad, took its departure and the members resumed the real business of life, which was support of their parties' policies.'

The *Daily Mail* dubbed her followers 'suffragettes'. They adopted tactics that were more aggressive than those of other groups: they interrupted political meetings with banner-waving and heckling; they organised rallies, marches and petitions; they set up a newspaper, and won a good deal of publicity. Failure to win success pushed the movement into illegal actions that led to suffragettes being imprisoned. Some of them went on hunger-strike and were forcibly fed. This forcible feeding attracted such bad publicity that the Liberal Government's 'Cat and Mouse Act' was passed to permit temporary release and arbitrary rearrest. From 1909 the WSPU's methods became more violent. Windows were smashed, properties set on fire, acid poured in letter boxes, golf courses and flower beds wrecked. In 1914 Mary Richardson tried to slash an important painting, Velasquez's *Venus*, but her activity was nothing in comparison to the tragedy of the previous year: during the Derby horse race of 1913 Emily Wilding Davison

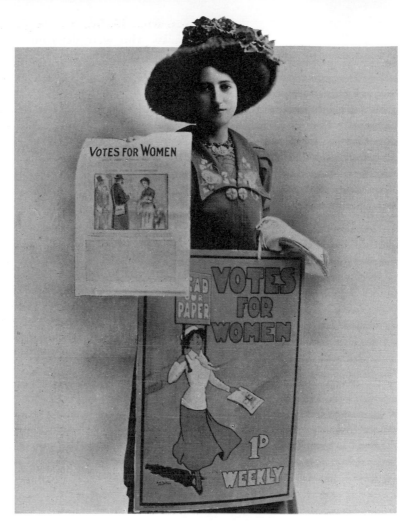

*An Edwardian appeal for support for the cause of female suffrage.*

rushed on to the course, attempting to seize the bridle of the king's horse, Anmer. The frightened animal fell, injuring her fatally.

By now the suffragettes knew that women in New Zealand and in South Australia had received the vote. Yet all efforts in Britain had failed. The increasing violence alarmed Conservatives especially. In 1912 the Labour MP George Lansbury resigned to fight his Bow and Bromley constituency again, specifically on the issue of female suffrage. His reward was to be soundly beaten by an anti-suffrage Conservative.

Fragments of the WSPU split off through differences with Mrs Pankhurst and her daughter Christabel about the use of violence and the leadership style of the Pankhursts. From 1910 the membership lists of the WSPU began to shrink.

In 1913 Asquith's Liberal Government proposed giving the vote to female householders and to the wives of householders. But the bill was wrecked by an alliance of Conservatives and Irish Nationalists who were determined to see Home Rule safely in place before there was any further reform of the franchise. This curious combination of enemies sprang from Irish fear that reform would drastically cut their Westminster representation: the average electorate in an Irish seat was by 1914 about half that of one in England. (Ireland's population had been falling, while England's had been expanding.) Asquith had been pushed into this proposal rather reluctantly by more enthusiastic colleagues who also pointed out that skilled fund-raisers and organisers from the NUWSS were now rallying to Labour to help it fight anti-suffrage Liberals. Asquith now dropped the measure and within a year the Great War had swept it aside.

Did the Pankhursts' tactics help the cause of votes for women? The historian Martin Pugh argues:

'The Pankhursts proved a highly divisive force within the women's movements . . . they inflicted a catalogue of splits among militant forces . . . There are no grounds for the view that the WSPU shifted public opinion in its favour, rather the reverse.'

(M. Pugh, *Women's Suffrage in Britain*, 1980)

However, the film maker Midge Mackenzie, who has produced a book on this issue, believes:

'Prior to 1914 it was the militant vanguard, the WSPU, that revitalised the question of votes for women with its tactics of political confrontations and the immense publicity that ensued.'
(M. Mackenzie, *Shoulder to Shoulder*, 1975)

The outbreak of war led Mrs Pankhurst to set aside her campaign in the interests of winning the war.

## ESSAY

Use the notes you have gathered for the task set at the beginning of this chapter to write an essay on one of the following:

1. Do you agree that 'parliamentary reform was largely a reflection of changes in the social and economic structure of the country'?
2. 'We must admit those whom it may be safe to admit' (Macaulay). Was this the principle that governed parliamentary reform in the nineteenth century?
3. Were Victorians right to be so suspicious of democracy?
4. 'In the 1860s Disraeli succeeded in reforming Parliament: Gladstone failed.' Why was this?
5. Who might have mourned the decline of corruption? Were they right to do so?
6. Why did the pressure for female suffrage fail before 1914?

# Winning the voters' support

In 1867 the Conservative politician Lord Carnarvon explained his worry that the 1867 Reform Act would make life impossible for his party:

> 'I am convinced that we are in a very critical position. Household suffrage will produce a state of things in many boroughs the results of which I defy anyone to predict. In Leeds, for example, the present number of electors are about 8500. With household suffrage they will become about 35,000. Is there anyone who dares to say what will be the character and tendency of that constituency? It may be good or bad; but it is a revolution. The Conservative party is in imminent danger of going to pieces now if indeed it does not disappear in the deluge that the Government are bringing on.'
>
> (D. G. Wright, *Democracy and Reform*)

He was right to be concerned. Giving the vote to far more people had a major impact on political parties.

The material in this section deals with how people who were eager to capture and control political power responded to the challenge of a changing society and a widening franchise. It is therefore concerned with the *ideology* of political parties, with the *authority* that party leaders tried to exert over their followers, and with the changing political *identity* of Britain. The main issue to be considered is: How and why did modern political parties develop at this time?

## TASK

Plan and write an essay on the following:

'It was during the period 1850 to 1914 that the modern political party was born in Britain.' Do you agree?

In order to do this, consider and make notes to answer the following questions:
- What are the features of a modern political party?
- Were any of these features present in the 1850s?

- Were they present in 1914?
- Why did developments take place between these dates?
- Who played a major part in bringing about changes?
- Do the changes justify agreement with the essay title?

Once your notes are complete, compare and discuss them with others. Then write out the essay. It may help to refer briefly to or quote from the views of historians and people at the time.

## Ministries 1859–1916

| Years | Political party | Prime ministers |
|---|---|---|
| 1859–65 | Whig-Liberal | Lord Palmerston |
| 1865–66 | Whig-Liberal | Lord John Russell |
| 1866–68 | Conservative | Lord Derby |
| 1868 | Conservative | Benjamin Disraeli |
| 1868–74 | Liberal | William E. Gladstone |
| 1874–80 | Conservative | Benjamin Disraeli |
| 1880–85 | Liberal | William E. Gladstone |
| 1885–86 | Conservative | Lord Salisbury |
| 1886 | Liberal | William E. Gladstone |
| 1886–92 | Conservative | Lord Salisbury |
| 1892–94 | Liberal | William E. Gladstone |
| 1894–95 | Liberal | Lord Rosebery |
| 1895–1902 | Conservative | Lord Salisbury |
| 1902–05 | Conservative | Arthur J. Balfour |
| 1905–08 | Liberal | Sir Henry Campbell-Bannerman |
| 1908–16 | Liberal | H. H. Asquith |

# The development of the Liberal and Conservative Parties

## *Parties in the 1850s: the need for change*

Politics in early Victorian times were 'a matter of government and administration rather than legislation' according to the historian Alan Beattie (*English Party Politics*, Vol I). The Whig-Liberal Party and the Conservative Party were both loose alliances of differing groups. The former included rich land-owning aristocrats; non-conformist industrialists like Titus Salt; intellectuals like John Stuart Mill; radicals keen to see all sorts of reforms; and a mass of men who belonged to no special groups, were cautious in out-look, and saw it as their duty to follow their leaders and support the good government of the country. The party leaders had only limited control over their MPs and might well suffer around fifteen defeats a year on their proposed legislation without feeling deep concern. The Conservative Party contained even more of the land-owning class than the Liberals (about half of their MPs, compared with one quarter for the Liberals). In 1846 the question of whether to repeal the taxes on imported corn so split the party as to drive out of it those who favoured this measure. Neither party enjoyed much control over such local party associations as existed. Conservatives especially saw little need for party branches in counties and small towns: the influence of major landowners seemed quite sufficient to guarantee success. In bigger places the job of organising votes at election time was commonly carried out in their spare time by local solicitors. When elections were held, little effort was made to present the ideas of the party leaders: local issues loomed largest. Certainly leaders did not consider that they should tour the land, rallying support.

Yet after the 1832 Reform Act had widened the vote, there were signs of change. The beginning of central organisations can be seen in two London-based clubs, the Tory Carlton Club (1832) and the Liberal Reform Club (1834). From 1835 to 1846 Frederick Bonham established and supervised a permanent committee to watch over Conservative election campaigns. Bonham supported the leadership of Robert Peel, who realised that the increase in voters changed the party scene, commenting:

> 'There is a new element of political power – namely the registration of voters. That party is strongest which has the existing registration in its favour.'

The need to make sure one's own voters were registered – and to try to block opponents' attempts to register their followers – led the Liberals to create a Registration Association in 1861 and the Conservatives to establish the Registration Society in 1864. The historian Robert Blake suggests that in the period up to 1867, although politicians struggled to get political office, their real differences were small:

> '. . . party differences had been only marginal. It was a political struggle for place rather than programmes.'

Nevertheless the increased number of voters stimulated the need for organisation for the struggle. The development of a national network of railways, of the telegraph system, and of cheap provincial papers (freed from stamp and paper duty and using steam presses) were significant changes that imaginative leaders could exploit. With a growing urban population the land-owning character of the parties needed to change. Thus, by the time of the 1867 Reform Act all sorts of factors were present that were to make change possible. But, for the moment, neither Liberals nor Conservatives were effectively organised in parliament or the country in the fashion followed by modern parties. There was no real continuity of effort in constituencies between elections and no developed party organisations to make that possible. The parties lacked the coherence of their modern equivalents.

## A BAD EXAMPLE.

Dr. Punch. " WHAT'S ALL THIS? YOU, THE TWO HEAD BOYS OF THE SCHOOL, THROWING MUD!
*YOU OUGHT TO BE ASHAMED OF YOURSELVES!*"

*The magazine* Punch*'s comment on the political battle waged between Gladstone and Disraeli.*

# The development of party 'image'

Many voters develop a strong attachment to a political party. During the later nineteenth century both the Liberal and the Conservative parties tried to develop their own special 'image', to push forward their own leaders as being especially suited to the country's needs. In the 1860s it was not easy to find major policy differences: both parties favoured free trade; both supported parliamentary reform in the later 1860s. But during the later nineteenth century attempts were made to distinguish between the policies of the two parties. Closely linked to this was a tendency to appeal to some groups in society rather than to others.

## Taking the party to the people

By the 1880s the canvassing of voters in boroughs, and the use of rallies, posters and propaganda were common. Party supporters wore the colour of their party, though there was some confusion in this, since neither party had yet developed exclusive claim to one colour in particular. In Suffolk, for example, Conservatives wore blue. Not far away, in Cambridge, Liberals also sported blue. By the late 1880s party leaders were beginning to tour Britain making major speeches, and to have their words not only reported in the provincial press, but also printed for distribution. In 1887 the Marquis of Salisbury, by then leader of the Conservatives, grumbled:

> 'This dirty business of making political speeches is an aggravation of the labours of Your Majesty's servants which we owe entirely to Mr Gladstone.'
> (M. Pugh, *The Making of Modern British Politics*, 1982)

William Ewart Gladstone had a major impact on the image of the Liberal Party. He served as Chancellor of the Exchequer in 1852 and from 1859 to 1866, and then as Prime Minister (1868–74, 1880–85, 1886 and 1892–94). He brought to politics a deep belief in the importance of moral causes. He also brought great skill as a speaker, and he was able to rouse huge gatherings of ordinary people. In 1879–80 he held his Midlothian campaigns, trying to stir up the country against the Conservative Government by a country-wide rail tour, stopping at key points to address the

*Gladstone pioneered new methods of political campaign by travelling around Britain to address mass rallies (1885).*

crowds who had been notified of his coming. One of his supporters, John Morley, later wrote a history of his hero's life in which he described these campaigns:

'Nothing like it had been seen before. "Statesmen" had enjoyed great popular receptions before, and there had been plenty of cheering and bell-ringing and torchlight in individual places before. On this journey . . . it seemed as if the whole countryside were up. The stations where the train stopped were crowded, thousands flocked from neighbouring towns and villages to main centres along the line of the route . . . All that followed in a week of meetings and speeches was to match. People came from the Hebrides to hear Mr Gladstone speak. Where there were 6000 seats, the applications were 40 or 50,000. The weather was bitter and the hills were covered with snow, but this made no difference in cavalcades, processions and the rest of the outdoor demonstrations.'

(John Morley, *The Life of William Ewart Gladstone*, 1903)

Gladstone's opponents were reluctantly forced to follow suit, and the age of the national leader touring the country to make speeches on national issues had been born. The Marquis of Salisbury's early efforts, one observer noted, were not very impressive:

'Lord Salisbury was forced to yield to the democratic spirit so far as to "go on the stump" and address popular audiences in great towns. It was an uncongenial employment . . . His voice was clear and penetrating, but there was no popular fibre in his speech. He talked of the things which interested him; but whether or not they interested his hearers he seemed not to care a jot. When he rolled off the platforms and into the carriage which was to carry him away there was a general sense of mutual relief.'

(George W. E. Russell, in F. E. Higgett)

With time, however, Salisbury's technique improved. It had become important to encourage voters to identify with their leaders.

## The Liberal 'image'

What did the Liberal Party stand for? Whose support did it attract?

One significant strand of support was provided by the many thousands of devout nonconformist church-goers. The religious census of 1851 showed that half the country's worshippers were nonconformist (that is, those who did not attend Church of England services). The historian Henry Pelling suggests:

'In small towns and country villages the ministers and the lay preachers were the backbone of Liberal strength.'

(H. Pelling, *The Social Geography of British Elections*, 1967)

This strength was especially to be found in the English Midlands and in Wales and Scotland.

In January 1880 the journal *The Nonconformist* observed that it was the Liberal Party which:

> '... has striven to be "the party of Christ", the party of moral principles as against that of selfish and corrupt interests, the party of peace as against that of violence, the party of popular improvement and reform as against that of resistance to progress, the party of justice... The strength of the Liberal Party is in the force of individual social conscience.'
> (P. Adelman, *Gladstone, Disraeli and Later Victorian Politics*, 1970)

Gladstone tapped such feelings. Though he was himself an Anglican, he was passionately concerned about moral causes. His return to politics (after retiring in 1875) was inspired by his loathing of Conservative foreign policy at a time when Turkish rulers had killed large numbers of Bulgarians living in their empire. Gladstone believed Disraeli was too concerned with propping up Turkey as a barrier to Russian expansion. His views led to the 1880 election involving a much clearer choice for voters than most earlier elections: foreign policy issues dominated. Moreover, Gladstone began to despair of the wealthy landowners' commitment to what he saw as right. He declared during the Midlothian campaigns:

> 'We cannot reckon upon what is called the landed interest, we cannot reckon upon the clergy of the established churches. We cannot reckon on the wealth of the country nor upon the rank of the country.'
> (P. Adelman, *Gladstone, Disraeli and Later Victorian Politics*)

Such views helped to push wealthy Whigs out of the party. This took some time, however, and was not really deliberate. Indeed rich titled landowners were more likely to be members of Gladstone's cabinet than were Radicals. When Gladstone retired (temporarily) in 1875, the problem of finding a leader and policies was clearly seen by the Whig leader, Hartington. In 1875 he wrote:

> 'My suggestion... was not exactly that we should do without a leader; but that the Whigs or moderate Liberals should have one, the Radicals another & the Irishmen a third. I think that there is hardly any important question on which the Whigs & Radicals will not vote against each other; Disestablishment, Household Suffrage in Counties, Education, Land Laws etc; & the position of a nominal leader seeing his flock all going their own way without attending to him, will not be comfortable. If each section had its own leader & its own organisation, it seems to me that there might be more real union & co-operation on points where we could agree than if we were nominally united;

when each section would complain & quarrel every time the
party organisation was not used to support its views...'

(M. Willis, *Gladstone & Disraeli: Principles & Policies*)

Gladstone himself recognised the problem of presenting a clear
Liberal image. In 1855 he complained:

'The problem for me is to make if possible a statement which
will hold through the election and not go into conflict with
either the right of the party, for whom Hartington has spoken,
or the left for whom Chamberlain spoke.'

Joseph Chamberlain had been pushing forward reforms that
would have changed the franchise, the distribution of seats, education and taxation. Hartington began to think, 'I see nothing for
the Whigs but to disappear or turn Tory.'

In 1886 Gladstone accelerated the departure of the Whigs by
declaring his support for home rule for Ireland. His Irish policy
had already upset them by attacking the authority of the landlords. By 1906 only 8 per cent of Liberal MPs were major
landowners. Those abandoning Gladstone included Chamberlain
who, though a Radical, opposed home rule as a vote-loser and as
an attack on the Empire. The Whigs and Chamberlainites became
Liberal Unionists. Together they mustered ninety-three votes,
enough to wreck home rule. In 1895 Chamberlain completed this
shift in politics by joining a Conservative cabinet.

Home rule provided a simple test as to whether one was a
Liberal. It reduced the party to 191 MPs in the 1886 election, and
left it searching desperately for able leaders behind whom to unite.
But it eased the way for those keen on reform. In 1891 the
National Liberal Federation (see p. 59) put forward its 'Newcastle
Programme' which asked for temperance reform; reform of the
House of Lords; taxation of land values and mineral royalties; the
disestablishment of the Welsh and Scottish churches; and home
rule for all appropriate areas of the UK. It was widely accepted in
the Party. Liberals still differed on issues – some opposed the Boer
War (as did Lloyd George); others were 'Liberal Imperialists' in
favour of a vigorous imperial policy. But, from 1903, they were
able to rally round a single cause; from this date Joseph
Chamberlain worked to convert the Tories to taxes on foreign
imports (tariff reform), and therefore Liberals were able to unite
round the policy of free trade. As Lloyd George put it in 1908:

'I am standing for Britain, Britain and the flag of freedom in her
markets. That flag has stood for free trade for 50 years and the
results are superb.'

Liberals did well in the 1906 elections by denouncing the
Tories. But in the 1910 elections they suffered heavy losses, and
historians debate whether, by this time, Liberalism had based
itself on too few sectors of the population to survive as a major

party. George Dangerfield speculated whether the problems of the time (the Irish question, the House of Lords, the suffragettes, and industrial troubles) were just too much for it. Others have pointed to the rise of the Labour Party and have noted the reluctance of Liberal constituency parties to rival it by picking working class candidates themselves. Henry Pelling has suggested Liberal decline might be:

'The result of long-term social and economic changes that were simultaneously uniting Britain geographically and dividing her inhabitants in terms of class.'
(H. Pelling, *A Short History of the Labour Party*, 1961)

But Paul Adelman argues:

'There is no hard evidence for the supposed demoralisation of the Liberal Party. Asquith's leadership was unquestioned, his government remained strong, unified and confident. It would be false to conclude that we are faced with a Liberal Party in decline in the years preceding the First World War.'
(*Modern History Review*)

Liberals stood for home rule, a minimal amount of social reform, and free trade. This was perhaps not enough, when, according to Alan Ball:

'At the end of the nineteenth century social class division replaced local issues and religious cleavages as the major dimensions of British politics.'
(A. Ball, *British Political Parties*, 1987)

## The Conservative 'image'

The key figure in the development of the mid-Victorian Conservative Party was Benjamin Disraeli. He appears at first to be an unlikely leader, as he was the son of a Jewish literary man; he was educated at obscure schools (and never went to university); he was almost arrested for debt; and he made such a disastrous maiden speech as an MP that it was howled down. However, Disraeli was very ambitious, he was highly gifted, and he was rather fortunate. He learned how to speak well, he befriended the wealthy Tory MP George Bentick and he married a wealthy lady. His attacks on Robert Peel's decision to scrap the Corn Laws brought him fame and party popularity and helped cause the split that removed the Peelite faction (including Gladstone) who would have barred his own progress. His political skills were displayed from 1867 to 1868, and in 1874–80 he finally led a Conservative ministry that had a clear majority. This ministry pushed through social reforms in public health and housing, in the safety of merchant shipping, and in trade union reform. Disraeli made much of his party's enthusiasm for the British Empire and for a vigorous foreign policy that placed British interests first. His biographer, Robert Blake, maintains:

'Disraeli made the Conservatives both the party of empire and the party of a strong, or as his enemies would have said, jingoistic foreign policy. There was nothing inevitable about this development. In Palmerston's day those were the attributes of the Whig/Liberal Party... From the 70s onwards, the Conservatives were identified with the cause of British nationalism, British ascendancy and the pursuit of purely British interests.'

(R. Blake, *Disraeli*, 1969)

Another historian sees further importance in Disraeli's career:

'Modern Conservatism['s]... electoral success since 1867 would have been impossible without its capacity to command a significant working class vote, and here it owes something to Disraeli's sense of the necessity of accepting the enlargement of the political nation and making the social condition of the people one of the prime objects of the party's concern.'

(P. Smith, *Disraelian Conservatism & Social Reform*, 1967)

However, not all historians are so enthusiastic. One of them has suggested:

'Disraeli held the Conservative Party together through a period of confusion in parliament. But the making of the Conservative Party... had to do with circumstances beyond Disraeli – with the death of Palmerston and the inevitable shift of his Conservative followers, with the disintegrating effect of Gladstone's leadership on the Liberals.'

(A. Tucker, *Canadian Journal of Economics and Political Science*, 1962)

In the 1880s the Conservatives benefited from the continuing drift to their ranks of wealthy men who had once been Whigs. They exploited the Liberal split over home rule and found their ranks swelled by Liberal Unionists. Indeed it has been suggested that the Irish question benefited them in other ways too, bringing support in Glasgow from anti-home rule members of the Orange Order and support in Liverpool from voters opposed to the flood of Irish Roman Catholic immigrants.

Parliamentary reform also helped. The redistribution of seats in 1885 was so managed as to create separate suburban Tory-voting constituencies in urban areas where such voters had once been swamped in larger electorates. As Salisbury himself suggested: 'there is a great deal of "Villa Toryism" that requires organisation.' Conservative leaders continued to stress that their party stood for the British Empire and for a vigorous foreign policy. They exploited Queen Victoria's Jubilee and Britain's eventual success in the Boer War.

But in the twentieth century these causes brought trouble. Firstly, Tories argued that Irish home rule attacked the empire and this led them to back Ulster's resistance to it. Eventually, as the official parliamentary opposition, they seemed to be supporting armed hostility to the policies of Britain's elected (Liberal) government. Then in 1903 Joseph Chamberlain led a campaign for tariff reform, which was intended to bind the British Empire more closely together, while taxing imports from foreign lands in order to protect British industries. But the campaign split the party and led to conflict outside parliament between the Tariff Reform League and the Free Food League.

Yet the Conservatives also remained aware that they needed to stand for reforms. The setting up of county councils, the limiting of shop hours, the Workmen's Compensation Act (for industrial injuries) of 1897, and the Education Act of 1902 were all signs of this continuing desire to be a party for more than just the wealthy.

Radical opponents like Lloyd George attacked the Conservatives as the party of the rich. In 1892 Lloyd George declared:

'What are the components of the Tory Party in our country? It contains practically the whole of the members of the privileged classes. Their numbers and far more their wealth and influence constitute the chief ingredients of its power. They must, therefore, wield its policy.'

(H. du Parcq, *Life of Lloyd George*, 1912)

It is certainly true that leaders like Lord Salisbury and A.J. Balfour came from aristocratic backgrounds. About a quarter of Edwardian Conservative MPs were wealthy landed gentry; and half came from industry and commerce, especially from certain trades like brewing (the consequence, perhaps, of the long-established pressure groups for temperance reform in the Liberal Party). But even the Liberals still had a few landowners and a good many businessmen, and the Conservatives were certainly well aware of the need for wider support. When a genuinely popular and cheap daily newspaper appeared – the *Daily Mail* – it supported them. And Salisbury understood the problem of finding policies to hold together the wealthy and the ordinary people. In 1886, he commented:

'The Tory Party is comprised of very varying elements and there is trouble and vexation of spirit in trying to make them work together. I think the classes and the dependants of class are the strongest ingredients in our composition, but we have to conduct our legislation so that we shall give some satisfaction to both classes and masses. This is especially difficult with the classes, because all legislation is rather unwelcome to them as tending to disturb the state of things with which they are satisfied.'

(P. Adelman, *Gladstone, Disraeli and Later Victorian Politics*)

In fact Salisbury led a party that had been very successful in widening its support from country towns and rural areas to include urban constituencies too. In 1900 Conservatives captured 177 borough seats in England and their strength in England remained formidable. Liberals became very dependent on Scottish and Welsh support.

## Party organisation

The increasing number of voters, the secret ballot, and anti-corruption legislation made it vital for a successful political party to develop an efficient and permanent organisation. The old ways of stitching together support were no longer enough. The spreading grip of political parties across the country can be seen in the fall in the number of seats that were not fought: in 1859 there were 383 uncontested constituencies, in January 1910 only seventy-five. The figures fluctuated, partly according to how united the Liberals were and how much money they could raise. The flight of rich people from the Liberals gave the Conservatives the edge here and Gladstone certainly regarded the heavy-spending brewers as serious opponents. Some of the uncontested seats were in Ireland where no one was prepared to stand against Nationalists. Nevertheless the general trend was down. More seats were fought regularly after 1880 than before, and such efforts required good organisation.

Voter registration played an important part in stimulating party growth. The electoral roll of voters was compiled in January (in England and Wales) and in November (in Scotland) from figures gathered earlier. When potential voters increased in number, making sure that one's supporters were registered developed into a major job. Registration took place before a revising barrister; and with him also objections could be raised about the voters one's opponents were attempting to register. In Newcastle in 1888–91, for example, Conservatives raised objections to 9500 names. Moreover regulations changed from time to time. In 1907 lodgers with their own front door key to a building were allowed to register as householders. Alert party agents were quick to boost their support by exploiting this. It thus became important for parties to have a large network of paid agents for this work, as well as to organise publicity, electioneering, and other tasks. By 1891 the agents of both the parties had formed professional bodies, with examinations, benevolent funds, and minimum salary scales.

Party agents worked alongside an expanding number of party clubs and branch associations. These clubs consisted usually of two or three rooms where drinks were served, billiards were provided and social events were organised. The clubs also served to help morale, recruit members, and provide volunteer labour.

The branch associations were made up of people seriously committed to their party's cause. Thus, while few MPs had to deal with organised parties in their constituencies in the 1860s, the situation had changed enormously by 1914. The Liberal Party especially experienced dramatic developments, which were spearheaded by Joseph Chamberlain's Birmingham Liberals. In 1865 this branch constructed a system of representatives elected by party members in wards, who came together in a general committee that decided policy and selected candidates for elections. Since the committee was large, an executive committee was formed, partly by ward-election, and partly from people nominated by the general committee. This was a far more organised system than had hitherto existed; it also threatened to push its policies at the party leadership, rather than doing meekly as it was told. Some leading Liberals were alarmed by it, finding it too American in style, and calling it rule by a caucus (i.e. minority). Nevertheless, numerous other urban Liberal associations copied that of Birmingham. In 1877 Chamberlain called a meeting of all such associations to establish the National Liberal Federation. Ninety-five branches took part. And this NLF threatened to be a very different organisation from the Liberal Central Association (set up in 1874 and run by party whips to raise money and to encourage the growth of loyal party branches). In 1877 the Whig leader Hartington complained of the NLF:

> 'It is almost certain to put the management into the hands of the most advanced men because they are the most active . . . to the exclusion of the more moderate and easy-going Liberals. There is a good deal of the American caucus system about it.'
> (P. Adelman, *Gladstone, Disraeli and Later Victorian Politics*)

The Birmingham caucus secretary from 1873, Frank Schnadhorst, emerged as NLF secretary too. Hartington had good reason to fear that the NLF was intended to be a Radical challenge to Whig power in the party. Chamberlain vigorously defended this new development, saying:

> 'Party is an instrument to achieve some more definite results than the return to office of a certain number of persons of undeclared opinions . . . At the present moment Liberals are at a loose end, each advocating some favourite reform.
> The Liberals of Birmingham have fully recognised the altered conditions under which they have to carry on their work. Owing to various causes, and notably to the extension of the suffrage and to the increased interest taken by the mass of the people in general politics, it is absolutely necessary that the whole of the party should be taken into its counsels and that all its members should share in its control and management. It is no longer safe to [accept] the nominee of a few gentlemen

... willing to subscribe something towards expenses... The object of a Liberal association should therefore be to secure a perfect representation of the opinions of the whole party.

Conservatism naturally works from above downwards while Liberalism best fulfils its mission when it works upwards from below.'

(A. Beattie, *English Party Politics*, Vol 1)

Certainly the Birmingham caucus proved to be very successful at winning all three local seats in general elections and at mounting effective campaigns in local elections. In the 1886 split the NLF remained loyal to Gladstone and drew closer to the Liberal Central Association. In the early twentieth century a new chief party agent, Hudson, emerged, and he worked well with his party's political leaders.

Liberal efforts had alarmed Conservative leaders, and even before the creation of the NLF had led them to form the National Union of Conservative and Constitutional Associations (1867). In 1870 Disraeli placed the very capable John Gorst in charge of this body and he developed the organisation that eventually became the Conservative Central Office. In 1881 he explained some of the work of this organisation:

'Enquiries are made as to the residence and qualification of the voters... Forms, instructions and advice are furnished. Local leaders are assisted in finding suitable candidates. Election literature is supplied. Formation of new associations is promoted and assisted. Speakers and hints for speakers are provided. Pamphlets, important speeches are printed and issued. All bills affecting the interests of the party are circulated amongst the local leaders.'

(A. Beattie, *English Party Politics*, Vol 2)

Whereas Liberal associations developed as pressure from below, seeking at times to influence policy, their Conservative counterparts were a response to orders from above and they were expected to do as they were told. In the early 1880s Gorst and Randolph Churchill made a brief attempt to give the National Union more power to challenge party leadership, but it came to nothing.

In 1881 the Conservatives established the Primrose League, named after what was thought to be Disraeli's favourite flower and colour. By 1910 it had two million subscribing members. The League did not indulge in detailed policy discussions; instead it rallied volunteer support for the party and, between elections, organised concerts, fêtes, outings and other social occasions. It proved invaluable in holding together party supporters and, especially, in drawing women to the Conservative cause. Nursing a constituency in between elections had become a very important activity. In 1892 the Wiltshire *County Mirror* observed that candidates won votes by:

> '. . . the visit to the village feasts, the chat in the village
> schoolroom, or pleasant friendly musical evenings in the
> winter.'
>
> (H. Pelling, *Social Geography of British Elections*, 1967)

The voters of the 1850s would scarcely have recognised the activities characteristic of the election in 1910. The number of voters, the relatively humble status of many of these voters, the secret ballot, the party efforts to turn out their supporters, the absence of large-scale open bribery, and the importance attached to party leaders and national issues were all signs of a transformed political world.

# The growth of the Labour Party

A voter going to the polls in mid-Victorian times would have looked in vain for a Labour Party candidate. No Labour Party existed. Yet, in a general election held in December 1910, forty-two Labour MPs were returned to parliament. This development raises two issues: Why did a distinct Labour Party emerge? And what did this Labour Party stand for? These issues imply questions about the *ideology* and *identity* of Labour.

Some historians suggest that the growth of the Labour Party was the consequence of conditions at the time. Others argue that its growth was far from inevitable.

## TASK

What arguments might have been put forward in 1914 at a meeting of their respective parties by
- a Liberal alarmed by Labour's rise?
- a Liberal unconcerned by Labour's rise?
- a Labour leader defending his party's record?
- a Labour member attacking his party's record?

Work in small groups to research some of the reasons for the rise of the Labour Party. Each group member should choose one of the roles just described; he or she should research the role from material already studied and from material in this chapter, by gathering, noting and organising relevant evidence. Then the group members should discuss their findings and draw upon them to list views and evidence relevant to the emergence of the Labour Party and what it stood for.

# *Favourable times*

Did conditions in the late nineteenth century produce the Labour Party? Certainly several socialist societies and labour clubs were set up at this time. Why? Some possible reasons follow.

## The spread of the franchise

By 1885 far more men could vote than twenty years earlier, and voting now took place in secret. Many working men, therefore, were encouraged to take an interest in politics. Some might even hope to become MPs, for in 1868 the rule requiring MPs to be considerable property owners had been swept away.

## Social and economic conditions

Changing social and economic conditions seemed more favourable for the rise of socialism in the late nineteenth century. Working people had more time for politics and there was a greater likelihood of their being able to read the numerous newspapers and magazines of the time. These publications included some, like Robert Blatchford's *Clarion*, that favoured reforms which would benefit the lives of ordinary people. In addition, it was easier to travel to meetings. It did not cost much to travel by the electric trams of the 1890s; and some skilled workers of the 1900s might even aspire to the ownership of a bicycle. As travel became easier and Britain's urban population grew, so the wealthier moved out to the suburbs. This left considerable areas – about ninety-five corresponded to parliamentary constituencies – which were dominated by working class housing. Amid this housing stood libraries where books were freely available, schools where education was provided, mechanics institutes where education was encouraged, and chapels where workers could develop public-speaking skills. Later Labour leaders like Philip Snowden were warm in praise of their chapel training.

## The spread of socialist thinking

Writers spread socialist thinking through a number of popular books. For example, though the American Harry George would not have called himself a socialist, he argued for large-scale land reform in *Progress and Poverty* (1883). He maintained:

> 'Everywhere you find distress and destitution in the midst of wealth, you will find that the land is monopolised; that instead of being treated as the common property of the whole people it is treated as the private property of individuals.'

Over 100,000 copies of George's book sold in Britain in the 1880s. The author made a triumphant tour too.

The poet, designer and artist William Morris also argued for the transformation of society. He became a socialist when he despaired of the Liberal middle class ever really committing themselves to reform, saying:

'as to real social changes, they will not allow them if they can help it. I can see no use in people having political freedom unless they use it as an instrument of leading reasonable lives; no good in education if, when they are educated, people have only slavish work to do. This release from slavery, it is clear, cannot come to people so long as they are subjected to the bare subsistence wages that are a necessity for competitive commerce.'

In a very popular work entitled *Merrie England*, Robert Blatchford described how life would be improved if only society were reorganised:

'I would set men to work to grow wheat and fruit and rear cattle and poultry for our own use. Then I would develop the fisheries and construct great fish breeding lakes. Then I would restrict our mines, finances, chemical works and factories to a number actually needed for the supply of our own people. Then I would stop the smoke nuisance by developing water power and electricity. In order to achieve these ends I would make all the land, mills, mines, factories, works, shops, ships and railways the property of the people. I would have towns rebuilt with wide streets and detached houses, with gardens and fountains. I would have public parks, public theatres. I would have all our children fed and clothed and educated at the cost of the State. I would have the people become their own artists, actors, musicians, solicitors and police.'

The enormously popular novels of Charles Dickens encouraged people to think about social conditions. And investigators like Charles Booth, William Booth and Seebohm Rowntree wrote different kinds of works, carefully conducting interviews and compiling facts and figures which showed the poverty and misery of many lives.

Karl Marx, the greatest socialist thinker of all, spent the last thirty years of his life living in London, although he was German. He died in 1883. His major work *Das Kapital* was not translated into English until 1887; and it remained largely unread even by most social reformers of the time.

Skilled workers were more likely than unskilled ones to read reformers' works. On the railways, for example, it was reckoned that the train drivers were far more radically-minded than the porters (– perhaps the latter were affected by their partial dependence on tips from wealthy passengers).

# *Socialist and Labour societies*

During the last twenty years of the nineteenth century a number of influential organisations emerged that favoured a drastic overhaul of society and government.

*A 1907 rally of the Social Democratic Federation: the crowd includes Robert Tressell, the author of the influential book* The Ragged-Trousered Philanthopist.

## The Social Democratic Federation (1881)

This was one of the most socialist-minded of these groups. Yet, curiously, it was led by a respectably dressed top-hatted wealthy ex-Etonian, H. M. Hyndman. Hyndman was one of the few political figures of the time who had actually read *Das Kapital* (in 1881 he worked through a French translation). He had little time for trade unions, and his forceful and dominant personality drove away some of his early recruits, including William Morris, and Karl Marx's daughter Eleanor. The SDF developed branches across Britain, but its main power base lay in London among skilled workers. By the 1890s its membership may well have been around 2500. Its efforts in parliamentary elections met with complete failure, but in local council elections it did better.

# The Fabian Society (1884)

The Fabian Society shared Hyndman's suspicion of trade unions, but otherwise had little in common with the SDF. It adopted the name of the Roman general Fabius who won a war by avoiding open battle and by slowly wearing down enemy strength; the society aimed to spread its socialist ideas gradually through discussions, lectures and publications. It produced a huge array of pamphlets (which even included worthy topics like 'Allotments and How to Get Them'). Its members included the playwright Bernard Shaw, the sociologist Graham Wallas and Sidney Webb

*Sidney and Beatrice Webb, formidable workers and organisers, who did much to shape the character of the early Labour Party.*

and his formidable (and wealthy) wife Beatrice. The Webbs were influential members of investigating committees. Sidney Webb came to believe strongly in the work of councils and of government as a means of spreading socialism by slow reform. He wrote:

> 'Important changes can only be (1) democratic and thus acceptable to a majority of the people and prepared for in the minds of all, (2) gradual, thus causing no dislocation, (3) not regarded as immoral by the mass of the people and (4) in this country at any rate, constitutional and peaceful.'

# The Independent Labour Party (1893)

The Independent Labour Party found its early strength in northern Britain. It emerged first in 1893 in Bradford, a Yorkshire textile town where industrial troubles were common, and where no less than twenty-three local labour clubs had been set up. Within two years the ILP had 305 branches, 105 them in Yorkshire, seventy-three in Lancashire and Cheshire, and forty-one in Scotland. The party stood for practical reforms that would benefit working people. Its leaders were eager to co-operate with the trade unions. Because of this it decided to exclude the word 'socialist' from its title, so that it would not frighten away trade unionists who were used to looking to the Liberals as their allies. The ILP programme included demands for an end to child labour; proper provision for the sick, the disabled and the unemployed; and 'the collective ownership of the means of production, distribution and exchange'.

The ILP even had an MP, the Scottish ex-miner Keir Hardie. In 1888 Hardie had vainly tried to win a by-election in Mid Lanark. His experiences convinced him of the need to develop a distinct party for Labour. The Scottish Labour Party emerged from his efforts. Hardie realised the need to win trade union support. He rarely read books of socialist theory. His temperance upbringing, however, remained very much with him: once he was in parliament, Hardie tried hard to keep fellow Labour MPs away from of the bar.

Ramsay MacDonald, an equally important figure, was drawn to Labour by a similar feeling of frustration with the Liberal Party. MacDonald came from the Scottish fishing port of Lossiemouth. Like Hardie he had to overcome a background of poverty and illegitimacy.

A third early ILP leader, Philip Snowden, recalled:

'many young men who were Nonconformist local preachers were attracted to the movement by the ethical appeal of Socialism. Their experience in speaking was a great help to the Party propaganda. The movement was something new in politics. It was politics inspired by idealism and religious fervour. Vocal Unions were formed which accompanied cycling corps into the country at weekends and audiences were gathered on village greens by the singing of choirs.'

(Philip Snowden, *An Autobiography*)

In 1892 Hardie won a by-election in West Ham, an area where the SDF was active. Two other ILP men won seats – John Burns in Battersea, and Havelock Wilson in Middlesborough. Hardie always remained loyal to the ILP, but the latter two MPs drifted over to the Liberals.

Socialist enthusiasm showed itself in many ways. There were socialist swimming clubs, socialist scouts and socialist cycling clubs. Aided by the invention of the pneumatic tyre in 1888, members of the latter sped about the country combining business with pleasure. Yet parliamentary success was hard to come by. In 1895 all twenty-eight ILP candidates were defeated. The handful of working men who sat in parliament following the break-through by Thomas Burt and Alexander MacDonald in 1874 were likely to be Liberals.

The ILP remained short of money and ramshackle in organisation. Nor were its social reforms necessarily popular. Reforms in Victorian times meant interfering officials; the loss to a family of children's earnings; the burden of school fees; and the hated poor-law guardians. The clearance of slums left poorer families even more crowded than ever, so inadequate was the building of new homes that they could afford.

It was little wonder that Hardie visited the TUC in 1887 to plead for it to support the separate political organisation that the ILP represented.

## Trade union support

Unions of mid-Victorian times had little to do with politics. Their limited aims were summarised in 1867 by one of their number:

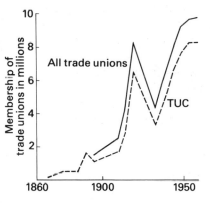

E. J. Hobsbawm,
*Industry and Empire*, 1968.

*Trade Union membership 1860–1960.*

"The South Yorkshire Miners Association has many objects. First, to raise from time to time by contribution among the members, funds for the purpose of mutual support. Secondly, striving to obtain better legislation for the efficient management of mines. Thirdly, compensation for accidents. Fourthly, to assist all members when unjustly dealt with by their employers. Fifthly, a weekly allowance to members when injured following their employment. Sixthly, a grant at the death of any member caused by accident while following their employment. Seventhly, to shorten the hours of labour. The benefits of our local lodges are, a weekly allowance to members when sick, and allowance at the death of any member [or] member's wife.'

(H. Browne, *The Rise of British Trade Unions*, 1979)

These benefits came from subscriptions that only well-paid skilled workers like engineers and carpenters could afford. Attempts to form unions among the less skilled were more difficult to sustain.

Nevertheless, the unions that did exist were alarmed by the bad publicity they were getting and concerned about changes in the law that might threaten them, so delegates from them came together in 1868 to form the Trades Union Congress. The TUC's Parliamentary Committee watched over their political interests. The TUC's secretary from 1875 to 1890, Henry Broadhurst, sat in parliament as an MP – but as a Liberal.

Hardie wanted the unions to support a separate political organisation. Events in the last twenty years of the nineteenth century drove some unions to respond to Hardie's appeals for help. These events were as follows.

## Foreign competition

This increasingly challenged the supremacy of British industry. It led employers to try to cut their costs by reducing wages and lengthening hours of work.

*In the late nineteenth century there was an upsurge of union activity: this meeting is a gathering of gas workers in London whom Will Thorne led with great skill.*

## New unions

New unions emerged which sought mass membership (rather than a membership of limited numbers of skilled workers), and which behaved aggressively in their battles to establish themselves. In 1888, for example, Will Thorne helped to develop a union for gas workers. In 1889–90 this union held strikes in the provinces that succeeded in reducing the length of shifts. Unskilled workers in building trades and on the railways began to get organised. The Seaman's and Fireman's Union swelled to 65,000.

Older unions changed too. Some of them merged to form more powerful bodies like the National Miners Association, organised by a Scot, Alexander MacDonald, and the National Union of Railwaymen (1913) formed from three separate unions. This whole development was encouraged by two successful strikes: in

*The Bryant and May match girls won widespread support with protest marches and petitions in their battle for better pay and conditions.*

*Dockers celebrating the triumphant end to the 1889 dock strike.*

1888 workers in Bryant and May's match factory won a battle about the dangerous, disgusting and ill-paid circumstances in which they toiled; and in the following year Ben Tillett and Tom Mann led a lengthy strike for better pay in the London docks.

## The spread of socialism among the unions

The attitude of employers (some of whom were Liberals) encouraged trade unionists to think of supporting socialism. In addition, trade unionists eager to enter politics found that, even at a local level, the Liberal Party preferred to choose wealthier candidates; and this encouraged such men to think of the need for a separate party. The changing mood of the times can be seen in the start of May Day celebrations in 1890 in London, when people marched along singing the new socialist song, 'The Red Flag'.

## Counter-attacks by employers

Employers mounted successful counter-attacks. By 1894 Tillett's union had been ousted from the docks. Employers also increasingly used non-union labour, helped by the setting up of an organisation to supply them, for in 1893 William Collison, an anti-union ex-bus driver, formed the National Free Labour Association. Moreover, employers began to group themselves. In 1894 the Federation of Engineering Employers was set up, and in 1898 a parliamentary committee was formed to protect employers' interests.

## Government and the law

An unsympathetic government and legal system seemed to be in control. The Conservatives tended to support the employers. The Liberals, badly beaten in 1895, seemed divided, and were chiefly concerned with imperial and church matters. In 1896 the attitude of the legal system was shown in the case of Lyons *vs*. Wilkins: through it union rights to picket were severely restricted.

All these factors led the TUC to vote in favour of a resolution put forward by a delegate from the Amalgamated Society of Railway Servants, a man who also happened to belong to the ILP:

### TUC resolution of 1899

'That this congress having regard to its decisions in former years and with a view in securing a better representation of the interest of Labour in the House of Commons hereby instructs the Parliamentary Committee to invite co-operation on lines mutually agreed upon in convening a Special Congress of representatives from such of the above-named organisations as may be willing to take part to devise ways and means for securing the return of an increased number of Labour members to the next Parliament.'

(H. Pelling, *The Origins of the Labour Party*)

In 1900 delegates from some unions met representatives from the ILP, SDF and the Fabians. The result was the setting up of a body for joint political action, the Labour Representation Committee. It was made up of seven trade unionists, two ILP delegates, two SDF delegates and a Fabian. It represented a triumph for Hardie's efforts to draw unions into backing a separate political organisation, and he thwarted SDF efforts to commit the LRC to openly socialist policies, for he felt that such policies might frighten away further union support. Yet the LRC was not strong. Its funds came chiefly from a levy on unions of 10s. for every thousand members. In the 1900 elections only two LRC men – Keir Hardie and Richard Bell – won seats. Bell proved to be a Liberal at heart, and in 1905 was expelled from the LRC.

# The emergence of the Labour Party

In 1901 the unions supporting the LRC represented 353,700 workers. By 1908 the number had grown to a million. Fear for their security lay behind this change. In 1901 the House of Lords upheld the Taff Vale Railway Company's case for damages and losses (because of a strike) against the Amalgamated Society of Railway Servants; the union was required to pay the full costs of the strike (totalling £42,000). Other unions were horrified at the implications of this, and LRC leaders were quick to declare that they would work to reverse this decision. The rush of new members also brought funds to fight elections.

*James Ramsay MacDonald during his time as Secretary of the Labour Representation Committee.*

These signs of strength helped the LRC's secretary, Ramsay MacDonald, to organise an electoral pact with the Liberal chief whip, Herbert Gladstone. Gladstone's secretary warned him:

'The LRC can directly influence the votes of nearly a million men. They will have a fighting fund of £100,000. Their members are mainly men who have hitherto voted with the Liberal Party. Should they be advised to vote against Liberal candidates and should they act as advised, the Liberal Party would suffer defeat. They would be defeated, but so also would we be defeated.'

By-election results seemed to bear out these fears. In 1901 the LRC split the anti-government vote in North-East Lanark and let in a Tory. In 1902–03 three by-elections (Clitheroe, Barnard Castle and Woolwich) were won by LRC men – David Shackleton, Arthur Henderson and Will Crooks. On major issues of the day, like free trade and Ireland, LRC and Liberals found themselves in agreement (especially since the SDF had left the LRC in 1901). Thus the LRC got a free run in a number of seats; and in return it agreed to give general support to the Liberal Party.

In the general election of 1906, what did LRC men stand for? In the view of one historian:

'The typical Labour candidate of the 1900s offered the electorate a battery of proposals including the 8 hour day, reversal of the Taff Vale decision, employers' liability, old age pensions, poor law reform, the feeding of necessitous school children, taxation of land values, free trade, Home Rule, nationalisation of mine royalties, payment of MPs, curtailment of the power of the House of Lords and universal suffrage. There was virtually nothing in this that was not acceptable to the new Liberals, or to the Gladstonians for that matter.'

(M. Pugh, *The Making of Modern British Politics*)

## Labour and the election of 1906

The election manifesto ran as follows:

'This election is to decide whether or not Labour is to be fairly represented in Parliament.
  The House of Commons is supposed to be the people's House and yet the people are not there.
  Landlords, employers, lawyers, brewers and financiers are there in force. Why not Labour?
  The Trade Unions ask the same liberty as capital enjoys. They are refused.
  The aged poor are neglected.
  The slums remain; overcrowding continues, while the land goes to waste.
  Shopkeepers and traders are overburdened with rates and taxation, whilst the increasing land values which should relieve the rate payers, go to people who have not earned them.
  Wars are fought to make the rich richer, and underfed school children are still neglected.
  The unemployed ask for work, the Government gave them a worthless Act and now the red herring of protection is drawn across your path.
  Production, as experience shows, is no remedy for poverty and unemployment. It seems to keep you from dealing with the land, housing, old age and other social problems.
  You have in your power to see that Parliament carries out your wishes. The Labour Representation Executive appeals to you in the name of a million Trade Unionists.'

Twenty-nine candidates met with success, twenty-four of them in seats where no Liberal opposed them. The movement now changed its name to 'Labour Party' and pressed the Liberals for reforms.

The Liberals of 1906–14 included men like Lloyd George who were eager to effect a number of reforms anyway. Certainly the 1906 Trade Disputes Act was directed at helping the unions by reversing the Taff Vale decision. Reductions in miners' working hours and control on certain 'sweated' trades – occupations like tailoring that took place in small workshops – pleased Labour too. Other Liberal social reforms were welcomed in general, but often sharply criticised in detail – generally for being too limited and mean.

It would be difficult to argue that the Liberal reforms were chiefly due to Labour pressure. By 1910 Labour found it difficult to know what to do. Elections were expensive, and it did not dare to risk bringing down the Liberals, yet the Liberals seemed chiefly concerned with matters other than those pressed by Labour.

A further threat to Labour came in 1909. A Liberal trade unionist, Walter Osborne, objected to his railway union using part of his union subscription to support Labour. The House of Lords decided in Osborne's favour, thus preventing unions from contributing to political causes from their general funds and threatening the whole financial security of the Labour Party. In 1911 the Liberal Government gave partial relief by introducing salaries of £400 a year for MPs. Lloyd George argued:

> 'The work of Parliament is greater, it is greater in quantity and volume of work, it is very much greater in the attention it demands at the hands of each individual member.
>
> In the old days we had only two classes here. We had the great country families and the legal profession. Since then you have brought in one class after another – the great middle class – the labouring population and factory representation. There is a large and growing class whose presence in this House is highly desirable, men of wide culture, of high intelligence and of earnest purpose whose services would be invaluable but whose limited means prevent their taking up a political career.'

*The Times* newspaper grumbled:

> 'It is perfectly well known that the Government have no conviction and that payment of members would never have been proposed by them were it not that they do not know how to meet the deficiency of dealing with the Osborne judgement. They know well that their expedient must have permanent and far-reaching consequences which will be evil. The whole thing is merely a gambler's throw. The Labour Party are quite ready to take the payment, but they have made it plain that they do not relinquish their demand for the reversal of the Osborne judgement.'
>
> (*The Times*, 10 August 1911)

By the end of 1910, a year in which two elections were held, the number of Labour MPs had risen to forty-two. This growth was especially due to the Miners Federation's decision to join the party. Could Labour look forward to an ever more effective role in the future?

# The failure of Labour?

The Labour Party's fortunes from 1910 to 1914 have made historians consider how secure and effective a party it really was. There are a number of points to think about.

## Labour's relationship with the Liberals

It took two years for the Liberals to offset partially the Osborne judgement by bringing in MPs' salaries. It took a further two years for them to modify the law itself through the Trade Union Act (1913). Even this did not wholly reverse the Osborne judgement. Unions that wished to back a political party financially had to keep separate funds for this purpose; and this could only take place after a ballot of their members on whether they wanted their union to affiliate to a party. Indeed members had to give their individual agreement to providing financial support. The Liberal leadership seemed to take little account of Labour needs, yet Labour did not dare to strike out on its own and end its electoral pact.

## Election results 1910–14

In these years Labour fought fourteen by-elections and came third in all of them. These by-elections included several contests for seats Labour had held; as a result the number of Labour MPs had shrunk by 1914 to a total of thirty-six.

## Quarrels in the Labour Party

The Party seemed divided and quarrelsome, especially on the issue of how far Labour should commit itself to socialism. A typical debate flared up in the Labour Party summer conference in 1907 from which this extract is taken:

'W. Atkinson moved
1. This annual conference of the Labour Party hereby declares that its ultimate object should be the obtaining for the workers the full results of their labour by the overthrow of the present competitive system of capitalism and the institution of a system of public ownership and control of all means of life.

2. To organise and maintain a Parliamentary Labour Party with its own whips and whose policy shall be in the direction of attaining the above and also of carrying out the decisions of the annual conference.

Pete Curran (Gas Workers) said that as a Socialist he opposed this amendment of the constitution. The socialist section was bound in honour to acknowledge that the delegates had not yet declared in favour of class conscious principles. Seven years ago they decided that the Trade Unionists, Socialists and Co-operators should form an alliance for the purpose of bringing into existence an independent political party. The idea that permeated this amendment was to switch the movement to what was called class-conscious lines. The Trade Unionists who made up the bulk of the movement and contributed the funds of the Movement would not pledge themselves in this class conscientiousness.

J. Keir Hardie (ILP), "Suppose this amendment were carried? What followed would be that only men who were Socialists could be MPs. Was it desirable that those MPs who were not Socialists should be cleared out?" '

(A. Beattie, *English Party Politics Vol. II*)

98,000 voted in favour, 835,000 against.

In 1907 Victor Grayson won Colne Valley for Labour and proceeded to attack MacDonald and his colleagues. In 1911 some frustrated ILP members joined with the SDF to form the British Socialist Party. Yet MacDonald led Labour for most of this period. He had to withstand intense criticism. Ben Tillett, hero of the 1889 dockers' strike wrote:

'I do not hesitate to describe the conduct of these blind leaders as nothing short of betrayal. They have displayed greater activity for temperance reform than for labour interests. A great many victims to destitution will be in their graves before the Liberal Government will have approached the subject of unemployment, which they will sandwich between the abolition of the House of Lords and Welsh Disestablishment. The temperance section in particular will be seizing on the other 'red herrings' and the winter will have passed and these unctuous weaklings will go on prattling their nonsense, while thousands are dying of starvation.'

(Ben Tillett, *Is the Parliamentary Labour Party a Failure?*, 1908)

And Beatrice Webb, one of the Fabian leaders, complained:

'J. R. MacDonald seems almost preparing for his exit from the ILP. I think he would welcome a really conclusive reason for joining the Liberal Party. Snowden is ill, Keir Hardie 'used up'. The rank and file are puzzled and disheartened. The cold truth is that the Labour members have utterly failed to impress the House of Commons and the constituencies as a live force and have lost confidence in themselves and each other. The Labour Movement rolls on. The Trade Unions are swelling in membership and funds, more candidates are being put forward, but the faith of politically active members is becoming dim or confused whilst the rank and file become every day more restive. There is little leadership but a great deal of anti-leadership.'

(*Beatrice Webb's Diaries*, 1914)

## Trade union developments

The years from 1911 to 1914 were a time of great industrial unrest, with strikes and lockouts on a sizeable scale. During this time trade union membership rose from two to over four million; a number of big unions were formed (like the NUR and the National Transport Workers Federation), and three of the bigger unions – the Miners, the Railwaymen and the Transport Workers – formed a 'Triple Alliance' to support one another. To some, it seemed that this was the way to change society – by the direct action of unions, not through the Labour Party. Tom Mann led such 'syndicalists', borrowing ideas from similar movements in France and Spain. The syndicalist views were expressed in a pamphlet in 1912 backed by the South Wales Miners and partly written by A. J. Cook, a man who was to trouble Labour leaders in later years. The aim of the authors was to create

'One organisation to cover the whole of the coal, ore, slate, stone, clay, salt, mining and quarrying industry of Great Britain, with one Central Executive . . .

[With the aim] That the organisation shall engage in political action both local and national, on the basis of complete independence of, and hostility to all capitalist parties, with an avowed policy of wresting whatever advantage it can for the working man.
**General**
Alliances [are] to be formed and trades organisation favoured with a view to steps being taken to amalgamate all workers into one national and international union to work for the taking over of all industries by the workmen themselves. The suggested organisation is constructed to fight rather than to negotiate.'

(W. H. B. Court, *British Economic History 1870–1917*, 1965)

However, the evidence shows that these years were not entirely gloomy for Labour.

## Union affiliation

Despite legal threats, union affiliation to Labour continued, and by 1914 covered a million and a half workers. In addition, the separate political funds required by the 1913 Trade Union Act may in fact have helped Labour: money for the Party was now specially laid aside – it did not have to compete with other demands in a general fund.

## Trade unionists' attitudes

Most trade unionists were not syndicalists. The Triple Alliance did not have political aims, and the disputes of the period were about the usual issues of wages, hours and conditions. The tensions of 1910–14 may even have helped Labour by widening the gulf between the Liberal middle classes and the trade unionists.

## Local politics

In local politics Labour was a growing force. As early as 1898 the Party captured West Ham council, and proceeded to give its workers two weeks' annual holiday, eight-hour working days and £1.10s. per week minimum wages. Election results show Labour's rise:

| Labour in municipal elections | | |
|---|---|---|
| **Year** | **Candidates** | **Number elected** |
| | **Labour** **SDF/BSP** | |
| 1907 | 274       66 | 86 |
| 1908 | 313       84 | 109 |
| 1909 | 422      133 | 122 |
| 1910 | 281       49 | 113 |
| 1911 | 312       32 | 157 |
| 1912 | 463       95 | 161 |
| 1913 | 442       52 | 196 |

## A new party

Labour was a very new party. Some of its problems were due to its very limited organisation. Paid party agents played a vital part in the complicated electoral procedures of the time by making sure that supporters were properly registered; but in 1912 Labour had only seventeen agents, while the Liberals had nearly 300! Given time, and the money that the unions eventually provided, progress might be made. Certainly MacDonald worked hard to develop the Party organisation.

## The *Daily Herald*

In 1911 Labour gained the support of a successful popular newspaper – George Lansbury's *Daily Herald*.

## Electoral reform

Some people thought that widening the vote to include all adults might benefit Labour. The Party supported suffragists, who sought the vote for women by peaceful means. It also demanded the vote for all adults. Yet whether this would really benefit Labour was not clear: MacDonald thought that

> 'in places like the Potteries where poverty and degradation is of the blackest kind, the Labour Party is bound to be weak.'
>
> (Quoted in M. Pugh, *Modern British Politics*)

The Great War, however, was to have a sharp impact on Labour fortunes.

## ESSAY

Historians have drawn different conclusions about the situation of the Labour Party before 1914. Choose one of the three following views and plan an essay that will discuss it.

1. 'The Labour Party's growth in the early twentieth century was inevitable, given the social and economic issues of the time.' (K. Laybourn, *The Rise of Labour*)
2. 'The end of this period (to 1914) found the Labour Party dependent upon the Liberals, dissatisfied with its achievements, unsure of its aim and apparently in decline.' (C. Brand, *The British Labour Party*)
3. 'There are no real grounds in voting behaviour for believing Labour to have been poised to take over from the Liberals in 1914, on the contrary, without the protection of the pact the Parliamentary Party would have been reduced to a handful.' (M. Pugh, *Modern British Politics*)

# Political power in action

By late Victorian times politicians who were in power had to face growing demands to improve British society. The material in this chapter deals with one of the issues that faced them: What should the state do for people living in great hardship?

This issue compelled politicians to consider if they thought it right to intervene, i.e. it is an issue concerned with *ideology*. It is also concerned with how far politicians were able to intervene, i.e. it deals with the *authority* of politicians in power. Politicians who considered this issue had to reach a view on the kind of *identity* they felt British society ought to have.

## TASK

Work through the sources in this chapter to
- list the reasons why some people believed that the state should intervene in people's lives as little as possible
- list the reasons why others argued that the state had to do far more

- indicate what the state had actually done by the end of the Victorian period
- decide why you think people differed on the issue of state interference.

# Differing views in late Victorian times

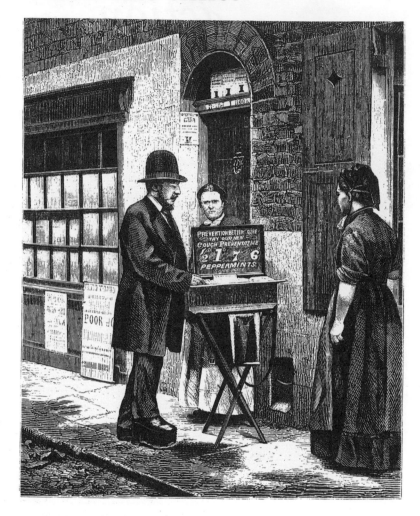

*A travelling salesman of the 1900s offers customers a pre-NHS range of cures for illnesses.*

## *Views that questioned state interference*

### Encouraging the poor?

A number of people argued that it would be wrong to encourage people in need to think that they could always count on the government to come to their aid. One of the most famous of these was Samuel Smiles. Smiles was born in Haddington near Edinburgh. He was not totally opposed to all state action, for he believed there had to be laws to stop the ill-usage of people and other laws to try to prevent the spread of diseases. He supported the educational reforms of 1870 (1872 in Scotland) that required the setting up of elementary schools for all children. John Stuart Mill, the philosopher, had suggested:

> 'Letting alone should be the general practice, every departure from it, unless required by some good, is a certain evil.'

So Smiles in fact saw reasons for a number of 'departures' from the policy of 'letting alone' (or *'laissez-faire'*). He might well not have gone as far as *The Times* in expressing hostility to government regulations and laws when it declared (10 August 1854) that it was better

> 'to run the risk of cholera and the rest than to be bullied into health'.

In an age when even Albert, the Prince Consort, was killed by typhoid, such views were decreasingly common!

In 1859 Smiles published *Self-Help*, a book that become popular reading for Victorians. In it he suggested:

> '"Heaven helps those who help themselves" is a well-tried maxim, embodying in a small compass the results of vast human experience. The spirit of self-help is the root of all genuine growth in the individual; and, exhibited in the lives of many, it constitutes the true course of national vigour and strength. Help from without is often enfeebling in its effects, but help from within invariably invigorates. Whatever is done *for* men or classes, to a certain extent takes away the stimulus and necessity of doing for themselves; and where men are subjected to over-guidance and over-government, the inevitable tendency is to render them comparatively helpless.
>
> Even the best institutions can give a man no active help. Perhaps the most they can do is, to leave him free to develop and improve his individual condition. But in all times men have been prone to believe that their happiness and well-being were to be secured by means of institutions rather than by their own conduct. Hence the value of legislation as an agent in human advancement has usually been much over-estimated. No laws, however stringent, can make the idle industrious, the thriftless provident, or the drunken sober. Such reforms can only be effected by means of individual action, economy, and self-denial; by better habits, rather than by greater rights.'

## Weakness of character?

A number of people believed that people who were very poor lived in this condition because of their weakness of character. Norman Pearson, for example, wrote an account, *The Idle Poor*, that maintained:

'It is to be feared that the confirmed loafer and the habitual vagrant are seldom capable of being reformed. It is a mistake to suppose that the typical pauper is merely an ordinary person who has fallen into distress through adverse circumstances. As a rule he is not an ordinary person, but one who is constitutionally a pauper, a pauper in his blood and bones. He is made of inferior material, and therefore cannot be improved up to the level of the ordinary person... Speaking broadly, pauperism is a token of the inferior capacity which belongs to an inferior stock. The hereditary nature of this incapacity may lighten the moral reproach against the loafer and the vagrant, but emphasises the necessity of protecting the community against them, and, in particular, of protecting it against the perpetuation of the degenerate stocks which they represent.

This is an aspect of the case which, till lately, has been too much overlooked, but it is really the most important factor in the problem, seeing that it affects not only ourselves but our prosperity. On this ground alone the proper authorities should be invested with the power of segregating and detaining – permanently, if necessary – those who burden the present and imperil the future of our race.'

(Quoted in J. R. Hay, *The Development of the British Welfare State*)

Some of those holding harsh views about the personalities of the poor pointed in particular to how much they drank. Even Seebohm Rowntree, who was sympathetic to the plight of the needy, noted that in York there was a public house to every 230 people. In fact there was probably a gentle downward trend in drinking alcohol during Victorian times. An average of around 162 litres (of beer) per person a year in the 1850s had fallen to about 135 litres by the end of the century. Scottish temperance workers spread a vigorous anti-alcohol campaign across Britain. Some who believed the poor to be weak-minded tried to cut temptation by such reforms as limiting the opening hours of public houses or by banning betting off race-courses (in 1906).

*The scene inside a late nineteenth century Salvation Army hostel, Liverpool. The boxes held mattresses for the homeless to sleep on.*

## Charity

Numerous wealthy people worked hard to raise money to help the poor. Some of them felt this charitable approach was the only correct one to pursue, and that even it had to be carefully handled. The Charity Organisation Society tried to co-ordinate the work of different groups. In its report of 1876 it suggested:

'. . . it is a hurtful missuse of money to spend it on assisting the labouring classes to meet emergencies which they should themselves have anticipated and provided for. The working man does not require to be told that temporary sickness is likely now and then to visit his household; that time of slackness will occasionally come; that if he marries early and has a large family, his resources will be taxed to the uttermost; that if he lives long enough, old age will render him more or less incapable of toil – all these are the ordinary contingencies of a labourer's life, and if he is taught that as they arise they will be met by State relief or private charity, he will assuredly make no effort to meet them himself. A spirit of dependence, fatal to all progress, will be engendered in him, he will not concern himself with the causes of his distress or consider at all how the condition of his class may be improved; the road to idleness and drunkeness will be made easy to him ... One thing there is which true charity does require the working man to be told, and it is the aim of this Society to tell him, not in words merely, but in acts that cannot be confuted. We desire to tell him that those who are born to easier circumstances sympathise with the severe toil and self-denial which his lot imposes upon him; that many are standing beside him ready and even eager to help if proper occasion should arise; and that if he, or wife, or child should be stricken with protracted sickness, or with some special infirmity, such as we all hope to escape, there are those at hand who will gladly minister to his necessities, and do their best at least to mitigate the suffering which it may be beyond their power to remove.'

Octavia Hill spent much of her life trying to provide decent homes for poorly paid workers. Yet in 1888 she argued that the idea that charity was readily available could be harmful because:

'You discourage the habit of belonging to clubs, the habit of saving, the habit of purchasing things: you bring side by side the man who had laid by nothing, and is well cared for at a time when misfortune comes to him, and the man who has sacrificed something through his time of steady work ... people should keep clear from any danger of holding out to the poor hopes that something can be done for them that cannot be done; even inquiries set on foot by the Government raise very great hopes in the people ... the Mansion House Relief Fund raised extravagant hopes ... The people are exceeding sharp and the more their homes look miserable, the more they expect to get: the drink following the distribution of the Mansion House Relief Fund was something fearful.'

(Evidence to the House of Lords Select Committee on Poor Relief)

## Friendly societies

Friendly societies grew up to help people to save in case of sickness, old age and widowhood. By 1910 friendly societies had thirteen million members. In 1894, for example, one of the largest friendly societies, the Foresters, argued:

'The aim of the working class ought to be to bring about economic conditions in which there should be no need for distribution of state alms. The establishment of a great scheme of state pensions would legalise and stamp as a permanent feature of our social life the chronic poverty of the age. The desire of the best reformers is to remove the conditions that make that poverty so that every citizen shall have a fair chance not only of earning a decent wage for today but such a wage as shall enable him to provide for the future . . . Employers have presented carefully organised barriers to the workmen getting more wages . . . We have always held that the only object of [reform] was to transfer the burdens from employer to labour . . . Man is a responsible being. To rob him of his responsibilities is to degrade him. The working class should rise to the occasion and insist upon being capable of using their own wages to their own advantage.

(Quoted in J. R. Hay, *The Development of the British Welfare State*)

In addition, profit-making assurance companies like the Prudential were worried that state action might harm their business.

## The status quo

There were plenty of people who believed that the existing system of helping the poor that had been set up in 1834 (1845 in Scotland) was sufficient. This system required that those in desperate need should prove their plight; they then had to enter a workhouse, where conditions were deliberately made harsh so that they seemed 'less eligible' than conditions endured by badly paid but independent workers. In 1895, faced with the argument that the

*Inside the Poplar Workhouse, London, 1905. The Labour leader George Lansbury took a particular interest in this institution: such places helped to inspire Labour campaigns for state welfare.*

elderly ought to be entitled to pensions that would enable them to live in their homes, a Royal Commission decided:

> 'While we fully appreciate the humane motives of those who wish for the general extension of outdoor relief in the case of the aged, we cannot but feel that grave risk would be incurred if no definite tests were imposed dependent on the individual circumstances of each case; such, for example, as the requirement of a clear measure of destitution, and evidence of respectability and a reasonable endeavour on the part of the applicant to make provision for his old age in accordance with his means during his life, and of general independence of the rates until the failure of physical faculties has deprived him of the means of support. We also feel that it would be undesirable to interfere with the discretion at present exercised by the guardians in cases where the applicants have relatives in a position to keep them, who are withholding the assistance they might fairly be expected to give. We do not advise that persons should be relieved who are not really destitute, but we feel that evidence of an industrious or independent life is presumptive proof of thrift, and entitles the applicant to better treatment than the wastrel or drunkard . . . dependence on the rates . . . as the proper condition of the respectable poor in old age . . . seems to us fatal to that hope so generally expressed that pauperism is becoming a constantly diminishing evil, ultimately to disappear before the continuous progress of thrift and social well-being . . .'
>
> (Report of the Royal Commission on The Aged Poor, 1895)

## Legal action

At times politicians felt compelled to act. Yet both Liberals and Conservatives often did so in the belief that minimal action to cure an abuse was all that was required. Legislation prevented women and children from working below ground in mines, or from working very long hours in the textile factories. Terrible diseases like cholera and typhoid compelled politicians to pass health reform acts that increased the power of local authorities to improve street cleaning and water supply services, and to clear away slums. Yet when the Conservative, Richard Cross, introduced his 1875 Artisans Dwelling Act which allowed local councils to purchase compulsorily and clear away unhealthy housing areas, he declared:

> 'I take it as a starting point that it is not the duty of the Government to provide any class of citizen with any of the necessaries of life, and among [these] we must include . . . good and habitable dwellings. That is not the duty of the state because if it did so it would inevitably tend to make that class depend not on themselves but upon what was done for them

elsewhere . . . Nor is it wise to encourage large bodies to provide the working classes with habitations at greatly lower rents than the market value paid elsewhere . . . there is another point of view from which we may look . . . No one will doubt the propriety and right of the state to interfere in matters relating to sanitary laws.'

(Hansard)

As a result some city centres became more pleasant as slum housing was cleared away; but working class urban lives became more cramped, confined and overcrowded than ever before.

## *Views that favoured state action*
### The investigators

Pressure for action came from a number of different directions. By late Victorian times a more literate public with better access to newspapers and magazines could be reached by investigators eager to enlighten richer people about the misery in which many poor people lived. A whole range of people explored the distinct slum areas that had developed in cities after those who could afford it had moved out to the suburbs. Some of these explorers compared their journeys to those being made by other Europeans 'in darkest Africa'. William Booth (1829–1919), the founder of the Salvation Army, drew such comparisons; and he demanded for the people he had encountered a standard of living at least equal to that enjoyed by cab horses.

The Reverend Andrew Mearns's pamphlet, *The Bitter Cry of Outcast London*, made an especially powerful impact in 1883. He went to

*A queue of Londoners awaiting their Salvation Army breakfast of tea and bread.*

'pestilential human rookeries where tens of thousands are crowded together amidst the horrors which call to mind what we have heard of the middle passage of a slave ship. To get into them you have to penetrate courts reeking with poisonous gases

rising from accumulations of sewage and refuse, courts which rarely know the virtues of a drop of cleansing water, every room on these rotten and reeking tenements houses a family, often two... The State must make short work of iniquitous traffic and secure for the poorest the rights of citizenship, the right to live in something better than fever dens.'

## The evidence

Some investigators proceeded by systematically gathering evidence. The pioneer in this work was Charles Booth, a wealthy Liverpool ship-owner who came to London to open offices there. He heard the SDF claims that a quarter of Londoners lived in great poverty and, unconvinced, began his own enquiries. His work took up seventeen years of his life, from the mid-1880s on, and he filled seventeen books with findings which greatly altered his views. The evidence was published as *Life & Labour of the People of London*. Booth tried to proceed calmly and scientifically, finding classifications for the many people he interviewed:

'The classes into which the population of each of these blocks and districts is divided are the same as were used in describing East London, only somewhat simplified. They may be stated thus:

A. The lowest class – occasional labourers, loafers and semi-criminals.
B. The very poor – casual labour, hand-to-mouth existence, chronic want.
C and D. The poor – including alike those whose earnings are small, because of irregularity of employment, and those whose work, though regular, is ill-paid.
E and F. The regularly employed and fairly paid working class of all grades.

The proportions of the different classes shown for all London are as follows.

| | | | | |
|---|---|---|---|---|
| **A** (lowest) | 37,610 | or | .9 per cent | In poverty |
| **B** (very poor) | 316,834 | " | 7.5 per cent | 30.7 per |
| **C** and **D** (poor) | 939,293 | " | 22.3 per cent | cent |
| **E** and **F** (working class, comfortable) | 2,166,303 | " | 51.5 per cent | In comfort |
| **G** and **H** (middle class and above) | 749.930 | " | 17.8 per cent | 69.3 per cent |
| | 4,209,970 | | 100 per cent | |

Inmates of
Institutions                    99,830

                                4,309,800

Booth concluded

'What might be an admissable state of things in days past is admissible no longer. It drags us back and has become a question of the first importance.'

Booth showed that low pay, lack of regular work, supporting large families, illness, and old age were major causes of poverty. (Around 15 per cent of the very poor were so placed, he suggested, because of drink, laziness and character defects.) Booth became an advocate of government action, such as the introduction of pensions for all.

Other investigators wondered whether London's conditions were unique. Seebohm Rowntree, a member of the wealthy York chocolate-manufacturing family, explored his native town. He concluded in 1901 in *Poverty, A Study of Town Life*:

'We have been accustomed to look upon poverty in London as exceptional, but when the result of careful investigation shows that the proportion of poverty in London is practically equalled in what may be regarded as a typical provincial town, we are faced by the startling probability that from 25 to 30 per cent of the town populations of the United Kingdom are living in poverty.'

Rowntree made careful use of recent scientific work to establish what a family needed to earn to buy adequate food and fuel and to pay the rent. He concluded that 52 per cent of the very poor were paid wages too low to sustain an adequate life. Around 21 per cent of families lived in misery because the chief wage earner had died, or was too ill or too old to work. Rowntree's statistics showed 2229 houses sharing 155 water taps, 353 houses sharing 58 closets, and 247 infants per 1000 people in poor areas dying before the age of one compared with 94 infants per 1000 in families wealthy enough to hire servants.

## The officials

Officials employed to make sure that factory or health regulations were obeyed, doctors hired as medical officers of health by local authorities, and school inspectors, all added their evidence to the case that more should be done.

Medical officers of health, for example, drew up reports like this one in Salford:

'Our medical officer's report to the education committee in 1905 noted outbreaks among children of "small-pox, typhus fever, enteric fever, scarlet fever and diptheria", only a few of the diseases mentioned. "A large proportion of the pupils", the report added, "show signs of rickets." There has been considerable distress during the winter, but the children had "much appreciated the free breakfasts provided". Some went hungry every day.'

(R. Roberts, *The Classic Slum*, 1971)

A Lambeth Schools inspector commented that in his view:

'Want of food, irregularity and unsuitability of food taken together are the cause of degeneracy in children. The breakfast that these children get is normally bread and tea, if they get it at all. There is bread and margarine for lunch and dinner is normally nothing but what a copper coin can purchase at the local fried fish shop. They supplement this with rotten fruit which they collect beneath barrows. One of the most important points is the absence of fresh milk.'

(Quoted in T. Barber (ed) *The Long March of Everyman*, 1975)

Parliament itself ordered a number of enquiries into social problems that were carried out by groups of experts called Royal Commissions.

So behind the changes, and pressures for changes, lay a growing quantity of information that could be popularised in newspapers and read by a better educated population.

## Employers

Some employers were persuaded of the need for action, including members of the Rowntree and Cadbury families; William Lever, a soap maker; and Sir John Brunner, a chemical manufacturer. For some it was a matter of Christian conscience; but others felt that having a capable, peaceful workforce meant making sure that workers were healthy and well cared for. Thus John Macauley, the manager of docks in south Wales, argued in 1907:

'A great deal could also be done to lessen the effect of occasional unemployment by making insurance against sickness and old age compulsory to the extent of a definite percentage of a man's or woman's earnings. For this purpose the many friendly societies might with advantage be amalgamated and placed under the control of the state. All forms of sweating labour should be abolished, as well as the employment of child labour.'

(Royal Commission on The Poor Laws 1905–09)

## The politicians

Victorian politicians acted from time to time: both Conservatives and Liberals introduced housing, health and educational reforms.

The socialist and Labour societies were particularly keen on state action. Sidney Webb, a leading member of the Fabian society, believed that by 1902 a great deal had been done (perhaps by accident) as a result of piecemeal steps taken to increase the

power of local authorities. He described how it was possible for a
councillor to

'walk along the municipal pavement, lit by municipal gas and
cleansed by municipal brooms with municipal water and seeing
by the municipal clock in the municipal market that he is too
early to meet his children coming from the municipal school
hard by the municipal hospital will use the national telegraph
system to tell them not to walk through the municipal park but
to come by the municipal tramway to meet him in the
municipal reading room by the municipal art gallery, museum
and library.'

(D. Fraser, *The Evolution of the British Welfare State*, 1973)

Webb regarded these as strong foundations on which to build.
But, in 1902 at least, he expected little from the Liberals. He saw
their leadership as still living in the past, unable

'to turn over a new leaf and devote themselves to obtaining the
greatest possible development of municipal activity, the most
comprehensive extension of the Factory Acts, or the fullest
utilisation of the Government departments in the service of the
public. They are aiming at something else, namely the abstract
right of the individual to lead exactly the kind of life that he
likes (and can pay for) unpenalised by any taxation for purposes
of which he individually disapproves.'

(K. O. Morgan, *The Age of Lloyd George*, 1971)

Eagerness for action was not simply felt by socialists. As early
as 1885 Joseph Chamberlain had put forward a Radical Programme
in which it was argued:

'The evil effects of overcrowding upon the poorer classes of our
large towns is now generally recognised, . . . [and] it is to the
interest of all in the community to do away with these evils . . .
For under such conditions of life the workman, even if looked
upon merely as an instrument to produce wealth, is not nearly
so valuable to the community as he might be . . . The result of
the improvements undertaken in Paris under Napoleon has been
to reduce the mortality by one-half. But medical statistics show
that for every person who dies in this way, six persons are ill,
and the consequential loss to the community of
wealth-producing power is enormous. The interests of one class
cannot be separated from those of another. "The advance of
pathological knowledge," writes Dr Bristowe, "proves that
most, if not all, epidemic disorders spread by contagion."

While re-housing may be looked upon as an insurance paid
by the better class against disease, it may also be regarded as an
insurance paid by the rich against revolution. It is in the interest
of all in the community that the workman should become a
better instrument of production, that his dwelling should not be

a hotbed of disease, that his degradation and misery should not be a constant source of danger to the state. The warning of Danton must be heeded, "If you suffer the poor to grow up as animals they may chance to become wild beasts to rend you."

The State has too long made itself the champion of the rights of the individual; it must assert the rights of the many – of all. It is apparent that in open competition the fittest obtain more than they deserve, and the less fit come too near perishing . . . The generation of workmen now coming to manhood will at least be able to read; no doubt they will quickly learn that their claims were long ago admitted to be right and equitable. For the privileged classes long to refuse payment of these claims is impossible; to refuse by instalments is equally impolitic and unjust.'

(Ed. H. W. Lucy, *Speeches of Rt. Hon. Joseph Chamberlain*, 1885)

In 1886 Chamberlain was in power, in charge of the Local Government Board whose task it was to oversee the work of local boards and councils. It was a period of high unemployment, and he urged local councils to run public work schemes that would provide paid employment for the out-of-work, free of the shame of the poor law. This marked a tendency that was to develop in later years.

The debate over how the poor should be helped was, by 1905, clearly expressed in the arguments offered to and by a Royal Commission that spent the next four years studying poverty, its causes and its remedies. Even at this late date it was possible to hear arguments that had raged through late Victorian times. J. S. Davy, head of the Poor Law division of the local Government Board spoke for the old system and its 'less eligibility' requirement. Paupers should suffer, he said

'the loss of personal reputation, second the loss of personal freedom which is secured by detention in a workhouse and third the loss of political freedom by suffering disenfranchisement.'

(Royal Commission on The Poor Laws, 1905–09)

On the other hand a Royal Commission minority made up of a church minister, a trade unionist, a Labour politician and Beatrice Webb, Sidney's wife, wanted the old system swept away; the setting up of a Ministry of Labour; the organising of labour exchanges; retraining and public works programmes in times of depression; and local authority control over a range of welfare provisions.

After 1905 the problem of deciding what to do fell to a Liberal Government.

# Action in the pre-war years

In 1905 the Conservative Government of the time resigned. A Liberal Ministry led by Sir Henry Campbell-Bannerman took its place, called an election in 1906, and swept back into office: 401 Liberals and their Labour and Irish allies faced 157 Conservatives. Men like H. H. Asquith and David Lloyd George served in this Government till Asquith became Prime Minister in 1908. Asquith's Chancellor of the Exchequer (Lloyd George) and President of the Board of Trade (Winston Churchill) were especially eager to tackle the issue of the hardship endured by so many British citizens.

## TASK

Consider these questions by working through the following material, bearing in mind what you have already learnt from the first part of this chapter:
- How effective were the Liberal reforms?
- Did they solve all the problems of hardship that were in need of attention?
- What kind of society were the Liberals trying to create?

- Could they have done more? What obstacles faced them?
- How might people at the time have criticised the Liberal reforms?

Now write a review of the actions the Liberals took as if you were one of the people referred to in the task in Issue 3 on p.61 and were writing in 1914.

## *Why did the Liberals decide to carry out so many reforms?*

### The evidence of poverty

By 1906 it was impossible to escape the great weight of evidence about poverty in Britain. Researchers had shown that it had many causes including low wages, lack of regular work, ill health, old age, and living conditions that brought about illness. This evidence was widely publicised and read. It included inescapable evidence of hatred of the workhouses. By the 1900s these buildings housed the elderly, the sick, the frail and the orphaned: few able-bodied people went there – indeed 90 per cent of the unemployed never touched poor relief despite living in circumstances that were desperate. Charles Booth commented of workhouses:

'Aversion to the "House" is absolutely universal and almost any amount of suffering and privation will be endured by the people rather than go into it.'

(Royal Commission on The Aged Poor, 1895)

Moreover the evidence pointed to a problem which was beyond the ability of charities to solve alone. Even Octavia Hill admitted that the housing that philanthropists had worked so hard to build over the previous thirty years provided homes for only 26,000 people. London's population alone rose by that number in six months!

## Fear for Britain's place in the world

The Boer War that ended in 1902 had shown up in horrifying detail the poor state of health of many people in Britain. A quarter of the urban male population were unfit to serve in the armed forces. In Manchester 8000 of the men who volunteered for the army had to be rejected as physically unsuitable at once; only 1200 were eventually accepted. At a time when other countries were building up their armed forces, Britain seemed potentially weak. The founder of the Boy Scout movement, Robert Baden-Powell, who was one of the Boer War's heroes, warned:

'Recent reports on the deterioration of our race ought to act as a warning to be taken in time before it goes too far. One cause which contributed to the downfall of the Roman Empire was the fact that the soldiers fell away from the standard of their forefathers in bodily strength.'

Others were concerned that in the economic battle with rivals like Germany and the USA, Britain's workers were insufficiently energetic and educated. In 1905 a group of experts reported:

'No country can permanently hold its own in the race of international competition if hampered by an increasing load of this dead weight of poverty.'

## Political pressures

By 1906 the trade unions and the Labour Party were sufficiently formidable to concern the Liberals. In addition by 1906 the wing of the Conservative Party led by Joseph Chamberlain was campaigning for tariffs on foreign imports. He argued that, behind this shield of taxes, British and imperial economies would prosper, creating wealth to improve society and cutting unemployment. The Liberals, therefore, had good reason to feel the need to produce their own policies. In any case their ranks now contained men like Charles Masterman and Charles Trevelyan who believed that social reforms were urgently needed because they were the right thing to do. Such men formed a group of 'New Liberals' who wished (in some respects at least) to abandon *laissez-faire* and to use the power of the state. One of their number, Herbert Samuel, explained the causes that

'combined to convert Liberalism from the principle of state

abstention. It was seen that the State had become more efficient and its legislation more competent. It was realised that the conditions of society were so bad that to tolerate them longer was impossible and that the *laissez-faire* policy was not likely to bring the cure.'

> (Quoted in K. Morgan, *The Age of Lloyd George*)

Another Liberal MP, J. M. Robertson, proclaimed:

'*Laissez-faire* . . . is quite done with as a pretext for leaving uncured deadly social evils which admit of curative treatment by state action.'

> (Quoted in M. Pugh *The Making of Modern British Politics*)

Prominent among such men were the surprising allies, David Lloyd George (who came from humble origins) and the recent convert from Conservatism, Winston Churchill (who was born in Blenheim Palace). The latter commented, bleakly:

'I see little glory in an Empire which can rule the waves and is unable to flush its own sewers.'

> (S. H. Wood, *The British Welfare State*)

These Liberals saw social reform as a way of heading off socialism. They hoped that a system that gave people a degree of social and economic independence would be an insurance against the spread of socialist ideas. In this way they were at one with Conservatives like A. J. Balfour who believed:

'Social legislation is not merely to be distinguished from Socialist legislation but it is its most direct opposite and its most effective antidote. Socialism will never get possession of the great body of public opinion among the working class or any other class, if those who wield the collective forces of the community show themselves desirous to ameliorate every legitimate grievance.'

When Lloyd George attacked the Conservative-controlled House of Lords for blocking the money for social reform, he showed that the Liberals too were conscious of the need to keep socialism at bay, declaring:

'If a Liberal Government tackle the landlords and the brewers and the peers and try to deliver the nation from the control of this [group], then the Independent Labour Party will call in vain upon the working men of Britain to desert Liberalism that is so gallantly fighting to rid the land of the wrongs that have oppressed those who labour in it.'

Behind Liberal politicians stood liberal thinkers like the Oxford philosopher T. H. Green (who taught Asquith) and J. A. Hobson. They argued for state action to secure a minimum standard of living for all citizens. They maintained that reforms could readily be financed by taxing land that had risen in value – perhaps because of urban development – and by other sorts of unearned income.

# What had the Liberals the ability to do?

A successful reform programme faced a number of problems.

## Cost

The programme would be costly. Increased taxes or duties would be required.

## Parliament

It would have to pass parliament. The Liberals lost their huge majority in the Commons in two elections in 1910, but their Labour and Irish allies still gave them a clear overall lead. However, in the House of Lords, the Conservatives dominated politics with a permanent majority.

Asquith raged against the existence of this obstacle, declaring:

'We are living under a system of false balances and loaded dice. When the democracy votes Tory we are submitted to the uncontrolled domination of a single Chamber. When the democracy votes Liberal, a dormant Second Chamber wakes up from its slumbers and is able to frustrate and nullify our efforts [many times]... They proceed to frustrate and nullify the clearest and most plainly expressed intention of the elective House.'

In 1909 the House of Lords went beyond all its previous actions and rejected the budget put forward by Lloyd George to find £16 million to finance both social reforms (£8 million for pensions alone) and a naval rebuilding programme. The budget sought to raise revenue in ways that New Liberals had been advocating for some years:

- Income tax was to rise on a sliding scale from 9d. to 1s. 2d. in the pound.
- A 'super tax' of 6d. in the pound was to be levied on incomes over £5000 a year (in 1914 this figure became £3000).
- Duties on tobacco, beer, spirits and petrol were increased.
- A tax of 20 per cent of the unearned increased value of land was to be levied when land changed hands plus a duty of a halfpenny in the pound on the value of undeveloped land and minerals. These taxes meant that a thorough survey and valuation of land was required, a prospect that upset landowners as much as the taxes did.

- Those earning less than £500 a year were allowed £10 tax free
  per child.

The Lords could not amend the bill introducing the budget but
they could in theory reject it. They now did so. Asquith declared
war on them, calling an election and asserting:

> 'The House of Lords have deliberately chosen their ground.
> They have elected to set at nought in regard to finance the
> unwritten and time-honoured conventions of our Constitution.'

Lloyd George dismissed the Lords as '500 men chosen acci-
dently from among the unemployed'. The election of 1910
produced 275 Liberal MPs and 273 Conservatives, with Labour
and Irish Nationalists votes increasing the Liberal grip on office.
The Lords gave way and passed the budget.

But the Liberals were now bent on cutting the power of the
Lords. A second election in 1910 was fought on the issue of the
power of the House of Lords. The upper house finally gave way
when faced with the threat that the king would create new Liberal
peers sufficient in number to swamp the Conservative majority,
and passed the Parliament Act (1911) which reduced its own
authority. Henceforth the Lords could only delay bills passed by
the Commons for two years, and they lost all power to alter or
reject money bills.

Thus social reform had contributed to bringing about constitutional change.

## Officials

Social reforms also required officials to carry them out. By
Edwardian times Britain possessed far more people in paid public
service than had been the case in the mid-nineteenth century. In
1841 there were 40,000 men and 3000 women engaged in such
work; by 1911 the numbers had risen to 271,000 and 50,000
respectively. Moreover from 1870 admission to the civil service
had to be by an examination, and this ended the old system of
obtaining office by influence and seniority. (The queen wondered
if men recruited under the new system would really be gentlemen!)

By Edwardian times, too, a range of local government services
overseen by local government officials had emerged. The
Victorians reformed local government, creating elected councils in
cities and towns, setting up county councils (1888), and parish and
district councils (1894). It was these bodies which were given
many of the tasks of earlier social reform either directly, or (as in
the 1902 Education Act) by shifting to them the work of separately
elected boards. Whole armies of officials bustled about Edwardian
Britain. One of the problems of the Liberals was that such officials
were not necessarily popular with ordinary people. One historian
has suggested that, in Victorian times as least,

'It would not be far wrong to argue that the postman was the only representative of authority encountered in ordinary daily experience who was generally regarded as benign and helpful.'
(F. M. L. Thompson, *The Rise of Respectable Society*)

Governments had cleared away slum housing – but without providing replacement homes. They had forced children to go to school from the age of five to twelve or thirteen, denying their much-needed earnings to their parents – and for a time they even charged fees for this compulsory education. They had put controls on working hours for women – and thus limited their earnings.

The Liberal Government could not assume that social reforms would be popular.

## *The Liberal reforms*
### School meals, medical inspections and the 'Children's Charter'

*Dirt and disease inevitably followed poor living conditions. These children are being 'processed' in Finch St Cleansing Station, London, in the 1900s. Particular attention was paid to head lice.*

During the 1906 election, social reform was not a major issue. Instead the Liberals preferred to defend free trade against Chamberlain's proposed tariffs. Nevertheless the pressures of the time and the views of the New Liberals led to legislation. Evidence turned up by the members of a committee examining the 'physical deterioration' of British people led the Committee to propose that school meals should be provided for needy children and that medical inspections of school children should be carried out. In 1906, therefore, when a Labour MP proposed a bill allowing local authorities to provide school meals, Liberal support enabled it to become law. Parents able to afford to pay were expected to do so. But

> 'where children are unable by reason of lack of food to take full advantage of education, they [i.e. the local authorities] may apply to the Board of Education and spend out of the rates.'
>
> (Parliamentary papers)

This rate could amount to a halfpenny in the pound. In 1914 the government agreed to supply grants to meet half the costs, yet by this date at least half the local authorities had still to respond to the opportunity of providing meals.

The medical inspection of school children was required by a law passed in 1907. The Board of Education set up a medical department, and the gloomy reports sent in by doctors checking children's health led to the introduction of school clinics from 1912. Identifying problems was easy, but curing them was sometimes impossible. The costs of medicines, hospital care, or spectacles – even of travel to a hospital – were heavy burdens for many parents. A pair of spectacles could well cost a quarter of the weekly income of families on around £1 a week. Where ill-health was the consequence of dreadful housing conditions and a wretched diet, doctors could only despair. Some workhouses had developed infirmaries, and in 1886 it had been agreed that visiting them for treatment did not make one, officially, into a pauper. Charities and voluntary societies created a number of clinics and hospitals, but constantly struggled for money.

In 1908 the Liberal MP Herbert Samuel put forward a bill that gathered together a number of measures that dealt with the welfare of children. The law this bill became was commonly called the 'Children's Charter'. It meant that children were not allowed to beg; could be tried for offences in special courts; and could be sent not to prisons, but to 'borstals' away from adult criminals. A probation service was introduced. Children under sixteen years old were not to purchase cigarettes or to enter public houses.

Social reformers welcomed the measures; others grumbled that too many rules and regulations were being imposed on people's lives.

## Old age pensions

Charles Booth was just one of the influential people who belonged to a pressure group that demanded that pensions should be paid to the elderly to help them to continue to live outside workhouses (and the Scottish poor houses). However, Liberal ministers hesitated: the costs of the reform alarmed them. A series of by-elections in which Labour candidates defeated Liberals may well have helped persuade Liberal ministers to act in 1908.

Pensions were made available to those who were over seventy, had lived in Britain for at least twenty years and had been out of prison for the last ten of these years (later shortened to two years). The pensions were paid through post offices, places free of the stigma of the old poor law. Entitlement, however, depended on income. A pensioner with a yearly income of up to £21 received the full 5s. a week. Those living on £31 10s. 0d. a year were not entitled to a pension. Between those two, a sliding scale adjusted the pension – 2s. for those incomes up to £28 17s. 6d.; 3s. for those receiving up to £26 5s. 0d., or 4s. for those living on incomes up to £23 12s. 6d. It was not generous, yet the £8 million it cost helped to precipitate the budget crisis of 1909.

A working class boy, whose family kept a tiny shop, observed:

> 'even these small doles meant life itself for many among the elderly poor. Old folk, my mother said, spending their allowances at the shop, "would bless the name of Lloyd George as if he were a saint from heaven". The government met with much opposition to the introduction of a pension scheme at all from both the middle and working classes. Free gifts of money, many urged, would dishearten the thrifty who saved for their old age, and encourage the idle.'
>
> (Quoted in R. Roberts, *The Classic Slum*)

## Employment

Surveys like Booth's and Rowntree's had shown that low wages, unemployment or irregular earnings were major causes of poverty. Other investigators commented on the damage done to health by the hours and conditions in which some people worked. In 1908 the actual working time in coal mines was limited to eight hours a day. In 1909 the Trade Boards Act set up boards to control wages and working conditions in the sweated trades. In 1911 the Shop Act introduced a legal weekly half-day holiday for shop workers (whose hours of work were usually very long).

Winston Churchill, President of the Board of Trade in 1908, took a keen interest in such reforms. To aid him in his work, he recruited the support of an Oxford academic, William Beveridge. Beveridge (like Lloyd George) visited Germany, and admired the arrangements in place there that required workers and employers to set money aside regularly as an insurance against accident and unemployment. Beveridge believed:

> 'The problem of unemployment lies at the root of most other social problems. Society is built up on labour; it lays upon its members responsibilities which in the vast majority of cases can be met only from the reward of labour; it imprisons for beggary and brands for pauperism; its ideal unit is the houschold of man, wife and children maintained by the earnings of the first alone. The household should have at all times sufficient room and air – but how, if the income is too irregular always to pay the rent? The children should be supported by the parents – but how, unless the father has employment? The wife, so long at least as she is bearing and bringing up children, should have no other task – but how, if the husband's earnings fail and she has to go out to work? Everywhere the same difficulty occurs. Reasonable security of employment for the bread-winner is the basis of all private duties and all sound social action.'

Some workers in Britain earned enough to be able to save through their trade unions. Around one and a half million managed this. The rest of the country's workforce made no provision at all for times of hardship. In 1905 the Conservatives allowed local authorities to raise rates of up to 1d. in the pound to be used to provide work for the unemployed when conditions (in winter especially) ended their usual occupations. Churchill and Beveridge wished to do more.

## Labour exchanges

Labour exchanges provided one answer. The necessary legislation in 1909 allowed eighty-three such places to open their doors in 1910 (and more were set up in succeeding years). But workers were not required to register there nor were employers compelled to notify the exchanges of any vacancies. The provision of washing facilities, clothes-mending services and refreshments were designed to make the exchanges attractive to workers: to the skilled they were probably very helpful; for the unskilled they had far less to offer.

## Insurance

Insurance was the other major policy initiative. Churchill argued that his 1911 bill offered a lifebelt to save those in temporary trouble; it did not rescue the long-term unemployed, and it excluded many occupations. Churchill explained:

> 'To what trades ought we as a beginning to apply our system of compulsory contributory unemployment insurance? There are trades in which seasonal unemployment is not only high, but

chronic, marked by seasonal fluctuations: house-building and workers of construction, engineering, machine and tool makers, ship and boat building, sawyers and general labourers. They comprise two and a quarter million workers. We propose to follow the German example of insurance cards to which stamps will be affixed each week.'

The contributions came from employees (2½d. a week), employers (2½d. a week) and the state (1⅔d.) The benefits amounted to 7s. a week, payable for up to fifteen weeks, with the entitlement to one week's payment for every five weeks' contributions. Workers who did not come into the scheme, or who had used up all their entitlement, were still driven, in the end, to turn to the poor law for relief. But the insurance fund prospered, and by 1914 it had a surplus of £23 million in it.

## Health insurance

Lloyd George had good reasons to feel strongly about the need for health insurance. Tuberculosis, a disease that flourished in deprived environments, claimed 75,000 lives a year. One of the victims had been his own father. Around six million people continued to set aside money for times of illness by saving with friendly societies and insurance companies. These organisations fiercely opposed insurance proposals that involved the state, fearing for their own survival. Yet Lloyd George was determined to do something for

> 'people who cannot be persuaded or cannot afford systematic contributions. No plan can hope to be really comprehensive which does not include an element of compulsion.'

An insurance scheme in operation in Germany influenced his thinking. So too did the view he shared with Churchill that insurance schemes gave workers a sense of self-respect: he felt that dependence on state handouts was both very costly and damaging to workers' morale.

The insurance societies were won over when Lloyd George modified his plans by reducing their threat to private insurance. Pensions for widows and orphans, for example, were scrapped. Moreover insurance societies that were 'approved' became the means (under state supervision) by which the 1911 insurance provisions were administered.

There were other critics too: on the one hand some of the wealthy objected to the insurance scheme in principle, and the Conservative Party delayed it as far as they were able; on the other hand Labour critics attacked the scheme as wholly insufficient. The final form of the act entitled insured workers to 10s. a week for a period off work for health reasons of up to twenty-six weeks. They were permitted free medical examination by doctors who agreed to care for a 'panel' of insured workers, and who in return received payment from the state. The funds for these benefits came in part from the workers themselves (4d. a week from those earning under £160 a year, employers 3d. a week, and the state 2d. a week). The scheme excluded insured workers' families, though it did allow a payment of 30s. for the birth of each child. It was intended to maintain an income for the bread-winner, not to provide a national health service. Nor did the scheme offer free hospital, dental, or other specialist services. The wealthier were still expected to provide for their own needs. And the insured who used up their twenty-six weeks' entitlement were compelled to seek poor law help.

All the Liberal reforms offered levels of support that were confined to the poor and gave low levels of aid that were really only a supplement to other resources. Supporting a family on 7s. or 10s. a week, or existing in old age on 5s. a week alone, was well nigh impossible. Nevertheless the Liberals had built up a network of support that did not involve people seeking poor law relief. Lloyd George and Churchill continued to consider further reforms that included a state house-building programme to free farm workers from living in tied cottages.

The Great War ended their planning, yet raised issues of social welfare by once again exposing weaknesses in British society.

# ESSAY

Write an essay on one of the following:

1. The historian G. E. Mingay has called the period 1870–1914 'an age of ever increasing government intervention when central investigation and control replaced the too often palsied hand of local initiative.' Do you agree with this view?

2. G. E. Mingay has observed of the period 1870–1914 'for an age often supposed to be marked by *laissez-faire*, the increase in the numbers involved in public administration was remarkable.' Why did this happen?

3. 'Broadly speaking, the state acted only to help those who could not help themselves. It left the ordinary citizen alone.' (A. J. P. Taylor) Is this all that social reform had achieved, or had meant to achieve, by 1914?

4. 'Until August 1914 a sensible law-abiding Englishman could pass through life and hardly notice the existence of the state beyond the post office and the policeman.' (A. J. P. Taylor) Is this really what life was like?

# A United Kingdom?

A single London-based parliament supervised the affairs of the whole of the mid-nineteenth-century United Kingdom. To Westminster went MPs elected by voters in England, Wales, Scotland and the whole of Ireland (i.e. the present Republic of Ireland and Northern Ireland). A separate Scottish parliament had ceased to exist at the beginning of the eighteenth century; a separate Irish parliament vanished at the start of the nineteenth century. Were United Kingdom citizens content with this arrangement? Did they feel part of a single country?

The material in this chapter considers such questions and is particularly concerned with the political *identity* of the country and with the following issue: Did a politically united United Kingdom seem an appropriate and acceptable structure to the citizens of the time?

## TASK

This chapter is organised in two parts. The first part outlines evidence suggesting that a single UK parliament was appropriate and acceptable to the citizens of the time; the second part suggests that not all the UK inhabitants were happy with this situation.

Work through the material, listing the main points. Discuss with others the views you have reached by the end of the chapter.

# Factors favouring a single UK political structure

The changes in the country's society and economy that were outlined in Issue 1 tended to tie together different parts of the kingdom and to emphasise the importance of England. By 1911 Greater London's population equalled that of Wales and Scotland combined. Scotland's population rose from about 1.5 million in 1801 to 4.75 million in 1911; England's shot up from 8.5 million to 33.5 million. Roads, steamer services, and above all railways, linked together the different parts of the country, helping to create national business, national newspapers, and national political parties. People became familiar with parts of the country that previously it would have been almost impossible for them to visit. Holidays in distant parts of the kingdom became common events for the better off. As early as 1846 that pioneer of the holiday business, Thomas Cooke, commented:

> 'It was in Scotland that I first began to combine tickets for railways, steamboats, and other conveyances under one system in order that passengers travelling under our arrangements might well be able to calculate the expense and foresee the engagements they would have to enter into.'
>
> (J. Simmons, in *Journal of Contemporary History*, 1984, Vol 19)

Increasingly people in different parts of the country wore similar clothing, ate similar food (though the Scottish affection for oats remained), and read similar books and newspapers. Addiction to the works of Charles Dickens was as strong in Scotland as in England – indeed Edinburgh had a Pickwick Club and was the first city to make the author a freeman. Letters criss-crossed the country in growing numbers: eight per person in the 1840s; sixty per person by 1900.

As the economy changed and expanded, so people moved from one part of the country to settle in another. Large numbers of Irish arrived in Liverpool and Glasgow, for example; many Welsh and Scottish people sought their fortunes in English cities. Growing businesses found their markets throughout the country, and not merely within their immediate locality. The management of the economy by the government mattered as much to Welsh coal-producers as to Lancashire cotton-workers or Scottish ship-builders. The issue of free trade or protection affected all: Scottish farming suffered from free trade and cheap foreign imports; English farming slumped too. Lord Rosebery, a very politically active peer, felt that features of the Scottish character were inevitably fading. He wrote:

> 'Much of that character has been taken away from us by the swift amalgamating power of railways, by the centralisation of

[an] Anglicising empire, by the compassionate sneer of the higher civilisation.'

(Quoted in K. Robbins, *Nineteenth-century Britain*)

Certainly it was clear that non-English languages commonly spoken in 1800 were in retreat by the 1900s. In 1840 two thirds of the population of Wales spoke Welsh – and half of them spoke only Welsh. By 1911 44 per cent were still able to speak Welsh, but Welsh-only speakers were confined to remote areas. In 1800 only one and a half million Irish could speak English. In 1900 a mere three quarters of a million were still able to speak their native Irish tongue. In Scotland Gaelic-speaking declined slowly, falling from 231,595 speakers in 1881 to 202,398 by 1911. The Registrar General of 1871 had no doubt as to the need for all to speak English. He wrote:

'The Gaelic language may be what it likes, both as to antiquity and beauty, but it decidedly stands in the way of the civilisation of the natives making use of it and shuts them out from the paths open to their fellow countrymen who speak the English tongue. It ought therefore to cease to be taught in all our national schools; and as we are one people we should have but one language.'

A number of people living at the time commented on the employment opportunities offered by the United Kingdom, its law and government, its armed services and empire. Writing in mid-Victorian times in a Free Church magazine, the Scot David Masson argued:

'Increased quiet, increased commerce and wealth, increased liberty, increased civilisation – these have been the consequences to Scotland of the once detested Union and since the Union Scottish talent and Scottish energy have had a wider and richer field to [expand] in than they would otherwise have possessed... There have been Scottish Prime Ministers, Scottish Chief Justices of England, Scottish Lord Chancellors, Scottish Generals of British armies and Admirals of British fleets, Scottish Governors of India. England is full of Scottish merchants and manufacturers. London is full of Scottish literary men and Scottish editions of newspapers.'

(Quoted in H. J. Hanham, *Scottish Nationalism*, 1969)

Certainly there were Scots, Welsh and Irish who grasped the opportunities not only for careers in another part of the kingdom, but also for the creation of businesses with a UK-wide presence. Thomas Lipton opened his first grocery stores in Glasgow; others soon began to appear in distant parts of the kingdom. Such shops stocked the products of firms producing goods for a UK market, thus increasing the sense of the emergence of a single country. When plans to establish a separate educational department to run

Scottish education were announced, an eminent Scottish scientist protested in 1884 that the proposal would

'accentuate the differences between England and Scotland for the future and tend to convert Scotland into a Province, with the narrow pecularities of Provincial existence. No country can less afford than Scotland to narrow the ambition of its educated classes or parochialise its institutions. If it separates itself from England in administration and education it need not be surprised if in time Scotland becomes less of an outlet for Scottish enterprise.'

(Quoted in H. J. Hanham, *Scottish Nationalism*)

An article in *The Times* went so far as to suggest that Scots who argued that their country was distinctive and should be treated differently were doing themselves harm:

'By their exclusiveness and provincialism the Scotch have not only kept out English influence which might have done them good, but they have driven the best of their own countrymen to England; it is not merely because Parliament sits in London that England drains away the best brains from the other two kingdoms but because Englishmen have thrown away those confined notions of nationality, which still prevail in Scotland and Ireland. We, south of the Tweed, have risen to the conception of a United Kingdom . . . but in Edinburgh, the cry still is "Scotland for the Scotch". Yet the more Scotland has striven to be a nation, the more she has sunk to be a province.'

(Quoted in H. J. Hanham, *Scottish Nationalism*)

Sir Henry Craik, head of the Scottish Education Department, and an MP from 1906, questioned the very notion of a Scottish nation:

'What is this national entity which you are going to cut off from the whole of Southern Britain and constitute a national item by itself? Is there that intimate sympathy of race and feeling between the remote fishermen of the Hebrides and the Orkneys and Shetland, and the Lanarkshire population or that population of Glasgow constituted very largely by an influx of 1,500,000 from Ireland? Is that exactly a homogenous population? Do you think the Northern parts of Scotland will be so pleased to be ruled by the packed population of the slums of Glasgow and the mining districts of Lanark?'

(Quoted in H. J. Hanham, *Scottish Nationalism*)

It was from Ireland rather than Scotland that the loudest demands came for political separation. Yet here too there were fierce arguments put forward against Irish nationalism. The lawyer A. V. Dicey suggested that if Irish people were given political control over their own affairs:

'Englishmen will find they have not attained the object which from an English point of view was the principal inducement to grant Home Rule to the Irish people, that is freedom from the difficulty of governing Ireland. The army in Ireland will be the British Army under the control of the British Government. The British Ministry remains at bottom responsible for the maintenance of peace and order throughout Ireland. The Gladstonian constitution cannot remove the admitted causes of Irish discontent. It cannot tempt capital towards Ireland; it cannot diminish poverty, it cannot assuage religious [prejudice], it cannot remove agrarian discontent.'

(A. V. Dicey, *England's case against Home Rule*, 1886)

*This cartoon shows Gladstone attempting to attack the many problems that Ireland posed for British politicians.*

THE IRISH DEVIL-FISH.

By the later nineteenth century there were plenty of signs that politicians were treating much of the kingdom as a single political unit. The English lawyer-politician H. H. Asquith represented Fife in Parliament. From 1879 Gladstone represented Midlothian, yet his main home, Hawarden, was in Wales. In 1872 Disraeli was elected to be Rector of Glasgow University. Even the queen established a home in Scotland, at Balmoral. Radical political reformers from non-English areas readily referred to events in England's past – like Magna Carta and the Bill of Rights – when making their demands. The Liberal, Conservative and Labour Parties operated throughout Britain, while no Welsh or Scottish Nationalist Parties campaigned for votes. In an article written in 1895, W. Jenkyn Thomas argued that Welsh interests were best served through a UK political party:

> 'The question of a separate Welsh party, independent of the Liberal Party is being more and more discussed in the Principality but . . . as yet, it is possible for a Welshman to declare himself opposed to the idea without forfeiting his character as a good Nationalist . . . I would have every good Welshman exert himself to spread the gospel of Welsh Nationalism . . . But, in my humble opinion, the best way to promote Welsh interests in Parliament is to leaven the Liberal Party from within and not to form a Welsh party distinct from and independent of that organisation . . . Disestablishment is the *"pièce de resistance"* of the present session . . . The University of Wales has been established. The home language of Wales has been placed in its rightful position in its elementary school system . . . Much quiet work has been done to secure more firmly the administrative unity of Wales – a step towards Welsh Home Rule.'
>
> (Quoted in K. O. Morgan, *The Age of Lloyd George*)

Socially, economically, and politically there were serious reasons for believing that a single UK-wide political structure best served the needs of the inhabitants.

# Factors working against a single UK political structure
## The Irish question

It was in Ireland that the issue of whether a United Kingdom was acceptable was most forcefully raised. Ireland's parliament had been extinguished as recently as 1800. The 100 MPs then allocated to Ireland to represent her at Westminster meant that they were a presence that could not be ignored.

Many Irish people felt strongly that they had major grievances. The established church in Ireland was Protestant, yet in twenty-eight of the thirty-two Irish counties the majority of the population was Catholic. Many Irish landowners were absentees and a significant number were English. The desperate poverty in which many Irish people lived could be blamed on the uncaring attitude of a far-away government in London, whether or not this was true. The Irish leader, Charles Parnell, declared in 1881:

> 'The reason the Irish do not succeed in Ireland is because a nation governed by another nation never does succeed.'

British governments attempted to deal with the Irish question by reforms that tackled specific grievances. In 1869 Gladstone ended the official Anglican-style church in Ireland. In 1870 and 1881 he pushed through land reforms for Ireland in order to give Irish tenants much greater security and fairer rents. Later Conservative governments pursued land reform further, helping tenants to buy their land on very favourable terms.

Yet this was not enough. For a time a Land League led by Michael Davitt used tactics that were sometimes violent and commonly involved boycotting anyone taking up the tenancy of a farmer evicted by his landlord. Sporadic bursts of violence occurred, and in 1882 even claimed the life of Ireland's chief administrator. In parliament, by 1885, a sizeable group (commonly eighty plus) of Irish Nationalist MPs used their strength to obstruct parliamentary business and negotiate deals.

By 1886 Gladstone was persuaded that Ireland did not fit neatly into the notion of a single political structure for the UK: Ireland would have to have its own parliament to run its own internal affairs. Moreover Gladstone realised the wider implications of his conversion to home rule for Ireland. In Parliament he argued:

> 'The principle I am laying down I am not laying down exceptionally for Ireland. It is the very principle upon which, to the immense advantage of the country, we have not only altered but revolutionised our method of governing the colonies . . . the colonies said "We do not want your good laws; we want our own". We admitted the reasonableness of that principle. We have to consider whether it is applicable to the case of Ireland. We stand face to face with Irish nationality [which] vents itself in the demand for local autonomy, or separate and complete self government in Irish affairs. Is this an evil in itself? Is it a thing that we should view with horror or apprehension? Sir, I hold that it is not.'
>
> (Hansard 1886)

In 1886 he wrote a pamphlet, *The Irish Question*, in which he developed his thoughts on the implications for Scotland and Wales:

'The sense of nationality both in Scotland and Wales set astir by this controversy may take a wider range than heretofore. Wales, and even Scotland, may ask herself whether the present system of intrusting all their affairs to the handling of a body English in such overwhelming proportions as the present Parliament is, is an adjustment which does the fullest justice to what is separate and specific in their several populations.'
(Quoted in H. J. Hanham, *Scottish Nationalism*)

Yet Gladstone's two attempts to bring in Irish home rule failed. Both in 1886 and 1893, not only did the Conservative Party oppose him, but also a considerable number of Liberal 'Unionists' did so too. These Liberal Unionists believed in the political union of the whole UK, and they were concerned for the fate of Protestants, especially in Ulster. Opposition to home rule rapidly developed in Ulster, and in 1912 took the form of signing a Solemn League and Covenant that included these words:

'Home Rule would be disastrous to the material well-being of Ulster as well as the whole of Ireland, subversive to our civil and religious freedom, destructive of our citizenship, and perilous to the unity of the Empire.'

But by 1911 the Liberal Government of the time needed John Redmond's Irish Nationalists to stay in power. The Home Rule bill passed the Commons in 1913, and in contrast to Gladstone's earlier experiences, the House of Lords had now had its powers cut and could only delay the bill for two years. Asquith's attempts to win Ulster over by offering a six-year delay in integrating the area into the rest of Ireland failed. An alarmingly tense situation developed as armed units of Ulster Volunteers on one side and Irish Volunteers on the other began to prepare for conflict. The outbreak of a far greater conflict – the Great War – swept all this to one side for the moment.

By 1914 John Redmond's home rule position seemed to some Irish people to be too moderate. In 1902 Arthur Griffiths established Sinn Fein, a party committed to Irish independence. Though the party met with no political success before 1914, it had in part grown out of movements in Ireland that believed the country to be distinctive, unique, and threatened with contamination by being tied in with the rest of Britain. The Gaelic League (1893) sought to spread the knowledge of Irish history and culture and the Irish language. And there was even a Gaelic Athletic Association which demanded that Irish people play distinctive Irish games, and not imports from over the Irish Sea.

# The Scottish experience

In his study of nineteenth-century Scotland, the historian W. Ferguson concluded:

> 'In spite of increasing cultural assimilation, Scotland, for most of her inhabitants, retained much of her individuality, and her outstanding problems – concerning church, poor law, education or public health – differed in substance from their English counterparts. Few politicians grasped this fundamental fact.'
>
> (W. Ferguson, *Scotland 1689 to the Present*)

Scotland had its own church, its own legal system and its own distinctive educational structure. And the Scots looked back to a time of independence, to victories over English forces, and to the ending of this independence by negotiation, not conquest.

Scotland, like Ireland, contained people with grievances. In 1850 the Free Church minister, James Begg, argued that Scotland was in decline and needed a Scottish administration and more Scots MPs in Westminster to put matters right. In 1852, the historical novelist James Grant supported Begg, suggesting Scots were not getting value for all they paid out in taxes:

> 'Vast numbers of respectable and well-educated young men pining for lack of employment are forced to emigrate to become private soldiers in India whilst their sisters must resort to the most humble means for subsistence – to labour with their hands or become poor dependents, teachers and governesses, amongst the very English people into whose pockets and Exchequer nine millions of our Scottish money are annually poured.'
>
> (Quoted in H. J. Hanham, *Scottish Nationalism*)

In 1853 Grant helped to establish the Association for the Vindication of Scottish Rights. The support this organisation attracted proved the existence of a mood of dissatisfaction, because literary figures, town councilors, liberal radicals like Duncan MacLaren, and even the Dukes of Hamilton and of Montrose supported it. So too did some businessmen, for there were people who believed that the Scottish economy was neglected by the London government. Few official orders came to Scottish shipyards, for example, and spending on army and navy installations in Scotland was scant compared with similar spending in England.

The Association held several successful meetings and drew up petitions. It sought seventy-one not fifty-three MPs for Scotland; an effective Scottish administration (instead of reliance on the Lord Advocate to fight for Scottish interests at Westminster); and a greater share for Scotland of government revenues. However, it did not seek independence, and with the outbreak of the Crimean War, it faded in importance, finally vanishing in 1856.

The Second and Third Reform Acts boosted the number of Scots MPs to seventy-two, and despite the strong support the Scots had given to the Liberal Party, Gladstone seemed to take Scottish support for granted. It needed a major upheaval like the Crofters' War of 1882 and the appearance of a separate, successful, Crofters' Party to produce action. Once the Crofters' Act (1886) was in place – giving crofters security and acceptable rents – this separate party collapsed back into Liberalism.

The Crofters' Party had undoubtedly been influenced by the success of the Irish Land League – and Irish events made a further impact in Scotland. Gladstone's conversion to home rule was welcomed by many Scottish Liberals, as well as by future Labour Party members like Keir Hardie. In 1886 a Scottish Home Rule Association was established. In 1888 the Scottish Liberal Association resolved:

> 'That this National Conference is of the opinion that Home Rule should be granted to Scotland so that the Scottish people could have the sole control and management of their own national affairs and suggests that the true solution of the question may be found in granting Home Rule Legislators on a federal basis to Scotland, England, Ireland and Wales.'
> (Quoted in H. J. Hanham, *Scottish Nationalism*)

But some Scottish Liberals were opposed to this policy and joined Liberal Unionists in campaigning against it. In the Glasgow area where Ulster influence and the Orange order were increasingly important, Liberal Unionists did well. In 1885, seventeen were voted into parliament as MPs.

For the moment, however, it was the setting up of a more effective Scottish administration that governments pursued, rather than home rule. On this at least the Liberals and the Conservatives agreed. Gladstone's appointment of Lord Rosebery as Under-Secretary for Scotland proved an inadequate solution. After a couple of years a frustrated Rosebery resigned in 1883. Lord Salisbury's Conservative Government created the post of Scottish Secretary in 1885. It first occupant, the Duke of Richmond, was not however in the cabinet. In the following year, Salisbury widened the new minister's powers, freeing him from subordination to the Home Office and giving him control over a wide range of matters including law and order, and local government. In 1888 the Chancellor of the Exchequer, Goschen, produced a formula entitling Scotland to a share of budget revenues dependent on the proportion contributed to the government. By 1892 the Scottish Secretary had joined the cabinet, and by 1905 a commoner was usually appointed to defend policy in the Commons. (Hitherto the Secretary had usually been a peer and the Lord Advocate had represented him in the Commons.) However, the Scottish Secretary was based in London.

Scottish MPs continued to grumble that Scotland received insufficient attention. In 1913 the MP for East Aberdeenshire declared:

'To my knowledge there has been a Scottish majority in the House in favour of temperance reform since 1885, a majority which has always been voted down by the English members. In the second place let me call attention to one urgent question – land reform . . . Scotland is being depopulated, emigration is double that from Ireland . . . a single Scottish official rules Scottish education with almost despotic sway . . . This House grudgingly allows to Scotland one day of 7 hours in each Parliamentary year for the discussion of Scottish estimates. Is it any wonder Scotland is tired and demands a Parliament of her own? That she demands her own legislation for land, for the liquor trade, for education, for housing, for fisheries, for ecclesiastical affairs?'

(Quoted in H. J. Hanham, *Scottish Nationalism*)

Perhaps just as significant as political affairs in stimulating a sense of a Scottish identify was the 1886 decision by the Scottish Football Association that Scottish teams should not compete in the FA Cup, following an incident in a third-round match between Preston North End and Queens Park. In sporting terms at least, Scotland developed as a distinctive nation.

## ESSAY

'It was the forces tending to develop a single United Kingdom identity that revived pressures for national separatism.' Do you agree?

# *Essays on Part 1*

1. 'Between the 1860s and the turn of the century, British politics . . . took on recognisably modern characteristics.' (M. Pugh) Do you agree?
2. 'The changes in British political parties 1850–1914 reflect the changes that were taking place in society.' Is this true?
3. 'Politicians only carried out social reforms in order to win votes'. Does a study of 1905–14 lead you to support this conclusion?
4. Why, and in what ways, was the political system reformed between 1850 and 1914?

# PART 2 *The Twentieth-Century Context, 1914–79*

# *How and why did British society change between 1914 and 1979?*

Between 1914 and 1979 life in Britain changed greatly. People's real incomes trebled yet the number of hours they worked fell by over ten a week by 1979. Far more people enjoyed holidays, and were more able to travel throughout the world during these holidays, than had been the case nearly seventy years earlier. By 1979 Britain's inhabitants could expect to live longer, and to receive free treatment for illnesses when once most had had to pay. All children in 1979 received education to the age of sixteen, not to twelve or thirteen, and had far more opportunities to enter higher education than had been the case in the century's opening years.

By 1979 the British citizen's knowledge of the wider world and his or her access to entertainment had been transformed by the technological revolutions that had created radio, television, and the record and cinema industries. Yet was it all change for the better? In 1973 Lord David Cecil looked back to the time when his grandfather, Lord Salisbury, had died in 1903, and described the following years as

> 'a period of spectacular catastrophe which entailed . . . the decline of most of what my grandfather had stood for. British greatness, aristocratic government, individual liberty and international peace.'
>
> (David Cecil, *The Cecils of Hatfield House*, 1975)

Whatever one's views on the merits of the changes in these years, there is no doubt that they were inextricably tied up with political changes in the period. The material in this section is, therefore, particularly concerned with issues that deal with Britain's changing *identity* such as: How and why did British society change between 1914 and 1979?

## TASK

Work in pairs.
   Choose one of the following statements.

- 'British society altered, above all, because of the effects on Britain of changes in the wider world.'

- 'It was developments within British society itself that really brought about the major changes of 1914–79.'

Work through the material in this chapter, noting down points that support your case. Discuss the results with your partner, sharing material to build up a overall view.

# The impact of the Great War

## The First World War itself

The First World War involved Britain and her French, Belgian, Russian and Italian allies in a terrible conflict against Germany, Austria–Hungary and Turkey.

Huge armies battered one another in gigantic and dreadful battles in Europe. At sea fleets clashed, and submarines hunted merchant shipping. The war spread to parts of the British Empire. It even involved conflict in the skies and brought to Britain the horrors of bombs falling upon the civilian population. For almost a hundred years Britain had experienced wars at a distance – small-scale events hundreds of kilometres away, fought by forces of volunteers. The First World War could not be managed in this way. It demanded men and materials on a vast scale; it threatened Britain with ruin and defeat. Though Britain eventually emerged victorious, success was bought at a high price, and the effort to win success seemed to people at the time to bring about many changes.

At first volunteers sustained the war effort. But in 1916 conscription was introduced. Men from the age of eighteen to the age of forty-one had to present themselves for military service, although those in essential jobs were excused duty in the forces.

In 1917–18 of the two million men who were examined for military service, only 36 per cent were passed as fit for full military duties. The depressing conclusion was that 41.1 per cent were either totally unfit or were described as 'unable to undergo physical exertion'. (The rest performed non-combatant duties or were in essential jobs.)

Between 1914 and 1918 the United Kingdom found 5,704,416 men to serve in the war. Never before had the country made so huge a military effort. Men were uprooted from their homes and thrown together. Leonard Thompson, a farm worker in Suffolk, volunteered for the army in 1914 and fought at Gallipoli and in France:

'We were all delighted when war broke out. We were all damned glad to have got off the farms. [After the war] the soldiers who got back to the village recovered very quickly. Generally speaking we were thankful that it was all over and we could get back to our work. Yet things had changed. The farm workers who had been soldiers were looked at in a new way. We felt there must be no slipping back to the bad old ways and about 1920 we formed a branch of the Agricultural Labourers' Union.'

(R. Blythe, *Akenfield*, 1969)

# The economy during the war

The war threw together men from quite different social classes. It brought together rich and poor in the same terrible conditions. Nearly three quarters of a million of them were killed and one million seriously wounded. The war was also very expensive, and pushed the government into changes in finance that would have been unthinkable in peacetime.

In 1913–14 1.2 million people paid income tax; by 1919 the figure was 7.8 million. Moreover the level of the tax shot up from 1s. 2d. in the pound to 6s. Indirect taxes also rose sharply, and duties on many imports were imposed. Yet despite these efforts the national debt rose to £7186 million and the government had to borrow heavily.

The huge scale of the war drove the government into increasing interference in everyday life.

## New ministries

The following ministries were established to manage this interference:

- Ministry of Food – to encourage food production and manage the 1918 rationing of food
- Ministry of Labour – to supervise manpower in Britain
- Ministry of Shipping – to organise and allocate space on shipping
- Ministry of Munitions – to produce the means of war
- Ministry of Reconstruction – to plan a better post-war Britain.

The government took control of the coal industry and the railways, and organised insurance of and allocated space in shipping. It imposed censorship on the press and even limited the previously lengthy opening hours of public houses in the belief that excessive drinking was hurting the nation's health. The new Ministry of Munitions (1915) created 218 factories that made explosives, aircraft, tools, chemicals and ball-bearings. Under wartime controls British finance poured into British enterprises instead of into its preferred peacetime destinations abroad. The generating capacity of British electricity doubled from 1914 to 1918; optical glass output increased sixty-fold; a new aircraft industry appeared; and the chemicals industry expanded rapidly. And in 1916 the government set up a Department of Scientific and Industrial Research.

Against this must be set the damage done to the British economy. Much shipping was sunk, and British shipyards which were working desperately to replace vessels lost export markets to foreign rivals. Other British industries also lost export markets to the USA, Japan, and to the neutral Scandinavian countries. In addition, the coal, railway, iron and steel, and textile industries worked to provide the urgently needed means of war, but had no time to overhaul and modernise their already out-dated methods of working.

## A *changing society*

Many who lived through these years detected a change in people's behaviour and attitudes. In working class Salford, Robert Roberts observed:

> 'The First World War cracked the form of English lower class life and began an erosion of its socio-economic layers that has continued to this day. In our own community, well before the war was over, we began to see basic alterations in certain habits and customs. Similar changes were taking place in every industrial corner of the land. "Things," people repeatedly told one another, "will never be the same again." Daily newspapers, magazines, periodicals, comics and, as people grew richer, even books made their appearance in homes almost bare of print before the war. Communications from husbands and sons, official forms, and, later, ration books all made hitherto unknown demands upon the unlettered.'

The war had a particularly noticeable impact on the place of women in British society. Their services were needed in a whole range of occupations to replace the men who had volunteered for or been conscripted into the armed forces.

To many women who had hitherto been badly-paid domestic servants, factory work brought better pay and more free time.

Margaret Morrison went to work in a west of Scotland shell factory:

'Until then I had worked as a laundry maid on a big estate. Most of us had never worked on machines before. We were given a week's instruction by one of the foremen. After a while they said we could do as well as any of the skilled workmen. Of course we didn't get the same pay. Working in the explosives section could be dangerous. We worked a twelve-hour shift, but the pay was good.'

(Quoted in A. Marwick, *Women at War*, 1977)

Munitions work may have been dangerous, but its weekly wage of £2 for women was better than the average pre-war wage for women of 11s. 7d. By 1918 nearly a million women worked in munitions and engineering. The number of women working in transport services rose from 18,000 to 117,000, and in clerical jobs from 33,000 to 102,000. The *Daily Mail* noted shorthand typists' wages rose in a year from £1 to £1 15s. 0d. and added:

'The wartime business girl is to be seen any night dining out alone or with a friend in the moderate-priced restaurants in London. Formerly she would never have had her evening meal in town unless in the company of a man friend. But now with money and without men she is more and more beginning to dine out.'

(Quoted in A. Marwick, *The Deluge*, 1965)

Robert Roberts noticed how the war changed women's attitudes:

'It undoubtedly snapped strings that had bound them in so many ways to the Victorian age. Even we, the young, noticed their new self-confidence. Wives in the shop no longer talked about "my boss", or "my master". Master had gone to war and Missis ruled the household, or he worked close to her in a factory, turning out shell cases on a lathe and earning little more than she did herself. Housewives left their homes and immediate neighbourhood more frequently, and with money in their purses went foraging for goods even into the city shops, each trip being an exercise in self-education. She discovered her own rights. The events in 1914–18, then, did not start, but they accelerated significantly, a movement already well developed, one which would go some way to release that other great social undermass of the time – the working-class women of Britain'.

(R. Roberts, *The Classic Slum*)

Historians may differ in detail, but in general they are agreed about the importance of the Great War. To Martin Pugh:

'The experience and response of the mass of people during the First World War were of major importance in shaping the modern pattern of British politics.'

(*The Making of Modern British Politics*)

Janet Roebuck suggests:

'The First World War marked the close of Britain's golden
century and brought the years of national prosperity,
confidence and world leadership to a stop with all the finality of
the fall of the guillotine. The age of disillusion and anxiety was
opened by the war.'

(*The making of Modern English Society since 1850*)

And G. E. Mingay writes:

'World War I marked the end of the old Britain, the beginning
of the new. Life was never quite the same again.'

(*The Transformation of Britain*, 1986)

# Between the wars

During the inter-war years the British economy expanded. By
1938 total industrial production was 63 per cent above the levels
of 1913. In many ways the British people became more prosperous. By 1939 two out of every three houses had been wired up to
the electricity grid – in 1920 the figure had been one in seventeen.
In the ten years after 1924 the number of licensed motor vehicles
on Britain's roads rose from 1.3 million to 2.4 million. By 1939
over eleven million people were enjoying paid holidays – yet in
1930 the figure had been a mere one and a half million. Britain's
towns and cities still bear witness to the surge of home-building
that took place in these years, as both council housing and private
house-building activities expanded vigorously. When Seebohm
Rowntree returned to study York in 1935–36, he found a better
housed population with more homes having their own bathroom.

Certain industries expanded. The numbers working in the
electricity industry more than doubled between 1924 and 1938 to
reach nearly a third of a million. The building industry employed
840,000 in 1920 but 1,159,000 in 1937. Motor vehicle production,
aircraft manufacture, chemicals, banking, insurance and distribu-
tive trades all took on more workers.

The inter-war population of Britain benefited from a fall in the
price of many goods. Food prices in particular fell sharply. And
the behavioural patterns of Britain's more prosperous people were
changing. Church attendances continued to fall. The spread of
methods of birth control meant that couples deferred having
children and limited the number of them. This made it easier for
families to buy houses and to purchase the increasing number of
electrical gadgets that were easing the burdens of housework.
Drunkenness declined, but smoking increased. Families living in
their more comfortable and hygienic homes were able to enjoy

listening to gramophone records (from 6d. each), listening to the radio (– by 1939 nearly three quarters of all homes had radio licences), and reading from the great range of cheap newspapers and magazines. The cinema developed into an enormously popular attraction, allowing people to escape into imaginary worlds, but also providing newsreels of events taking place all round the world.

Yet the inter-war years are often most vividly recalled as an era of poverty and misery. Against the many signs of prosperity must be set high levels of unemployment. From the mid-1920s there were about 1.2 million to 1.5 million unemployed; in the 1930s this figure rose. In the 1920s it had accounted for 10–11 per cent of the workforce; but by 1932 it had exceeded 22 per cent. Rowntree found that of those York inhabitants living in poverty, 28.6 per cent were so placed because of unemployment. There were parts of Britain where in the early 30s 50 per cent, 60 per cent or even more of the workforce had no job. Behind these figures lay factors that contemporaries wrestled to understand. In 1931 a foreign visitor to Britain commented:

'manufacturing costs are among the highest in the world. If this situation continues, any economic structure based on exports is faced with inevitable ruin . . . Old England has been living in a fool's paradise, fondly imagining that she could still rely on the spirit and methods of the nineteenth century. Such reforms as have been attempted are insignificant; at any rate, up to the War no serious efforts were made to transform coal mining, the metal industry, or textiles – the three bases on which exports and prosperity were founded. England is like a venerable mansion which though well and solidly built, has for years lacked repairs both in and out.'

(André Siegfried, *England's Crisis*, 1931)

Export industries were particularly hard hit. In 1913 Britain had taken over 25 per cent of world trade in manufacturers; by 1937 this share had slumped to 19.1 per cent. Coal production fell from 287 million tonnes in 1913 to 227 million tonnes in 1938. The amount of shipping tonnage produced halved from 1913 to 1938; and the cotton industry's output fell drastically. Unemployment, therefore, was heavily concentrated in certain areas. In 1932 a third of all coal miners were without work; 43 per cent of the cotton workers, 48 per cent of the iron and steel workers, and 62 per cent of the shipyard workers had no employment. All these were industries that had relied heavily upon export markets.

The decline was, to some extent, inevitable. The war had damaged British exports and helped those less heavily involved – or neutral – to take advantage. By 1914 several other countries had more than caught up with the industrial lead Britain had once possessed, and this trend was bound to continue after the First

*A branch of the NUWM on the march in the 1930s.*

World War. Moreover world conditions for trade were not consistently healthy during these years. The 'Great Depression' of 1929–33 was a world-wide phenomenon that hit the USA severely, struck a number of European countries harder than Britain, and even reached the Far East. World trade shrank 25 per cent in three years. The collapse of banks, of share values, and of companies led many countries to erect tariff barriers: trade in the mid-30s was even more difficult, as governments tried to protect their economies by taxing imports.

Historians have tended to conclude that even so British industry did not perform well. G. E. Mingay has suggested:

'In the end, it seems likely that at bottom there was a fatal weakness in the attitudes and values of British industrialists... They were cautious, attached to familiar forms of production, and fearful of risks that might jeopardise their control of the business. Few, if any, had technical training.'

(*The Transformation of Britain*)

Contemporaries also struggled to understand what was happening. The writer J. B. Priestley travelled round the country in 1934 noting over and over again circumstances like these:

'The export trade of such places as Bradford was declining long before the war. We used to sell textile machinery to other countries and send out managers and mechanics with those machines. You cannot expect to teach other people to make goods and then expect them to go on still buying those goods from you. The war was a sharp break in this process of decline, a brief golden age of profits. Then reality broke in again in the early nineteen-twenties. The export trade, dependent on countries that had not the money to spend, rapidly dwindled. The very tide of fashion turned against the West Riding, which was still making solid fabrics for a world that wanted flimsy ones. Prices sank lower and lower. One firm after another staggered and then crashed.'

(J. B. Priestley, *English Journey*, 1934)

The contrast between the prosperity in some parts of Britain and the poverty in others faced politicians of the inter-war period with a massive challenge.

# The impact of the Second World War
## *The economy*

From 1 September 1939 to 14 August 1945 Britain was again at war. The fight against Germany, Italy and Japan took British servicemen all over the world.

The speedy success of German forces in 1940 drove the British out of mainland Europe: for the army at least there were not to be the huge and costly conflicts of the First World War. But for Britain's airmen and sailors the war was at times desperate. They fought to prevent invasion in 1940, to reduce German air-raids on Britain; and to stop German ships and submarines starving Britain into defeat by sinking shipping. 270,000 members of the armed forces and 35,000 merchant seamen were killed in the conflict.

The bombing of Britain meant that 60,000 civilians died. Many factories and shipyards, railways and bridges were damaged. Air-raids totally wrecked 475,000 houses, and badly damaged around four million more.

The struggle demanded great sacrifices by the British people: by 1945 nearly eight million Britains were in the armed forces or in the uniformed groups who supported the forces. Government spending and borrowing rose sharply. In 1937–38 defence took £197.3 million, 21.5 per cent of total spending. By 1944–45 defence costs had climbed to £5125 million, 82.94 per cent of total spending.

Government power increased too, by means of an Emergency Powers Act (1939). New ministries of food, supply, economic warfare and information were established and the numbers of civil servants swelled from 387,000 in 1939 to 704,700 by the end of

*The Aberdeen Home Guard practise their skills.*

the war. Conscription for those not in employments defined as essential came promptly in 1939. A new Minister of Labour, the trade union leader Ernest Bevin, took responsibility for the huge task of organising the British people for the war effort. The conscription of men aged between eighteen and forty-one was extended to unmarried childless women aged between twenty and thirty; and by 1943 the age range for women had been widened to between eighteen and fifty years old. Some women joined the forces, and thousands were drafted into jobs left vacant by men recruited to fight, or into jobs created by new demands on production in wartime. Taxes rose too. Income tax reached 10s. in the pound. Even this yielded insufficient money, and so the government plunged Britain more deeply into debt, increasing the pre-war figure seven-fold.

Some industries suffered. Activities regarded as less urgent – like building new houses and making clothes – suffered a 50 per cent fall in labour force size. Other industries boomed, including chemicals, aircraft manufacture, farming (the total tilled area increased 66 per cent) and machine tools. The war stimulated scientific research and its practical application, as in the development of jet engines, better radar, and antibiotics. The old industries – like coal, iron and steel, and shipbuilding – found their products once more in demand; but their out-of-date working conditions were ill-suited to the pressures of a crisis which left no time for modernisation.

# The social effects of the Second World War

In 1939, fearful of the slaughter they feared would come, the government organised the evacuation of 1,500,000 children from places likely to be targets of bombing to more remote areas. Another two million children were moved privately. By the end of 1939, 900,000 had drifted back to the towns as the German bombers failed to come – they were busy in Poland. Many children from city slums had habits that horrified their new hosts. The writer-diplomat Harold Nicolson noted in his diary:

> 'many of the children are verminous and have disgusting habits . . . This is a perplexing social event. The effect will be to demonstrate to people how deplorable is the standard of life and civilisation among the urban proletariat.'
>
> (Quoted in A. Kendall, *Their Finest Hour*, 1972)

Though the Luftwaffe's raids did not devastate Britain as dreadfully as pre-war politicians had feared, life in target areas (like major cities) became a tense and often distressing experience – though some felt that, in curious ways, life improved. A Londoner observed:

> 'People were much more together. They met in the air-raid shelters, in the tubes at night, they were in the Home Guard, or they queued for spam or whatever it was they could get hold of, one egg a week. Everybody really lost a lot of their inhibitions about talking to their next-door neighbours. When the raids were over they used to almost celebrate in the early morning and this was the spirit that I think a lot of people hoped would continue after the war . . .'
>
> (P. Addison, *Now The War is Over*, 1985)

Although wages rose and unemployment virtually vanished, there was little for the population to spend their wages on, as rationing was introduced and then spread to cover clothing, petrol, and many items of food.

Once again, as in the First World War, women found that their labour was urgently required. The number of women working in vehicle building and engineering, for example, rose by 770,000. 65,000 women joined the Land Army to help with farm work, and they had to be allowed to carry out jobs that had hitherto been the exclusive preserve of men. Many women hoped these new opportunities would continue in peacetime. This was not necessarily what their employers wished, as this factory manager's comment on one employee indicates:

> 'This girl has so taken to machinery that she'd like to become an apprentice and go right through the works. This of course is

*A female welder at work in wartime. Women proved that male prejudices against their employment in certain trades were wholly misplaced.*

not possible on account of Union agreements. There's a feeling among the men at the moment women must be in the factory solely because of the war but really women's place is the home.'

The end of the war found British people subject to higher taxes and more extensive government controls than ever before. War had damaged and distorted the economy, wrecked overseas trade, and drastically cut overseas investment. Yet the war had also brought an unprecedented awareness of the need for social reform – and a sense that such reforms were needed urgently.

# The post-war years, 1945–79
## *The years of austerity*

*Bringing up a large family in 1945.*

The shattered state of the British economy meant that wartime controls continued into peacetime. The food ration of 1948 actually fell below the wartime average. The Labour Government of 1945–51 sought to channel scarce resources into rebuilding British industry and pushing up exports. Barriers to this ambition included a shortage of manpower, and a shortage of funds for investment. The former was tackled by encouraging inhabitants of the Empire and the Commonwealth to come to Britain: in June 1948 the *Empire Windrush* docked with 492 persons on board, and this was the start of a sizeable movement of people from the Caribbean

*Some of the immigrants from the Caribbean area who came to Britain in the 1950s.*

area whose labour was much needed in Britain. The cash crisis was met partly by a loan of 3750 million US dollars (to be repaid over fifty years at 2 per cent; partly by $3,189,800,000 from the USA in Marshall Aid in 1948, as the Americans sought to revive the European economies; and partly by squeezing as much as possible out of the British economy.

*A terrible winter in 1946 hampered Britain's recovery.*

Thus life at home remained bleak, but the export drive boomed. Between 1946 and 1950 exports increased in real terms by 77 per cent. The motor industry did especially well, producing 903,000 vehicles in 1950, far exceeding the pre-war peak of 526,000.

This period of recovery was impressive, yet deceptive. Several industries were nationalised, notably coal, gas, electricity, the railways, and iron and steel. With the exception of the latter, there

*Official recognition of the nationalisation of the post-war coal industry.*

was only half-hearted opposition to these reforms, for these industries needed expensive overhaul. That they worked as fully as they did was a sign of post-war shortages that other countries could not supply either, and was certainly not a tribute to their efficiency. The textile industry also prospered, with its out-of-date equipment churning out products to meet desperate needs. But even the motor industry was not all it might have been: a report in 1950 pointed out that Britain built too many different models, thought too little of the needs of customers abroad, and neglected after-sales service.

Moreover the promising condition of the economy in 1950 was damaged by the onset of the Korean War and the undertaking of a vast rearmament programme in response to the Cold War that ate up resources, finance, and skilled manpower.

## The age of affluence

For thirteen years from 1951 the Conservatives ruled Britain. Total manufacturing production rose; and a vast house-building programme was undertaken that provided a quarter of all families with the homes they inhabited by 1964. The numbers of doctors and teachers rose. Rationing was swept away and, in innumerable ways, there were clear signs of increased affluence. The number of private cars in Britain rose, from 2.5 million in 1951 to over eight million in 1964. Over the same period, television ownership increased from one million to thirteen million. This prosperity marked the overcoming of the immediate consequences of the war, the reward for the efforts made in these years, and the recovery of world trade in general.

But by the 1960s there was a growing awareness in Britain that, though the country seemed to have done well, others had done even better. British exports had increased 29 per cent from 1951 to 1962, but West German exports had risen by 247 per cent and Japanese exports by 378 per cent.

*A family at home in the 1950s: radio brought news with an immediacy never known before.*

By 1960 the Prime Minister, Harold Macmillan, and a growing number of other people were beginning to think that Britain had been wrong to ignore developments in Europe. After the war several of the countries of Western Europe – France, Germany, Italy, Holland, Belgium and Luxembourg – had discussed linking their economies more closely to each other. From 1951 they treated coal and steel as goods to be freely traded between them. And in 1957 the Treaty of Rome created the European Economic Community.

Attlee's government had not been interested in the early stages of this development. One of the Europeans who came to try to persuade Labour Ministers to join the new development was Étienne Hirsch:

> 'They said that it was very good for all the countries of the continent of Europe who had been defeated or invaded, but that the situation was quite different for Britain who had not been defeated, who was still a country with its Commonwealth.
>
> I am not sure that Bevin and Cripps had a precise understanding of what we meant by "community". They certainly hated the idea of having an organisation which would have powers in some instances above the national governments. I think that was the crux of the decision.'
>
> (A. Thompson, *The Day Before Yesterday*, 1971)

After 1951 the Conservatives had showed no desire to join in creating the EEC. R. A. Butler, a Cabinet Member, believed

> 'We never had any great drive towards Europe in the early 1950s, and it's rather an extraordinary thing that neither

Macmillan, myself, nor Anthony Eden really pressed for entry
into Europe in the 1950s. I can't quite explain it, but all I know
is that the whole of Whitehall – I mean the Treasury, and the
Foreign Office – were not in favour of us pressing the matter at
that time. I think it was due to jealousy of the idea that Europe
might be a federal republic in which we had to sacrifice
sovereignty, and that is, I know, what Eden felt himself at the
Foreign Office.'

(A. Thompson, *The Day Before Yesterday*)

*A cartoonist's view of the unsuccessful attempt by Harold*
*Macmillan to take Britain into the European Community.*
*The French leader, de Gaulle, and the German Chancellor,*
*Adenauer, are not impressed by Britain's desire to alter the*
*Community.*

But by 1959–60 Britain's troubles and the EEC's success
persuaded Macmillan to apply for entry. Two years of discussions,
from 1961 to 1963, ended when the French leader, de Gaulle,
blocked Britain's application. Macmillan had hoped that joining
the EEC would shake up Britain's industry. By 1956 Britain had
lost her well-placed position in motor manufacturing: Germany
produced and exported more cars. Despite mergers between firms,
the decline of Britain's motor industry had begun. Its fate was
repeated in other industries too. The cotton industry crumpled
before competition both from abroad and from man-made fabrics.
The iron and steel industry struggled to match more efficient
foreign competitors, and in the shipbuilding industry closure after
closure took place.

*The sad sight of a shrinking cotton industry. Looms in a Lancashire weaving shed of the 1960s await their journey to the scrapyard.*

Efforts to improve economic planning in Britain were made. A second effort to join the EEC once more failed before de Gaulle's hostility. It was only after the fall of the formidable French leader that Britain was able to sign, in January 1972, the Treaty of Rome that finally admitted her to the European Community. And the exploitation of North Sea oil did something to offset the general mood of decline, helping Britain to sustain her prosperity.

During the 1960s and 70s a fierce debate developed as to what Britain's role in the world should be and as to what kind of society the country ought to have. By then little remained of the once massive British Empire. Even those who regretted this – and many did not – had to recognise that post-war Britain lacked the strength to maintain her empire against the actions of freedom movements that were active in seeking independence. The cost of modern weaponry made Britain increasingly dependent on American military might. By the 1970s many inhabitants of former colonies had settled in Britain, particularly peoples from India, Pakistan and the Caribbean area. Some of these newcomers found themselves facing hostility and abuse – even violence. And by the late 1970s the need for labour that had led governments to encourage immigration had turned to worries about rising un-employment.

In concluding his survey of these post-war years, the historian Arthur Marwick comments:

'There were new sources of conflict and tension, but for the great majority horizons were wider, aspirations higher and opportunities for their fulfilment larger. The most desperate problem was that economic set-backs and technological change meant intolerably high levels of unemployment... the war ...did bring change, but also complacency and a reinforcement of older structures (while other countries were forced to build anew).'

(*British Society since 1945*, 1982)

# ESSAY

Write an essay on one of the following.

1. Look again at the two quotations in the task at the beginning of this chapter. Now write an essay to comment on either the first or the second.

2. What sort of policies would you expect to be offered to the electorate by politicians eager to exploit the circumstances of 1918–45 in order to win votes?

# *Towards democracy?*

| Year | Population | Population over 21 | Total | Electorate as % of Adult Population |
|------|-----------|-------------------|-------|-----------------------------------|
| 1900 | 41,155,000 | 22,675,000 | 6,730,935 | 27 |
| 1910 | 44,915,000 | 26,134,000 | 7,694,741 | 28 |
| 1919 | 44,599,000 | 27,364,000 | 21,755,583 | 78 |
| 1929 | 46,679,000 | 31,711,000 | 28,850,870 | 90 |
| 1939 | 47,762,000 | 32,855,000 | 32,403,559 | 97 |
| 1949 | 50,363,000 | 35,042,000 | 34,269,770 | 98 |
| 1959 | 52,157,000 | 35,911,000 | 35,397,080 | 99 |

Butler and Freeman, *British Political Facts*, 1964.

*The electorate 1900–60.*

In 1914 all women and about 40 per cent of men were unable to vote in parliamentary elections. By 1970 all adults of both sexes were able to vote, and the age at which they were permitted to do so had been cut to eighteen. The 'votes for women' campaign had finally triumphed in 1928; but, as evidence in Part I has shown, this campaign was only one part of a wider movement to improve women's circumstances. Fifty years after obtaining the vote on equal terms with men, many women still felt that they suffered from numerous disadvantages. The campaign for women's rights took forms other than that of seeking the vote and persisted once the vote had been obtained.

The material in this chapter is particularly concerned with Britain's political *identity* and with the issue: What should people's rights be in British society?

## TASK

Use the material in the previous chapter and in this chapter to draw up detailed plans (300 words) showing how you would answer one of the following essays:

1. In what ways and for what reasons was the British electoral system reformed between 1918 and 1969?

2. '"Votes for Women" formed but one strand in a campaign to change their place in society and by itself was insufficient.' Do you agree?

# Reform in 1918

With the outbreak of war suffragettes and suffragists alike ceased campaigning. Mrs Pankhurst turned her magazine *The Suffragette* into the vigorously pro-war *Britannia*. She devoted her formidable energies to supporting the drive to recruit soldiers. Her daughter Christabel declared to an American audience in 1914:

> 'You must not suppose that because the suffragettes fight the British Government for the sake of the vote . . . that on that account the suffragettes are not patriotic. Why should we fight for British citizenship if we do not most highly prize it? . . . We want to see the strength of our country maintained because we believe that strength is more and more going to be used for the good of the whole world. Our country has made mistakes in the past . . . But we are going to do better in the future – above all when British women co-operate with the men in the important work of Government.'
>
> (Quoted in M. Mackenzie, *Shoulder to Shoulder*)

Sylvia Pankhurst pursued social work in the east end of London and adopted an increasingly anti-war viewpoint. So too did Emmeline Pethick Lawrence. Her campaigns in the USA helped to create the Women's Peace Movement and led to the holding of a Women's Peace Conference in The Hague. And members of suffragist groups tended to be rather more critical of the war than followers of the Women's Social and Political Union (WSPU).

Because electoral reform (including votes for some women) emerged at the end of 1918, it is easy to assume that the war did much to bring it about. The historian Arthur Marwick suggests that in this, as in other matters,

> 'It is difficult to see how women could have achieved so much in anything like a similar time span without the unique circumstances arising from the war.'
>
> (Ed. H. Winkler, *Twentieth-century Britain*, 1976)

His fellow historian, Martin Pugh, is more cautious, commenting that 'careful study tends to show how little change resulted from the war, not how much'. He does note that the eventual decision of 1918 for giving women the vote was:

> 'the vote of the suffragist majority elected in 1910 but for whom the Party considerations that had proved an obstacle before now ceased to apply.'
>
> (*Women's Suffrage in Britain*, 1980)

The need to re-examine the electoral system emerged in 1916. The war meant that a fresh general election was deferred until the conflict was over, but it was clear that the upheaval of the times had thrown the old system into disarray. Men called up or volunteering for war service inevitably moved, and thus lost their right to vote, since that depended on a year's occupation of a particular property. It was reckoned that in 1916 less than 20 per cent of men were in the places where they had originally registered to vote. Some politicians, such as Sir Edward Carson, pressed the case for servicemen's right to vote.

Once discussion of suffrage had recommenced, it was impossible to exclude the question of votes for women too. The suffragist leaders who set out their case to Asquith, the Prime Minister, found that there were three cabinet members who supported them – Lloyd George (Liberal), Arthur Henderson (Labour), and Lord Robert Cecil (Conservative).

Asquith presented the problem to a conference of thirty-two MPs and peers convened by the Speaker of the House of Commons. Some of these politicians feared that enfranchising women on the same terms as men would produce a register in which female voters outnumbered male voters with damaging results. As Martin Pugh observes:

> 'While hypocritically paying fulsome tribute to their war work, politicians had no intention of allowing the female majority to dominate the electorate, or industry.'
> (M. Pugh, *The Making of Modern British Politics*)

The conference also considered the views of both those who wished to allow votes to servicemen who were under twenty-one, and those who wanted to deny votes to those who were conscientious objectors. A shift to a system of proportional representation won wide support, but unlike most of the rest of the proposals died before reaching the statute book.

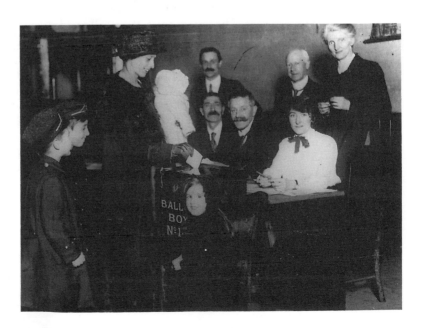

*A woman casts her vote at the general election of 1918*

The Act that was finally passed included these provisions:

1. The vote was given to all adult males aged twenty-one or over who satisfied a six-month residence qualification. Peers, prisoners and the insane were excluded, but those receiving poor relief were no longer disqualified.

2. Women aged thirty or over could vote, provided that they were householders, or wives of householders, or university graduates.

3. Voting was to take place on one day only, and was not be spread over several weeks.

4. Electoral administration was reformed. Candidates had to deposit £150, which they lost if they polled under an eighth of the votes cast. Party agents no longer decided who was on the register; this task went to local government officials who annually made up lists of voters. Returning officers' expenses and election costs were to be met from public funds, and not by candidates.

5. Servicemen of nineteen and over were permitted to vote in the immediate post-war election. And by 209 votes to 171, the Commons decided to disqualify for five years all those who had been conscientious objectors.

6. Certain people continued to have more than one vote, but the number of votes anyone could possess was now limited to two. Those entitled to two votes were either university graduates who could vote in one of the twelve university seats, or owners of business premises. University electors could vote by post, but business electors had to vote in person. Between 1922 and 1945 the Conservatives owed about nine seats to university electors, and between seven and eleven seats to business electors.

7. Constituencies were reorganised so that each was as near 70,000 votes as was reasonably possible. Ten double-member borough seats were allowed to survive, but otherwise the old borough/county division disappeared.

8. As a result of suffragist pressure, voting by women in local government elections was put on the same footing as in parliamentary elections. This widened the franchise in local elections, for up till now the only women who had been able to vote were those who were householders in their own right.

There were grumbles. The suffragist leader Millicent Fawcett noted of the 'householder' clause for women:

> 'There was some outcry against this on the part of ardent suffragists as being derogatory to the independence of women . . . I felt, on the contrary, it marked an important advance that it recognised in practical political form a universally accepted and most valuable social fact – namely the partnership of the wife and mother in the home. We did object to the absurdly high age.'
>
> (M. Fawcett, *The Women's Victories and After*, 1920)

The Act's effect was to deny the vote to many women war workers.

Debates were also marked by public confessions of changes of mind by some who had once opposed female suffrage. Herbert Asquith was the most prominent of such people:

How could we have carried on the War without [women]? Short of actually bearing arms in the field, there is hardly a service which has contributed to the maintenance of our cause in which women have not been at least as active and as efficient as men. But what . . . moves me still more . . . is the problem of reconstruction when this War is over. The questions which will then necessarily arise in regard to women's labour and women's activities in the new ordering of things are questions which I feel it impossible to withhold from women the power and right of making their voice directly heard.'

(*House of Commons Debates*, 1917, Vol. 92)

The bill passed comfortably through the Commons. In the House of Lords it faced the hostility of the Leader, Lord Curzon, although he publicly recognised that resistance was pointless. The Lords passed the bill by 134 to 71 votes. 8.4 million women now gained the right to vote – women who were regarded, by the men who had carried out the reform, as being stable and mature family women who were likely to be influenced by their husbands. In any case they were outnumbered by the thirteen million male voters. The total (male) electorate in the last pre-war election had been a mere seven million!

A separate Parliamentary Qualification Act allowed women aged twenty-one and over to stand for election to parliament.

# Between the wars

The Great War ended on 11 November 1918. Just over a month later a general election provided a good test of the new electoral system. The results removed the fears of those apprehensive of the consequences of enfranchising women and working class men. The victorious wartime coalition won a massive majority. No separate women's party emerged in parliament, despite the efforts of Christabel Pankhurst to fight this cause in the constituency of Smethwick. One woman managed to become elected: Constance Gore Booth, Countess Markiewicz, won the St Patrick division of Dublin. But since she was a fervent Irish Republican, she did not recognise Westminster's authority in Ireland, and refused to take up her seat. The first woman actually to attend the Commons as an MP was an American who had never fought the female suffrage cause. Nancy, Lady Astor, captured the constituency of Plymouth when her husband moved from the seat to take up a peerage in the Lords. She found the House ill-organised to receive her – indeed the only women's lavatory was a half-kilometre walk from the debating chamber! In 1921 she was joined by Margaret Wintringham, a Liberal who fought Louth when her husband, the previous MP, died.

During these years it was possible for a woman who was not entitled to vote in elections to become an MP, for the rules governing the circumstances of those who could stand for election differed from those determining who could be an elector. The Labour MP Ellen Wilkinson told the Commons:

> 'When I was first elected to this House I happened to live in furnished rooms and having neither a husband nor furniture I was not eligible for a vote . . . independent wage-earning women should be represented in this House where so much of our legislation directly concerns them.'
>
> (*House of Commons Debates*)

The post-war electoral scene led politicians to conclude that there was nothing to fear from giving women the vote on the same terms as men. The Conservative Stanley Baldwin promised to tackle this issue during his successful electoral campaign in

*Evidence of changing times: young female voters going to the polls for the first time in 1929, having been given the vote the previous year.*

1924. He honoured his pledge in 1928, and received support from all parties – though hostility from two of his own party, Churchill and Birkenhead. The reform added to the register about 3.5 million women aged between twenty-one and thirty and 1.8 million hitherto unenfranchised women over thirty years old.

In the general election of 1929 women formed 52.7 per cent of the electorate, and the Labour Government which emerged from this episode contained the country's first woman cabinet minister. Margaret Bondfield, Minister of Labour, began work as a shop assistant at the age of fourteen and, through her trade union activities, rose in the Labour movement.

In the opinion of the historian A. J. P. Taylor, the successful campaign for adult suffrage had very modest political consequences:

> 'In the long run more women voters probably benefited the

Conservatives and more voters altogether probably injured the Liberals who were the least suited to become a mass party.'

(*English History 1914–45*, 1965)

The WSPU disbanded. The National Union of Women's Suffrage Societies turned itself into the National Union of Societies for Equal Citizenship, and launched campaigns to improve women's rights in law, in employment, and in social conditions. The historian Martin Pugh regarded their efforts with a critical eye when he wrote:

'The bulk of the movement had been too socially conservative to embrace the feminist objectives which remained to be taken up by a later generation of women for whom the franchise campaign was a distant memory.'

(M. Pugh, *Women's Suffrage in Britain*)

Yet the inter-war years did witness a number of achievements in the battle for women's rights. This struggle came at a difficult time. Once the war was over, trade unionists had expected women to step aside from wartime work and resume their domestic duties. From the mid-1920s economic depression added to the gloomy employment scene. At least the light industries that developed at this time often employed women (frequently because of the low wages that they could pay them). The economic circumstances and many of the attitudes of the time made the struggle for equal pay for equal work very difficult: the best that could be managed in the teaching profession, for example, was a promise to pay women five sixths of the equivalent male salary. However the doors to a number of hitherto closed occupations were prised open. The 1919 Sex Disqualification Removal Act provided women with the opportunity to enter professions like law and accountancy. 1921 saw the qualification of the first woman barrister, Helena Normanton. In 1920 Oxford University agreed to award full degrees to women. (Cambridge did not carry out the same reform until 1947.) In 1921 the government gave way to pressure to let women sit examinations for entry to all grades of the civil services; and in 1925 three women won admission to the highest (administrative) grade.

Women were to be found playing an increasing part in public affairs. In 1919 they became liable for jury service. By 1923 there were about 4000 women magistrates, mayors, councillors and poor law guardians.

Reforms in 1926 and 1935 allowed married and single women to hold and dispose of property on the same terms as men. The 1923 Matrimonial Causes Act made grounds for divorce the same for women as for men, and a further act in 1937 added cruelty, desertion, or the insanity of one's partner as reasons justifying divorce. In 1925 wives were granted guardianship rights over their children on terms equal to those of their husbands. In the event of a split, the courts were to decide who had custody. Social reforms like widow's pensions (1925) of 10s. a week, the development of clinics for pregnant women, and easier access to birth control brought some improvement to women's lives.

Nevertheless the mood of the inter-war years was unsympathetic to providing full equality for women. The advertising and the magazines that boomed in these years stressed women's roles as wives and mothers. The increasingly numerous branches of the Women's Institute (from its beginning in 1915 in Anglesey) placed most emphasis on women's domestic activities. Women's pay was markedly lower than men's; not till 1942 did the TUC pledge itself to fight to achieve equal pay. In the words of the historian, John Stevenson:

> 'Many of the high hopes of the early feminist pioneers for full equality had not been achieved . . . A measure of equality and an element of independence had been obtained, but only within a culture and economy which remained male-dominated in all important features.'
>
> (J. Stevenson, *British Society 1914–45*, 1984)

# Since 1939

Once more warfare showed the importance of female labour and the ability of women to take over male occupations. Once again war prevented the normal operation of democracy and delayed a general election. And by the time an election took place in 1945, parliament had passed the House of Commons Redistribution Act (1944). This established separate boundary commissions for England, Scotland, Wales and Northern Ireland, which were charged with the duty of reviewing constituency boundaries to equalise the numbers of voters between them (in so far as geographical factors and local community ties made this possible).

The Labour Government elected in 1945 passed the 1948 Representation of the People Act to abolish the second votes hitherto possessed by university graduates and owners of business premises; to cut the length by which the House of Lords could delay a bill it disliked from two years to one; and to abandon the six-month residence qualification for voters. The Lords opposed the proposal to cut its delaying time, and, in a final exercise of its former power, delayed the Act for two years!

The final reform of the franchise in these post-war years came in 1969. As part of a more general improvement in the status of eighteen to twenty-one year-olds (which included allowing them to marry without parental consent; to make legal contracts; and to take out mortgages), they were granted the right to vote. This added 800,000 new voters to the register.

The distinctive British electoral system resisted pressure from reformers who wanted to see proportional representation. In 1951 Labour achieved 230,684 votes more than the Conservatives, yet lost the election. Its votes tended to be piled up in certain places – in fact seventeen of its victories were won with majorities of over 25,000. The more general spread of Conservative votes produced narrower victories, but more of them. There were also occasional criticisms that Irish citizens living in Britain were able to vote here. Others noted that Scotland and Wales were over-represented at Westminister in terms of population. In 1979 Scotland had seventy-one MPs, although fifty-seven would have reflected its relative population size more accurately. Northern Ireland, however, was under-represented. The argument that this was justified by its having its own assembly at Stormont collapsed in 1972 when direct rule from Westminister replaced the authority of the assembly. In 1978 it was agreed that representation from Northern Ireland should rise from twelve to seventeen MPs.

In 1975 the Conservative MPs elected Margaret Thatcher to lead them. In 1979 her party won electoral victory. These events might seem to mark the final achievement of equality with men. In 1955 women had won the right to equal pay for equal work if employed as teachers, civil servants, or local government officials. The establishment of life peerages in 1958 produced opportunities for women as well as men. In 1963 hereditary peeresses were allowed to sit in the Lords. And women in post-war Britain have found educational opportunities more open to them than ever before.

In addition better health provisions, more readily-available methods of birth control, and easier grounds for divorce have given women more control over their own lives. A married woman of the 1890s was likely to see fifteen years of her life occupied by pregnancies and the nursing of infants: By the late 1970s only four years, on average, were so employed. Rising divorce rates suggest that women are perhaps less prepared to put up with miserable marriages – though it has also been pointed out that the proportion of marriages now broken in middle life by divorce corresponds closely to the number that, 100 years ago, were broken by death.

In the late 1960s a movement developed that demanded major improvements in women's rights. The movement stressed particularly the need for easier abortion; the misery of numbers of women who suffered rape and other forms of physical abuse; the continuing failure of employers to recognise and promote women; and the derogatory ways that women were represented in the media. The movement was not confined to Britain, but developed in the USA and in much of Western Europe too. Writers like Simone de Beauvoir, Germaine Greer and Betty Friedan provided widely-read analyses of the ways in which women were unfairly treated. Women's groups, women's centres, and feminist publications multiplied.

In 1969 a member of the movement explained:

'We are economically oppressed: in jobs we do full work for half pay, in the home we do unpaid work full time. We are commercially exploited by advertisements, television and the press. We are brought up to feel inadequate, educated to narrower lengths than men. This is our specific oppression as women. It is as women we are organising.'

(M. Rowe, *Spare Rib Reader*, 1982)

An Act in 1967 made abortion easier to obtain, and in 1969 divorce became possible on the grounds of the irretrievable breakdown of marriage. The 1970 Equal Pay Act promised equal pay for women and men doing the same work – to be implemented within the following three to five years. From 1976 the Sex Discrimination Act banned discrimination against anyone on the grounds of sex, in education, employment, and advertising. An Equal Opportunities Commission was established to watch over the operation of the Act. Women were allowed time off work to have babies with the guarantee of their jobs back within a specified period.

Yet in 1975 the average earnings of women were still little more than half those of men. The 1979 election that brought Margaret Thatcher to power also saw the number of women MPs fall from twenty-seven to nineteen. One in eight families in the late 1970s was cared for by a woman living alone. In his review of the 1970s Norman Shrapnel concludes:

'Seen as a cause, women in the seventies were triumphant. They achieved vast publicity and debate, produced heroines of note, established important and belated principles. That, as far as practicalities were concerned, they ended the decade much as they began it was more than disappointing. It was infuriating ... At the end of the decade it was as difficult to get adopted as a woman parliamentary candidate as it had been at the start, and that was difficult indeed.'

(*The Seventies*, 1980)

The winning of true equality for women proved to be a far more complex matter than merely obtaining the vote.

# ESSAY

Write an essay on one of the following.

1. Choose one of the essay plans from the task at the beginning of this chapter. Discuss it with others who have chosen the same plan, then develop it into a full essay of around 1000 words.

2. 'It is important to ask why was it in 1918 that women got the vote and not, let's say, in 1938.' (Arthur Marwick) How would you answer this point?

# Winning the voters' support

During the twentieth century the organisation of political parties developed further as they responded to changing conditions – both social and economic – and to the widening of the franchise. The sociologist A. H. Halsey sees this period as one of

> 'a massive development of working class political and industrial combination and a parallel response by the dominant classes... we have seen the rise of Party and between them they have created a vast proliferation of the organs of state.'
>
> (A. H. Halsey, *British Social Trends Since 1900*, 1988)

Halsey is describing the Labour and Conservative Parties. Yet many voters of 1914 might have argued that the most important party was the Liberal Party. After all it formed the government. Just twenty-one years later, however, the Liberal Party lay in ruins with a mere twenty-one MPs. And most voters in 1914 would never have predicted that in ten years' time a Labour government would hold office. The changing fortunes of the political parties form the focus of this chapter, and raise the issue: Which party responded best to the widening of the franchise and to changes in British society from 1914 onwards?

It is necessary to consider the *ideology* of the parties, the *identity* they established in society, and the *authority* they sought to wield.

## TASK

Work in groups. Each group member should research and argue for one of the following statements and should be ready to criticise the other points of view.

- The Great War wrecked the Liberal Party.
- Liberal behaviour in post-war years ruined Liberalism.

- Liberal decline was inevitable as social and economic conditions changed and as the franchise was extended.
- Labour's rise ruined the Liberals.

Discuss your findings. Can you agree on an overall conclusion?

## Ministries 1908–79

| Years | Political party | Prime ministers |
|-------|----------------|-----------------|
| 1908–16 | Liberal | H. H. Asquith |
| 1916–22 | Coalition | David Lloyd George |
| 1922 | Conservative | Andrew Bonar Law |
| 1923 | Conservative | Stanley Baldwin |
| 1924 | Labour | James Ramsay MacDonald |
| 1924–29 | Conservative | Stanley Baldwin |
| 1929–31 | Labour | James Ramsay MacDonald |
| 1931–35 | National | James Ramsay MacDonald |
| 1935–37 | National | Stanley Baldwin |
| 1937–40 | National | Neville Chamberlain |
| 1940–45 | Coalition | Winston Churchill |
| 1945–51 | Labour | Clement Attlee |
| 1951–55 | Conservative | Winston Churchill |
| 1955–57 | Conservative | Anthony Eden |
| 1957–63 | Conservative | Harold Macmillan |
| 1963–64 | Conservative | Sir Alec Douglas-Home |
| 1964–70 | Labour | Harold Wilson |
| 1970–74 | Conservative | Edward Heath |
| 1974–76 | Labour | Harold Wilson |
| 1976–79 | Labour | James Callaghan |

# General factors

The historian Peter Pulzer has defined a political party as

'a means of justifying the actions of its leaders to the electors and a means of discovering the wishes of the electors.'
(*Political Representation and Elections in Britain*, 1967)

The circumstances in which political parties played both roles changed between 1914 and 1979. The popular press expanded, with newspapers often devoted to supporting particular parties, according to the views of the owners of the papers. Radio broadcasting emerged in the 1920s. By 1939 there were nine million licensed radios, and this meant that there were sets in about three quarters of British households. The setting up of the BBC did not mean that broadcasts were free from political control. In 1926, for example, the BBC excluded from its broadcasting people who were highly critical of government behaviour during the General Strike. Cinema newsreels were a further source of information about affairs, and these too were sometimes controlled. For example, the impact of German bombing on Clydebank was filmed, but it was thought that this was not suitable to be screened. The post-war spread of television has increased popular access to 'instant' news, though it has not ended the debate about censorship.

So the mass media emerged at the same time as a mass electorate obtained the vote. Political leaders cut back on their great speech-making tours and developed skills to suit the microphone and the camera. Advisers and 'image-makers' began to have their impact on how post-war politicians presented themselves. Professional advertisers were hired to 'sell' a political party. The parties they 'sold' built up their headquarters and their national staff; developed systematic fund-raising; and set up youth movements. Independent MPs rarely survived in such conditions.

A mass electorate meant that parties had to rethink their policies. What did most voters want? Opinion polls eventually provided glimpses into voters' thinking about issues.

Parties in power increased the grip of government on daily life, using an army of officials to implement parliament's decisions.

# The decline of the Liberals

| Liberal MPs and the Liberal share of the vote | | | |
|---|---|---|---|
| **Election year** | | **MPs** | **Percentage of the votes** |
| 1918 | Coalition | 133 | 13.5 |
|  | Independent | 28 | 12.1 |
| 1922 | Coalition | 62 | 11.6 |
|  | Independent | 54 | 17.5 |
| 1923 |  | 159 | 29.6 |
| 1924 |  | 40 | 17.6 |
| 1929 |  | 59 | 23.4 |
| 1931 | National Liberal | 35 | 3.7 |
|  | Liberal | 33 | 6.5 |
|  | Lloyd George Liberal | 4 | 0.5 |
| 1935 |  | 21 | 9.0 |
| 1945 |  | 12 | 9.0 |
| 1950 |  | 9 | 9.1 |
| 1951 |  | 6 | 2.5 |
| 1955 |  | 6 | 2.7 |
| 1959 |  | 6 | 3.9 |
| 1964 |  | 9 | 11.2 |
| 1966 |  | 12 | 8.5 |
| 1970 |  | 6 | 7.5 |
| 1974 (February) |  | 14 | 19.3 |
| 1974 (October) |  | 13 | 18.5 |
| 1979 |  | 11 | 13.8 |

In 1914 Britain was ruled by a Liberal government. The authority of its leader, Herbert Asquith, was unchallenged. The party faced problems (as dealt with in Part I), but it had good reason to expect to survive as a major political force. Yet within ten years its strength in parliament had shrunk to a mere forty MPs. Subsequent years saw yet further decline – through the 1950s only six Liberals sat at Westminster.

Historians have long discussed the reasons for this rapid collapse. Some have pointed to pre-1914 difficulties and wondered whether the Liberals were perhaps a doomed force already. More commonly historians have focused on post-1914 affairs and considered a number of possible factors.

## Was Liberal decline due to the Great War?

Asquith viewed the probable impact of war with alarm. He noted

'suppose a good three quarters of our own party in the House of Commons are for absolute non-interference at any price. It will be a shocking thing if at such a moment we break up.'

In fact the German invasion of Belgium helped Asquith to hold together most of his followers. When war was declared, two ministers, Burns and Morley, resigned. A small group of men such as Charles Trevelyan and Arthur Ponsonby were highly critical of the conflict and of its conduct. They helped to form the Union of Democratic Control (UDC): this body brought together Liberal and Labour followers who opposed the conflict and tended to pull such Liberals to an eventual political home in the Labour Party. In contrast another group plunged into the war with zeal. They were led by Lloyd George, who was Chancellor of the Exchequer in 1914. In 1915 he moved to the new Ministry of Munitions to sort out a supply crisis, and then he went on to the War Office. This group sought military victory, even if that involved measures that jarred the Liberal conscience. Wealthy Liberal businessmen like Mond and Guest rallied to this cause.

The bulk of Liberal MPs drifted along uneasily. Asquith represented them well, for he proved a war leader who was reluctant to act decisively. Yet the needs of war pushed him into actions that inevitably upset some in his party. Moreover the war hurt the party organisation: it decayed as attention focused elsewhere, after the resignation of Hudson, secretary of the National Liberal Federation.

The war did not go well, and in May 1915, Asquith agreed to a coalition with Bonar Law's Conservative Party. The Gallipoli campaign of 1915 damaged Churchill's reputation for, as First Lord of the Admiralty, he was heavily involved in this disaster, and he was pushed out of office once a coalition was formed.

So Liberal MPs felt buffeted by a series of setbacks in the early years of the war. The Defence of the Realm Acts gave the government emergency powers; Irish Home Rule had passed the Commons, but was suspended; censorship was imposed. Reginald McKenna, Chancellor in 1915, broke Liberal commitment to free trade by taxing a number of imports. A growing demand for conscription as the only way to build up British forces showed Asquith vainly trying to fend off this attack on individual liberty, by using alternative, but unsuccessful, schemes. In 1916 conscription for men from eighteen to forty-one years old was imposed. The Home Secretary, Sir John Simon, resigned.

Still the war went badly, and pressure for reform of the government from Conservatives and from Lloyd George Liberals eventually brought about Asquith's fall from office in December 1916. About 120 Liberals backed Lloyd George, who now led a coalition in which the Conservatives actually had more MPs. The rest of the Liberals followed Asquith, who was still the party leader and in control of the party finances and organisation. Asquith refused offers of office under Lloyd George. Exchanges between them became increasingly bitter, culminating in the 1918 Maurice Debate when Asquith attacked the accuracy of government figures for British troop numbers in France.

Several historians, seeing the divided state of the Liberals by 1918, have concluded that the Great War did them immense harm. Robert Blake, for example, has written:

'The Liberals were fatally handicapped. On almost every issue that came up Conservative tradition and ideology were better suited than Liberal to meet the needs of the hour . . . The necessities of a prolonged war tended to create doubts and divisions in the Liberals.'

(*The Conservative Party from Peel to Churchill*, 1970)

Even more bluntly, Trevor Wilson has observed:

'The Liberal Party can be compared to an individual who, after a period of robust health and great exertion, experienced symptoms of illness (Ireland, Labour unrest, the suffragettes). Before a thorough diagnosis could be made he was involved in an encounter with a rampant omnibus (the First World War) which mounted the pavement and ran him over. After lingering painfully, he expired.'

(T. Wilson, *The Downfall of the Liberal Party*, 1966)

*David Lloyd George at the peak of his political powers in 1918.*

# Was Liberal decline due to events after 1918?

It was a divided Liberal Party that fought the 1918 election, though it was still officially one organisation. Lloyd George led a coalition campaign in which candidates who were officially approved by himself and Bonar Law received a 'coupon'. 159 Liberals obtained this document; and 133 of these were elected. Asquith's followers were victorious in only twenty-eight constituencies, and Asquith himself was beaten by an obscure Conservative, Colonel Sprot. One of his key supporters, Herbert Gladstone, observed despairingly:

> 'The results of 1918 broke the Party, not only in the House of Commons, but in the country. Local associations perished or maintained a nominal existence. Masses of our best men passed away to Labour, others gravitated to Conservatism or to independence. Funds were depleted and we were short of workers all over the country. There was an utter lack of enthusiasm.'
>
> (In P. Clarke, *Lancashire and the New Liberalism*, 1971).

From 1918 to 1922 Lloyd George remained in office. His forceful style, his use of a small group of personal advisers, and the open and vigorous way in which he sold honours to boost his funds (and Conservative funds too) gave increasing offence to more conventional MPs. His policies upset Liberals too. The positive programme of social reform that his ministry had promised had faded away by 1921. An economic slump meant cuts in spending that damaged proposed educational reforms. The coal industry – supervised by the state in wartime – was hastily handed back to private enterprise, despite a report in favour of nationalisation produced by the Government-appointed Sankey Commission. One of Lloyd George's keenest Liberal supporters, Christopher Addison (Minister of Health), had to watch as his programme of state-subsidised council housing was killed off. Blame was heaped on Addison's head; he resigned and was soon to be found in the Labour Party's ranks. The use of force (particularly by the brutal Black and Tans) to try to crush the Irish uprising caused distress to many Liberal consciences. Lloyd George's final deal of 1922 created a divided Ireland. The old Irish Nationalist support for Liberalism was now gone for ever. Irish Unionists backed the Tories.

By 1922 most members of the Conservative Party were weary of Lloyd George's style, alarmed by a foreign policy that risked war with Turkey, and felt they no longer needed him. A sign of Conservative strength was the successful capture of Newport in a by-election in 1922; it had previously been a Coalition Liberal seat. At a meeting at the Carlton Club the Conservatives turned against their current leadership, rallied behind a junior minister, Stanley Baldwin, and their former leader, Bonar Law, and voted to abandon the Liberal alliance.

This left the Liberals still divided, and now struggling to find distinctive policies. Lloyd George's bid to fuse his Liberals with the Conservatives in a kind of Centre Party had failed, for his followers insisted they were still Liberals. Yet many of them were ineffective politicians, and between 1919 and 1922 seven Coalition Liberal seats were lost to Labour. The Liberals had their own party organisation, but it was weak. And it was not easy for the party to reunite. A Liberal fought a Liberal in the Spen Valley by-election, and this let in a Labour candidate; and distrust between the leaders remained intense.

Even so, 29 per cent of the voters chose Liberals in the 1922 and 1923 elections – a total little different from those voting for Labour. The historian Martin Pugh has pointed to Liberal success in places where there were large numbers of newly-enfranchised voters, such as Bethnal Green and Birkenhead. He suggests that the new mass electorate did not mean that the Liberal Party was necessarily doomed, nor unable to cope with new political conditions, but rather that

> 'Liberal decline must be attributed less to structural changes than to wartime political changes which, by 1918, had begun to push existing Liberal supporters towards Labour and indeed towards Conservatism.'
>
> (*History VI*, Vol. 5)

Liberal troubles remained. Asquith was seventy in 1922 and a far from effective leader, but he did not give up leadership till 1926. Lloyd George brought ideas, energy, and even money from the fund he had built up, yet suspicion of him remained. Liberals reunited and seemed to recover in 1923 and 1924 – only to find that Labour, whom they put into office, treated them with hostility. Then the Conservatives reunited; abandoned dangerous flirtation with a policy of protection; and swept back to power in 1924.

After 1924 the Liberals suffered heavily as the third party in a system designed to suit two parties. For most of the time they were short of money, and able to field far fewer candidates than the other two parties. The Liberal ability to fight local government elections dwindled too. Increasingly local parties were driven to doing deals with the Conservatives.

A huge effort in 1929 offered voters policies that were more constructive and imaginative than those of their rivals, and 513 candidates to vote for. 5.3 million people voted Liberal (over 8 million voted for each of the other parties), but only 59 MPs emerged from this great effort. After this the party declined further. The economic slump led some to follow Sir John Simon and become National Liberals – in effect Conservatives. Lloyd

George went his own way, supported only by members of his family; the rest of the party floundered feebly, increasingly dependent on rural constituencies, and increasingly unable to hold industrial seats. In 1935 the Liberal peer, Lord Lothian, deplored the Party's lack of

'a soul, a body of principles and emotion, vague, but powerful with great masses of people . . . The Liberal Party suffers from the fact that most of the causes for which it fought – suffrage, social reform, individual liberty, the supremacy of the House of Commons – are already achieved.'

(Quoted in J. R. M. Butler, *Lord Lothian*, 1960)

In addition the old causes of the disestablishment of the Church of Wales and the winning of home rule for Ireland were no longer effective mobilisers of support.

To pre-war troubles, the impact of the war, and post-war problems must be added a further factor – the impact on Liberalism of the rise of the Labour Party.

# The Labour movement

| Labour's electoral fortunes | | |
|---|---|---|
| **Election year** | **MPs** | **Percentage of the votes** |
| 1918 | 60 | 22.2 |
| 1922 | 142 | 29.5 |
| 1923 | 191 | 30.5 |
| 1924 | 151 | 33.0 |
| 1929 | 288 | 37.1 |
| 1931 | 52 | 30.6 |
| 1935 | 154 | 37.9 |
| 1945 | 393 | 47.8 |
| 1950 | 315 | 46.1 |
| 1951 | 295 | 48.8 |
| 1955 | 277 | 46.4 |
| 1959 | 258 | 43.8 |
| 1964 | 317 | 44.1 |
| 1966 | 363 | 47.9 |
| 1970 | 287 | 42.9 |
| 1974 (February) | 301 | 37.2 |
| 1974 (October) | 319 | 39.2 |
| 1979 | 268 | 36.9 |

# The impact of the First World War

The start of the First World War split the Labour Party even more seriously than it did the Liberals. The Party Chairman (MacDonald), Snowden and a cluster of mainly ILP members opposed the war; but the majority of the party supported British involvement in the conflict, and a senior member, Arthur Henderson, even joined the coalition government. Those hostile to the war joined the Union of Democratic Control where they met Liberals who shared their high-minded views on the proper conduct of foreign affairs. They had, at first, a hard time of it, as they were abused at meetings and persecuted by the popular press.

**Number of trade unions**

**Number of trade union members**
**Figures in millions**

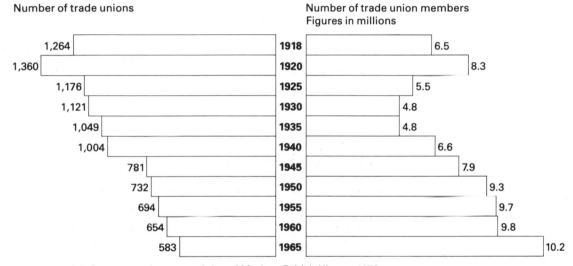

| | Number of trade unions | Year | Number of trade union members (millions) |
|---|---|---|---|
| | 1,264 | 1918 | 6.5 |
| | 1,360 | 1920 | 8.3 |
| | 1,176 | 1925 | 5.5 |
| | 1,121 | 1930 | 4.8 |
| | 1,049 | 1935 | 4.8 |
| | 1,004 | 1940 | 6.6 |
| | 781 | 1945 | 7.9 |
| | 732 | 1950 | 9.3 |
| | 694 | 1955 | 9.7 |
| | 654 | 1960 | 9.8 |
| | 583 | 1965 | 10.2 |

C. Cook and J. Stevenson, *Longman Atlas of Modern British History*, 1978.

However, the wider Labour movement benefited from the war. Trade union membership stood at 4.145 million in 1914; by 1919 it had risen to 7.926 million, as unions pulled back from the pre-war years of conflict with the state. Ministers listened more readily to union leaders, negotiated with them to obtain temporary relaxations of rules about employing skilled men and placed them on committees. Though not all the unions were affiliated to the Labour Party, affiliated members doubled, and this growth greatly helped Party finances. Interest in social issues like food and rent prices seemed to come more from the Labour movement than from Liberals. This helped establish a mood that eventually drew over to Labour several Liberals who cared about social reform, such as Christopher Addison, William Wedgewood Benn, and Charles Trevelyan. The latter commented, 'All social reformers are bound to gravitate as I have done, to Labour.' Nor were pro- and anti-war Labour supporters totally divided. In the War Emergency Workers National Committee contacts between them were kept, with agreement on issues like the need to raise wages and control rents. Lloyd George's dismissive treatment of Arthur Henderson, who wished to go to Stockholm to a conference of socialist delegates from countries involved on both sides of the conflict, drove that key Labour figure from the government. Henderson now concentrated on reuniting and developing the party. He worked in an optimistic atmosphere, as the Russian Revolution toppled the Czar, and socialism seemed to be on the march.

In 1918 the party created a new constitution for itself. The chief architect of this was the Fabian, Sidney Webb. Webb believed in peaceful social reform, and stressed the importance of the power of the state to transform ordinary lives. Wartime events encouraged him, for state power expanded to control rents, bring in rationing, and take charge of the economy. The most distinctive feature of the new constitutions was clause 4. In it the party aimed

> 'to secure for the producers by hand or by brain the full fruits of their industry, and the most equitable distribution thereof that may be possible upon the basis of the common ownership of the means of production and the best obtainable system of popular administration and control of each industry or service.'

This was the closest Labour came to clearly declaring itself to be a socialist Party. Several historians have commented that, though Labour included enthusiastic socialists, the bulk of the members were not really very interested in or committed to such a creed. As Martin Pugh has written: 'Socialism was for Labour a symbol sufficiently vague to be impervious to mere day to day policies and events.' It served as a badge to mark out the party's distinctive character. The historian A. R. Ball observed; 'Ideology was subservient to the important tasks of organising electoral success.' (*British Political Parties*, 1981).

Before the 1918 election Henderson had set to work to transform the party organisation. He developed local constituency parties and ward party branches based on individual memberships. The party's annual conference elected an executive of eleven representatives from unions, five from constituency parties, and four from women's sections. This cut into the power of the ILP and other socialist groups, for the trade union block vote dominated conferences. Thus equipped, Labour pulled out of the coalition just three days after the armistice ended the war. Although its organisation was just emerging, it managed to field 361 candidates. The newly widened electorate gave it over two million votes, though anti-war candidates like MacDonald tended to suffer defeat. Fifty-one Labour MPs were union nominees – twenty-five of them from the Miners' Federation – and prone to adopt a line as patriotic as Lloyd George's ministry.

Labour also gained support from the Co-operative Movement. During the Victorian period considerable numbers of shops that were owned by their customers were set up, and these paid out a 'dividend' from annual profits to each member according to how much he or she had purchased there during the year. The Co-operative Movement extended its activities into wholesaling (from 1863), and even began to produce foods. It was especially strong in northern England and in urban Scotland. In 1917 the movement's annual Congress agreed to found a political party. One Co-op MP triumphed in the 1918 election, and joined the Labour group of MPs. Labour and Co-op candidates avoided fighting one another in elections, and in 1926 the two movements reached a formal understanding. From 1946 Co-op candidates offered themselves as Co-operative and Labour.

## Co-op's electoral success

| Election year | MPs | Election year | MPs |
|---|---|---|---|
| 1918 | 1 | 1935 | 9 |
| 1922 | 4 | 1945 | 23 |
| 1923 | 6 | 1950 | 18 |
| 1924 | 5 | 1951 | 16 |
| 1929 | 9 | 1955 | 18 |
| 1931 | 1 | 1959 | 16 |

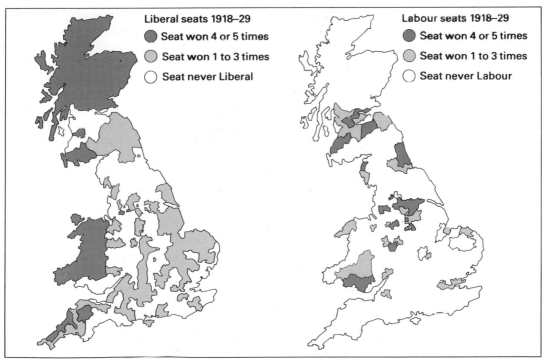

Liberal seats 1918–29
- Seat won 4 or 5 times
- Seat won 1 to 3 times
- Seat never Liberal

Labour seats 1918–29
- Seat won 4 or 5 times
- Seat won 1 to 3 times
- Seat never Labour

C. Cook and Stevenson, *Longman Atlas of Modern British History*, 1978.

# Labour's rise to power

Although the Labour Party was well organised by 1918, it did not really expect to be in office within six years. But in the immediate post-war years it seemed possible that the Labour movement might pursue a different strategy from the slow peaceful route to power advocated by leaders like MacDonald. The years 1919–21 were marked by widespread major industrial upheavals – through strikes by miners, railwaymen, dockers, and even by some members of the police. Voices in the movement were heard to urge 'direct action' by workers as the way to change Britain.

The government was especially alarmed by events on Clydeside. In 1919 six tanks were based in the city and soldiers manned machine-guns in Glasgow hotels. Behind this fear of 'Red' Clydeside lay a period of upheaval. Local people had suffered a sharp swing in employment. During the war the rise in house rents had led to strikes by the housewives of Govan and Partick that spread to 20,000 households and had helped to force the stoppage of increases during wartime. Some employers angered workers by the forceful way in which they tried to break traditional working practices and to bring in new machines. Shop stewards in the area began to lead workers' actions when their official union leaders seemed to be too timid. Socialist leaders were active in the area, including James Maxton of the ILP, and John Maclean, a Govan schoolteacher and a member of the Social Democratic Federation (SDF). Maclean had opposed the war and had so alarmed the authorities that he had spent much of the war in prison. But the efforts of the Clyde Workers' Committee (of local shop stewards) to call a general strike in 1919 failed. The ILP certainly did not seek revolution. The upheaval owed much to resentment at the tactless and aggressive behaviour of remote politicians and employers. In 1920 dockers opposed to the government policy of sending weapons to help Poland to fight the USSR, refused to load the arms ship *Jolly George*, and thus thwarted Lloyd George's policy.

By 1922 the fear of the Labour Party leaders that the movement they sought to guide might lurch out of control was fading. On 15 April 1921 a key event took place: the miners struck against wage cuts; the other major unions refused to back them, and the miners were eventually compelled to return to work. Rising unemployment helped to dampen union activities too. Many unions reorganised themselves into larger units, such as the Amalgamated Engineering Union (1920) and the Transport and General Workers (1921). They strengthened their links with the Labour Party through a National Joint Council representing the TUC General Council, the National Executive of the Labour Party, and the Parliamentary Labour Party. The Liberal Party had no links to workers such as Labour had with the unions.

Labour Party leaders pursued cautious policies, refusing to allow the newly formed British Communist Party to affiliate with them, and rejecting involvement with the Third International through which the USSR sought to guide socialists in other lands. Labour was able to exploit Lloyd George's retreat from social reform and his harsh policies towards trade unions.

In addition Labour also offered an idealistic foreign policy, attacking the old system that had led to conflict in 1914. The Labour Party absorbed the old UDC beliefs that the war was due to secret diplomacy, the arms race, and a mistaken pursuit of the theory of the balance of power. Labour stressed the value of the new League of Nations. These were attractive ideas to a war-weary nation. ILP leaders like MacDonald and Snowden returned to Parliament, no longer blamed for opposing a war which was now widely seen as dreadful in its impact. MacDonald's wartime stand helped him to win sufficient left-wing support to secure him the leadership of the Party. The historian Martin Pugh believes that events after 1914 allowed 'Labour to inherit the mantle of radicalism and to rally middle class and working class progressives under its wing.' (*History VI*, No. 5)

Labour's organisation improved too. Dr Marion Phillips led the new Women's Section. Four Standing Committees served the National Executive, and these dealt with organisation and elections; policies; literature and research; and finance and general purposes. By 1922 the *Daily Herald* relied upon financial support from Labour and preached the party's policies. Henderson's drive to set up local party branches was taking effect in industrial areas. In Bradford, for example, a party branch was formed in 1919 from the ILP, the Trades Council and the Workers' Municipal Federation. Branches like Bradford, Leeds, and Huddersfield were able to support full-time agents. Michael Savage has suggested that:

> 'The Labour Party underwent a fundamental change in character in the early 1920s in many areas; it changed from a party based on certain trade unions to one based on neighbourhood organisation.'
>
> (*The Dynamics of Working Class Politics*, 1987)

Ramsay MacDonald now played a key role in establishing the character of the Labour Party. His aim was to edge out the Liberals and make Labour the second party. His impressive appearance, effective oratory, and winning personality made him the dominant force in the party till its split in 1931. MacDonald was adept at describing a socialist utopia, using the vaguest of language, whilst actually advocating the most cautious of policies designed to win the widest support.

MacDonald's opportunity for office came in 1924. In 1922 a Conservative government took power, but plunged into an election in November 1923 in which choosing between the policy of free trade or that of protection formed the main issue. Liberal and Labour alike rallied to the cause of free trade. As a result, they together outnumbered Conservative MPs. Baldwin resigned and MacDonald (as leader of the bigger opposition party) was asked to form a ministry. He did so, in the knowledge that it would be brief, but eager to establish Labour's moderation and its independence of the Liberals. Thus Liberals who were ready to help Labour found themselves snubbed – not least because MacDonald shared Baldwin's loathing of Lloyd George. Lloyd George commented:

> 'Liberals are to be the oxen to drag the Labour train over the rough roads of Parliament, and when there is no further use for them they are to be slaughtered. That is the Labour idea of co-operation.'

He rightly assessed what MacDonald was up to, saying to his daughter that Labour leaders

> 'are all engaged in looking as respectable as lather and blather will make them. They are out to soothe ruffled nerves . . .
> Ramsay is just a fussy Baldwin and no more.'
> (K. O. Morgan, *Lloyd George Family Letters*, 1973)

It is not easy to know how far Labour's rapid rise was due to the widening of the franchise in 1918. Certainly new voters had no special reason to feel allegiance to the Liberal Party, and Labour had long had links with those who were fighting for women's suffrage. Martin Pugh argues that the evidence is unclear: voters divided roughly equally between the two parties in the early 1920s.

In 1924 the Labour Prime Minister MacDonald himself took control of the Foreign Office. His efforts here boosted the Party's claims to be working for a new and peaceful world order. He was the only British leader to attend the League of Nations. He helped calm a crisis between France and Germany, sharing in the work that produced a deal which ended French occupation of the Ruhr. He played a major part in working out the Dawes Plan, which tackled the vexed question of reparations to be paid to France by Germany for the havoc caused by the war: annual amounts were agreed that Germany was ready to pay and France to accept. MacDonald also worked out a plan (the Geneva Protocol) to increase League power to enforce its decisions (though his Conservative successors killed off the idea). Imperial policy was managed by J. H. Thomas, a man who had made his career through railway unionism. It was indistinguishable from that of his predecessors, and involved using the RAF to bomb Iraqis hostile to their British-backed rulers.

Labour's claims to be a party of social reform were severely constrained by their Chancellor of the Exchequer, Philip Snowden. Snowden supported free trade, and he cut and abolished a range of import duties; few Labour men knew enough about economics to stand up to the Chancellor's savage oratory. Nevertheless the ministry did return to the need for inexpensive housing: John Wheatley worked out a scheme of Treasury subsidies to local authorities that made possible the building of half a million council homes for rent. And at the Board of Education, the ex-Liberal Trevelyan increased free places in secondary schools, and restored the state scholarships that enabled ordinary children to afford a university education – scholarships that had been stopped by Lloyd George's cuts.

Strikes in 1924 showed that Labour was as ready to use emergency powers – and even to deploy troops – as any Liberal or Conservative government would have been. In a way it was helpful to MacDonald that his Ministry fell as it did, for it helped him retain his image as a man of the left. His government recognised the Russian government and worked on plans for treaties to improve trade and financial arrangements between the two countries.

Weary of Labour hostility, the Liberals planned to join the Conservatives in opposing a proposed loan to Russia. Then came a new opportunity for a break. The government abandoned the idea of bringing a charge of incitement to mutiny against J. R. Campbell, a Communist journalist who had written an article urging British troops not to fire on workers involved in the 1924 industrial upheavals. MacDonald was defeated by 364 to 191 votes, and he called an election. During the campaign the *Daily Mail* published a letter supposedly from the Russian Communist leader Zinoviev. The letter asked Communists to stir up workers to revolution with the aid of MacDonald's Anglo-Soviet treaty. These events helped to rally left-wingers behind MacDonald, as he seemed to be a man who was being persecuted by the establishment.

The 1924 election saw votes for the Labour Party increase, though it lost forty seats to a reunited and revived Conservative Party. But at least MacDonald had the satisfaction of seeing Liberal representation slump, and his own party clearly established as second to the Conservatives. MacDonald was able to comment to the king:

'They have in fact demonstrated that they, no less than any other Party, recognise their duties and responsibilities and have done much to dispel the fantastic and extravagant belief that they were nothing but a band of irresponsible revolutionaries intent on wreckage and destruction.'

# Troubles in the 1920s and 30s

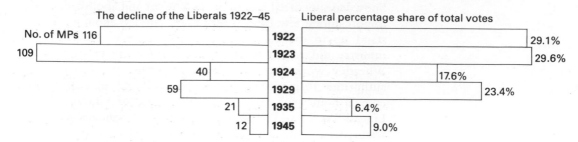

The decline of the Liberals 1922–45

| No. of MPs | | Liberal percentage share of total votes | |
|---|---|---|---|
| 116 | **1922** | 29.1% | |
| 109 | **1923** | 29.6% | |
| 40 | **1924** | 17.6% | |
| 59 | **1929** | 23.4% | |
| 21 | **1935** | 6.4% | |
| 12 | **1945** | 9.0% | |

The Labour Party had displaced the Liberal Party as Britain's second biggest political party. In 1929 it became the biggest party in the Commons (though without a clear overall majority), and for two years formed the government. The 1931 election, however, cut it down to a mere fifty-two MPs; and on the eve of the Second World War it had only 154 representatives in Parliament.

There were those on the left of politics who complained that Labour was too cautious and that it ought to be offering much bolder policies. The ILP, led by James Maxton, despaired of its former members, MacDonald and Snowden. In 1925 the ILP produced proposals called *Socialism in Our Time* that suggested a range of practical reforms. MacDonald was horrified; indeed he thought that the very title threatened his efforts to recruit wide support. By 1927 the ILP had cut its connections with the Labour Party. While in office from 1929 to 1931, Labour continued down the cautious path on which MacDonald had set it. The government improved unemployment benefits; cut miners' working hours; began a slum clearance programme; and set up marketing boards to control prices in branches of agriculture. To the main issues of the time – unemployment and economic depression – Labour had no answers as positive and imaginative as those offered by Lloyd George.

In 1932 a new left-wing pressure group emerged – the Socialist League. It also found that its ideas were frustrated: its demands for a 'Popular Front' alliance of Labour with the ILP and Communists in order to fight Fascism led to the League being disaffiliated from the party in 1937. Even after MacDonald's fall in 1937, Labour leadership remained in cautious hands. Arthur Henderson was succeeded in 1932 by the elderly pacifist George Lansbury. In 1935 Clement Attlee replaced Lansbury. Attlee came from a public school background; his control of the party rested heavily on backing from trade unionists, especially from the formidable Ernest Bevin.

But progress along the path of cautious policy-making did not go smoothly. Events in 1926 seemed to threaten the party with the return of 'direct action' – the belief that trade unionists could use their power to alter society. The nine-day General Strike of 1926 had its roots in the troubles of the coal industry. Coal's inability to prosper stemmed from the growth of rival forms of power, the high cost of British exports, and the inefficiency of over 1400 separate mining companies that ran the industry. The owners' solution – to cut wages, scrap a national wage structure, and increase hours – was delayed by the government's nine-month £23 million subsidy. When that subsidy ended and the crisis returned, the Conservative government was ready to fight the inevitable strike. Other unions, and the TUC, rallied to the miners' support, but their efforts failed, and they abandoned the battle. The miners struggled on until they were driven back by hunger.

The language used by some union leaders – especially by the miners' fiery secretary, A. J. Cook – alarmed the Labour leadership. Labour politicians vowed support for the miners, yet the episode was not the kind of event they relished. They argued that it was simply a struggle for decent conditions for miners, but MacDonald later wrote that a general strike was

> 'clumsy and ineffectual . . . I hope that the result will be thorough reconsideration of trade union tactics. If the wonderful unity in the strike . . . would be shown in politics, Labour could solve the mining and similar difficulties through the ballot box.'
> (A. Bullock, *The Life and Times of Ernest Bevin,* Vol. 1, 1960)

The TUC paper *The British Worker* insisted that 'The General Council does not challenge the constitution', but the government-financed *British Gazette* argued differently. It maintained that the TUC was challenging the constitution and was trying 'to force upon some forty-two million British citizens the will of less than four million others'. In 1927 the Trade Disputes Act declared general strikes illegal; banned civil servants from joining the TUC; and hit Labour Party income by requiring that union members wishing to subscribe to the party should do so separately instead of automatically through their union subscriptions.

A further source of Labour troubles at this time came from the collapse of its government in 1931. MacDonald and his ministers faced a world slump that aggravated the existing troubles of the British economy. Exports fell, unemployment rose, and foreign investors withdrew gold from Britain. Though ministers were agreed on pay cuts and other measures to tackle the troubles, serious reductions in unemployment benefits were more than some could accept. MacDonald, Snowden and a handful of Labour MPs agreed to remain and join a coalition: the rest resigned and suffered heavy defeat in a general election. The result was an upsurge of bitterness towards the old leadership.

Labour's struggles to recover were based on sturdy foundations.

*MacDonald arriving to accept the seals of office from the king in 1929.*

*This small group consists of Labour's women MPs in 1929.*

The unions were strongly committed to work for a Labour government; and the General Strike had driven home that need. Labour success in local elections even brought control of London County Council to Herbert Morrison's Labour group. In the 1935 General Election, Labour polled a mere 64,000 votes less than in 1929, but its relative lack of success was due to the frequency with which Labour candidates faced National Government candidates, and were therefore not able to enjoy the benefits of votes split between Liberals and Conservatives.

The double menace of Hitler and Mussolini helped the party to rally anti-fascist feeling, and by the late 1930s the party was voting for a rearmament programme. At the same time Attlee insisted that his party should develop detailed domestic policy programmes. Morrison and Hugh Dalton drew up plans for the reform of the social services, of electricity, banking, and transport, and of the cotton, coal, and iron and steel industries.

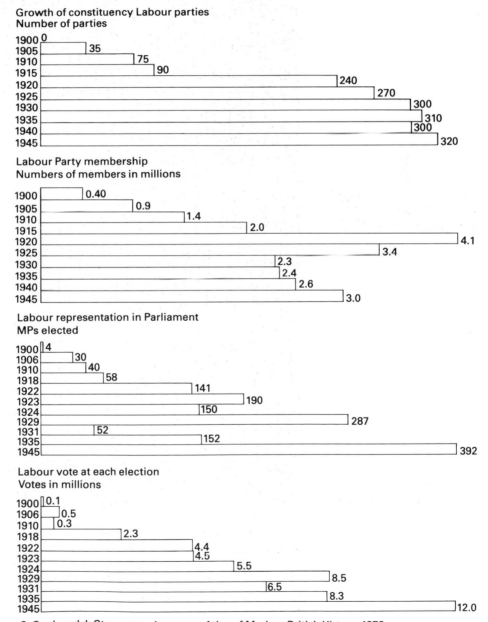

**Growth of constituency Labour parties**
**Number of parties**

| Year | Value |
|---|---|
| 1900 | 0 |
| 1905 | 35 |
| 1910 | 75 |
| 1915 | 90 |
| 1920 | 240 |
| 1925 | 270 |
| 1930 | 300 |
| 1935 | 310 |
| 1940 | 300 |
| 1945 | 320 |

**Labour Party membership**
**Numbers of members in millions**

| Year | Value |
|---|---|
| 1900 | 0.40 |
| 1905 | 0.9 |
| 1910 | 1.4 |
| 1915 | 2.0 |
| 1920 | 4.1 |
| 1925 | 3.4 |
| 1930 | 2.3 |
| 1935 | 2.4 |
| 1940 | 2.6 |
| 1945 | 3.0 |

**Labour representation in Parliament**
**MPs elected**

| Year | Value |
|---|---|
| 1900 | 4 |
| 1906 | 30 |
| 1910 | 40 |
| 1918 | 58 |
| 1922 | 141 |
| 1923 | 190 |
| 1924 | 150 |
| 1929 | 287 |
| 1931 | 52 |
| 1935 | 152 |
| 1945 | 392 |

**Labour vote at each election**
**Votes in millions**

| Year | Value |
|---|---|
| 1900 | 0.1 |
| 1906 | 0.5 |
| 1910 | 0.3 |
| 1918 | 2.3 |
| 1922 | 4.4 |
| 1923 | 4.5 |
| 1924 | 5.5 |
| 1929 | 8.5 |
| 1931 | 6.5 |
| 1935 | 8.3 |
| 1945 | 12.0 |

C. Cook and J. Stevenson, *Longman Atlas of Modern British History*, 1978.

1945 Labour Party
campaign poster.

# Labour from the 1940s

The Labour politician Ernest Bevin seeks to impress a voter
of the future (1945).

The election of 1945 finally brought real power to the Labour
Party. It had more MPs than those of all the other parties
combined. This success had its roots in the recovery of the later
1930s; it also owed something to the suspicion felt by many
voters towards the Conservative Party that had pursued appease-
ment at that time; and finally wartime itself had brought further
benefits.

   The arrival in office of Winston Churchill in 1940 had led to the
creation of a coalition. Attlee became, in effect, Churchill's
deputy; and Labour men took up several ministerial positions of
real importance – such as Ernest Bevin, who became Minister of
Labour. So the Labour Party that faced the polls in 1945 was led
by experienced people. Churchill concentrated on military and
world affairs, leaving Labour to take the lead in home affairs.

The triumphant figure of
the new Labour Prime
Minister of 1945,
Clement Attlee, amid
supporters.

Wartime social reforms, and the plans for further changes embodied in the Beveridge Report, linked Labour in voters' minds with an improved post-war Britain. Certainly Labour showed more enthusiasm than Churchill did for implementing William Beveridge's ideas for a national health service and a comprehensive national insurance scheme: Churchill was more concerned about the costs of such plans at a time when there were other demands on the economy. The historian A. R. Ball suggests:

> 'The Labour victory was a product of the movement of British opinion and expectations arising from the war. The 1945 election was a retrospective judgement of Conservative attitudes and policies in the inter-war years.'
>
> (*British Political Parties*, 1981)

In the 1945 election Labour offered state control of the Bank of England, of the fuel and power industries, of inland transport, and of iron and steel. It promised to implement the plans of the Beveridge Report and to improve education. The historian Paul Addison has noted how the election showed that Labour had widened its appeal:

> 'the working classes of the declining areas of heavy industry joined forces, through the ballot box, with much of the more prosperous working class in the Midlands and South Coast and a substantial section of the urban middle classes.'

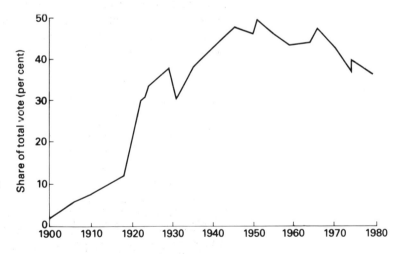

*The Labour Party's varying fortunes as shown by its share of the vote in general elections 1900–79.*

The party's wide appeal was evident in Parliament too. Most MPs were no longer trade unionists – members of the professions were more numerous. The Labour politician Arthur Greenwood asserted:

> 'We are a cross-section of the national life, and this is something that has never happened before.'
>
> (Quoted in P. Addison, *The Road to 1945*, 1975)

*The Labour Party attracted many female supporters. This is a meeting in 1949 of the Dulwich Labour Party's Women's Section.*

Labour's welfare policies will be dealt with in the next chapter. In part they had their roots in earlier programmes, in wartime coalition policies, and in the thinking of the Liberal, Beveridge. They proved to be policies that – till 1979 at least – the Conservative Party did not seek to reverse. The party's nationalisation programme focused on troubled areas of the economy, provided substantial compensation for private owners and followed a management structure that excluded workers' control of the industries in which they were employed. Conservatives were able to accept this programme too – with the exception of the nationalisation of the profitable road haulage business and of the iron and steel industry.

Abroad, the policies of Attlee and Bevin built up a western alliance against Stalin's Russia, equipped Britain with nuclear weapons, retained a form of conscription for the forces, and sent British forces to Korea to assist American efforts to repel an assault by the Communist North on the non-Communist South. There were Conservative critics of the government's withdrawal from parts of the Empire – especially from India; but most recognised, however, that Britain no longer had the strength to be a great imperial power.

Labour lost office in 1951, yet polled more votes than ever before (and over 200,000 more than the Conservatives). It therefore seems surprising that the party then remained in opposition for thirteen years. This period was marked by deep divisions, as Labour struggled to establish a clear identity to which voters would respond in preference to their opponents. The Conservatives, meanwhile, enjoyed the benefits of world economic recovery and of the capable leadership of men like Butler, Macleod, and

Macmillan. The Labour Party split, especially on issues of defence (see the last section of this chapter on p. 176), chiefly about the use of nuclear weapons. It was also divided over how much further it should pursue a programme of state control of the economy. Hugh Gaitskell, who led the party from 1955 to 1963 even attempted in 1959 (in vain) to persuade his followers to abandon clause 4 (see page 154). For a time Aneurin Bevan, Minister of Health from 1945 to 1950, provided a focus for discontent.

*Three Labour leaders: Harold Wilson, Hugh Gaitskell and George Brown.*

Both in opposition, and even more so when in office in the 1960s and 70s, the relationship of the party to the trade union movement emerged as an issue. Party leaders detected a growing popular unease about trade union power, but efforts to control the unions and reduce their grip on the party were not a success. Unions insisted they must be free to bargain as they thought best, and they wrecked the Labour government's 1969 *In Place of Strife* proposals. J. E. Cronin has argued that the unions' refusal to change, coupled with their retention of power over the party through finance and votes at party conferences, has hampered Labour's need to modernise and widen its appeal.

In addition the pro-Labour press did not fare well in the post-war years. In the 1940s 40 per cent of the sales of major newspapers were made by papers sympathetic to Labour. By the 1980s papers supporting the Conservatives attracted three times the readership of pro-Labour papers. The Labour/TUC-owned *Daily Herald* had vanished completely, transformed by various financial and takeover crises into *The Sun*. The historian Keith Laybourn has wondered whether 'the most fundamental reason for Labour decline, underpinning most other factors, has been the unwillingness of the party to adapt to the changing nature of British society.' The old industries like coal, iron and steel, and shipbuilding declined in the 60s and 70s. But these areas provided the heartland of Labour strength. The struggles of these workers to defend their industries contributed heavily to the numbers of strikes that so damaged Labour at the polls. In 1979 nearly 30,000 days' work were lost through strikes: in the same year James Callaghan's Labour government lost office to Margaret Thatcher's Conservatives, and polled only 11.5 million votes, compared with 14 million in 1951. Party membership fell too, slipping officially by 1976 to under two thirds of its 1950 figure. According to the sociologist A. H. Halsey, 'Labour parties now are even more deserted than the chapels to which they owed so much of their early education.'

# Conservative fortunes

| Date | CONSERVATIVES | | | LABOUR | | | LIBERALS | | | OTHERS | | Total MPs elected |
|------|----------------------------|---------------|-------------|----------------------------|---------------|-------------|----------------------------|---------------|-------------|----------------------------|-------------|---|
| | Total vote (millions) | % of votes cast | Seats won | Total vote (millions) | % of votes cast | Seats won | Total vote (millions) | % of votes cast | Seats won | Total vote (millions) | Seats won | |
| 1945 | 10.0 | 39.8 | 213 | 12.0 | 47.8 | 393 | 2.2 | 9.0 | 12 | 0.9 | 22* | 640 |
| 1950 | 12.5 | 43.5 | 298 | 13.3 | 46.1 | 315 | 2.6 | 9.1 | 9 | 0.4 | 3 | 625 |
| 1951 | 13.7 | 48.0 | 321 | 13.9 | 48.8 | 295 | 0.7 | 2.5 | 6 | 0.2 | 3 | 625 |
| 1955 | 13.3 | 49.7 | 344 | 12.4 | 46.4 | 277 | 0.7 | 2.7 | 6 | 0.3 | 3 | 630 |
| 1959 | 13.7 | 49.4 | 365 | 12.2 | 43.8 | 258 | 1.6 | 5.9 | 6 | 0.1 | 1 | 630 |
| 1964 | 12.0 | 43.4 | 304 | 12.2 | 44.1 | 317 | 3.1 | 11.2 | 9 | 0.3 | 0 | 630 |
| 1966 | 11.4 | 41.9 | 253 | 13.1 | 48.0 | 363 | 2.3 | 8.5 | 12 | 0.5 | 2 | 630 |
| 1970 | 13.1 | 46.4 | 330 | 12.2 | 43.0 | 287 | 2.1 | 7.5 | 6 | 0.9 | 7+ | 630 |
| 1974 (Feb) | 11.9 | 37.9 | 297 | 11.6 | 37.1 | 301 | 6.1 | 19.3 | 14 | 1.8 | 23** | 635 |
| 1974 (Oct) | 10.5 | 35.9 | 277 | 11.5 | 39.2 | 319 | 5.3 | 18.3 | 13 | 1.9 | 26++ | 635 |
| 1979 | 13.7 | 43.9 | 339 | 11.5 | 36.9 | 269 | 4.3 | 13.8 | 11 | 1.8 | 16= | 635 |

*General elections 1945–79.*

Although the Conservative Party contained people who had disliked the extension of the franchise in 1918, there is no evidence to show that this harmed the party, and indeed some historians believe that newly-enfranchised female voters in particular were inclined to vote Conservative. By 1928 Conservative fears of the impact on them of a wider franchise had gone; and it was the Conservative leader, Baldwin, who provided women with the vote on the same terms as men. The struggle between the Liberal and Labour Parties for the anti-Conservative vote helped the party too. The Liberal peer Lord Lothian commented in 1935:

> 'Toryism appeals to the instinct for conserving the traditions of the past, it prefers experience to theory . . . it has the immense interests of property and social privilege almost wholly behind it as a source of funds and influence.'
>
> (J. R. M. Butler, *Lord Lothian*, 1960)

*Stanley Baldwin, Conservative Prime Minister and one of the most skilful of inter-war politicians, stands (front left) outside Chequers with his family. His son, Oliver, joined the Labour Party.*

Certainly Liberal decline helped Conservative leaders to rally behind them those who had wealth and property. And although in fact Labour showed few signs of trying to implement socialist policies, Conservatives commonly described Labour leaders as socialists, and exploited fears of Communist Russia by trying to link Labour men to that country's beliefs.

The First World War helped Conservatism to recover and to leave behind links to anti-government military movements in Ireland. When Lloyd George's coalition no longer served their party's interests, the Conservatives broke with him in 1922. This

*The new Prime Minister of 1937 – Neville Chamberlain.*

divided the Conservatives, but Baldwin's skilful leadership had reunited the Party by 1924. Baldwin's character and achievements show another strength of the Conservative Party – it responded effectively to changing social and political conditions. Baldwin and Neville Chamberlain carried out a range of social reforms and preached the merits of the Conservative Party as the party of capable economic management. Baldwin, like Macmillan in the 60s, presented his party as a movement concerned with the whole nation, not just with one sector.

The Conservative Party of this period was more affluent than its rivals. It could afford to pay more party agents than either the Liberal or the Labour Party could do; it developed skilful advertising; and its leaders adapted well to the age of radio and the newsreel. The party organisation of the inter-war years improved the pay and training of its party agents; developed a flourishing women's section; and used volunteers to offset the constraints on spending at election time – in short adapted well to the new conditions in which voter registration was no longer the key.

Though the party organisation decayed during the Second World War, it was soon revived by Lord Woolton. Heavy spending on advertising brought a professionalism to Tory campaigns that their rivals found hard to match: for example, in 1964 Conservative spending in the run-up to the election was treble what Labour could afford. The Young Conservatives, founded in 1949, proved a highly successful movement. Swinton College was set up to polish further the training of party agents. By 1950 the party had twice the number of agents that it had deployed in the 1945 election. Further reforms (suggested by Sir David Maxwell Fyfe) made it easier for candidates to be selected even if they lacked great wealth. Candidates were not allowed to contribute more than £25 to election costs (£50 if a sitting MP): this scrapped

*The Conservative leader, Winston Churchill (1951).*

the old system which had encouraged constituencies to choose wealthy candidates who were able to dig deeply into their purses to pay electoral costs. Lord Woolton's efforts lifted party membership from 1.2 million in 1947 to a million more in 1948.

*The Conservative leader Harold Macmillan as seen by cartoonist Vicky. His success in restoring party fortunes after the Suez crisis of 1956 impressed many at the time.*

"I TOLD YOU THIS SORT OF STUFF WILL FETCH 'EM BACK INTO THE OLD CINEMA . . ."

Sir Alex Douglas-Home, leader of the Conservative Party, was in office for the briefest of periods in 1963–64.

Harold Macmillan in one of his favourite roles – that of country gentleman.

The Conservative Party allowed its annual conferences little power. Until the 1965 election of Edward Heath, its leaders 'emerged' after an obscure period of consultation, influence, and pressure from party grandees. But from 1965 a complex system of voting by MPs was adopted.

The Conservatives exploited the period of post-war prosperity, retaining Labour's social reforms of 1945–51, yet sweeping away some controls and making much of the success of their policy of pouring resources into a house-building programme. This helps to account for their success in being able to attract votes from the working class as well as from the more affluent. In 1970 the party took about 45 per cent of the votes of the manual working class.

During the 1970s the party evolved policies that were increasingly critical of the post-1945 strategies of state interference in everyday life. It caught the mood of many people weary of trade union behaviour in the 1960s and 1970s, and it swept Margaret Thatcher into office in 1979.

From 1914 to 1979 the Conservatives had shown their ability to respond to changing conditions and to offer policies with wide appeal. Their reward was to dominate these years.

# Pressure groups – peace movements in the twentieth century

## *The Great War*

In August 1914 Bertrand Russell was an eminent lecturer at Cambridge University. The outbreak of the First World War horrified him. He wrote a letter to a magazine declaring:

> 'All this madness, all this rage, all this flaming death of our civilisation and our hopes, has been brought about because a set of official gentlemen living luxurious lives, mostly stupid, and all without imagination or heart, have chosen that it should occur rather than that any of them should suffer some infinitesimal rebuff to his country's pride. And behind the diplomacy . . . stand vast forces of national greed and national hatred . . . concentrated and directed by Governments and the Press, fostered by the upper class as a distraction from social discontent, artificially nourished by the sinister influence of the makers of armaments, encouraged by a whole foul literature of glory and by every textbook of history with which the minds of children are polluted.'
>
> (*The Nation*)

Russell's active opposition to the war lost him his lectureship. He was offered a post at Harvard University in the USA, but the British Government would not issue him with a passport, and before the war was over he had served six months in prison for his anti-war writings.

Russell was just one of a number of people totally against the Great War. Some were pacifists opposed to any conflict, others (like MacDonald) believed that this particular war was unjust. That individuals should attack a government's foreign and military policies was nothing new; but the Great War saw the emergence of organised opposition, of pressure groups eager to alter those policies. As twentieth-century warfare became more dreadful and devastating through the development of ever more effective ways of bringing death to the enemy, so organised opposition to war expanded. Policies of this period may have been determined by the political parties in power, but pressure groups sought to affect those policies. The spread of popular education and of magazines and newspapers, together with greater wea' and more opportunities for travel, made it easier for pre groups seeking popular support to operate.

The outbreak of war in 1914 led to the establishment in December of the Union of Democratic Control. Within a year this body had about a hundred branches. It included ILP men like Keir Hardie, Ramsay MacDonald and Philip Snowden, and it also attracted Liberals who opposed the conflict. The UDC attributed the war to the secret nature of diplomacy: it preached that foreign policies should be open and democratically controlled. It feared that the pressures of war would transform society by 'prussianising it', that is by increasing the power of the state at the expense of individual liberty. The passage of the Defence of the Realm Acts seemed to UDC members to prove this point. But the biggest fear that lurked in the minds of those against the war was that the government would introduce conscription. Unlike other European countries, Britain had an army made up of volunteers. As the conflicts of 1914–15 killed and crippled those volunteers, cries for conscription became increasingly loud.

Clifford Allen and Fenner Brockway founded the No Conscription Fellowship (NCF) to resist these cries. The Prime Minister, Asquith, sought in vain to find an alternative to conscription. On 5 January 1916 he reluctantly put forward a bill to introduce conscription and saw it successfully through, with only thirty-six MPs voting against – thirty of whom were Liberals. In May 1916 the Universal Conscription Act established that all able-bodied men between the ages of eighteen and forty-one were liable for military service. The NCF, having failed to halt conscription, now focussed its efforts on seeking exemption for those who were opposed to the war: such opponents included members of certain religious groups, notably the Quakers, Jehovah's Witnesses, Christadelphians and Plymouth Brethren, while others opposed the war on moral or political grounds. In total about 16,000 men registered that they were conscientious objectors.

The government established tribunals to consider their cases. Those who were able to satisfy the businessmen, policemen, officers, clergymen and civil servants who made up these tribunals, were commonly offered alternative work or non-combatant duties with the forces. Quakers, for example, could often be found on battlefields working as ambulancemen, and sometimes risked their lives to rescue the wounded. The NCF held meetings and published a paper, and it also began coaching men who had to face a tribunal. Its ranks included Bertrand Russell and Dr Albert Salter (a bacteriologist); its chairman was Clifford Allen; and much of the detailed organisational work was done by Catherine Marshall.

It was difficult to help men totally opposed to any kind of wartime work. Such men were often called up, arrested when they refused to appear, or court-martialled and imprisoned, released after their sentence, then rearrested when they were called up once more and they refused to obey orders. Lloyd George, who had endured unpopularity for his opposition to the Boer

War, was especially hard on conscientious objectors. In 1916 the government tried a short-lived experiment with 'absolute refusers', sending them to work ten-hour days and six-day weeks in granite quarries near Aberdeen. The handful of anti-war MPs did their best to pester ministers, and *The Manchester Guardian* supported the committed conscientious objectors; but the mood of parliament was such that the objectors were even denied the vote in the 1918 general election.

## *The inter-war and Second World War years*

By the 1920s the mood among many British people had turned away from enthusiasm for forceful foreign policy. The Great War was seen as an appalling episode that must never be allowed to occur again. At such a time organisations seeking new forms of foreign policy that would avoid conflict in the future were able to flourish. Movements emerged such as the Women's International League of Peace and Freedom, the Fellowship of Reconciliation, and the No More War Movement. Such bodies held meetings, created festivals, published leaflets, and set up youth movements. Those who felt that the Scouts were too militaristic developed an alternative organisation – the Woodcraft Force.

The emergence of the League of Nations and the signing of the 1928 Kellogg Briand Pact by 115 states prepared to renounce war as an instrument of policy added to this mood of optimism. A flood of anti-war books poured off the presses; and the film *All Quiet on the Western Front* (1929), with its bleak portrayal of the reality of battle, attracted huge audiences. In 1932 a World Disarmament Conference took place; and in 1933 the Oxford Union debated whether 'this House will in no circumstances fight for King and Country', and agreed with the motion by 275 votes to 153. In the same year a by-election in Fulham East was won by J. C. Wilmot, a Labour man who stood for disarmament and co-operation with the League of Nations. For a while, from 1932 to 1935 the Labour Party itself was led by the pacifist George Lansbury. And during the early 1930s a clergyman, Dick Sheppard, organised the Peace Pledge Union.

But by the mid-30s this mood of optimism was fading. Mussolini's attack on Abyssinia, Hitler's rise to power, the power of militarism in Japan, and the Spanish Civil War all affected attitudes. Bevin's brutal attacks on Lansbury helped to oust him from the Labour leadership. Attlee, the new leader, was ready to support rearmament by the late 1930s.

The peace movements of the inter-war years took many forms and reflected revulsion at the events of the Great War. They faded as it became clear that fascist leaders responded only to force. Nevertheless the Second World War found 60,000 British men and women refusing to fight. Conscription came in at the start of the conflict, but was not the issue that it had been in 1915–16. Opponents of the war generally based their views on religious and moral beliefs, though some argued that fascism was the result of the needlessly harsh treatment of Germany after 1918. Tribunals operated more fairly than in the Great War, and indeed the whole issue of conscientious objection seemed less intense, dramatic, and emotional.

## Peace movements in a nuclear age

On 6 August 1945 an American B29 bomber, the *Enola Gay*, flying high above the Japanese city of Hiroshima, released a single bomb nicknamed 'Little Boy'. Three days later another American aircraft dropped a similar bomb ('Fat Man') on Nagasaki. By the end of the year 210,000 people had died as a result of these two atom bombs. These events opened up a whole new dimension to warfare. The development of nuclear bombs threatened a degree of devastation hitherto undreamed of. During 1949 the Soviet Union exploded an atomic bomb; Britain and France developed their own nuclear devices; and at the same time further research dramatically increased the destructive power of these terrible weapons. All this produced, in response, a pressure group more formidable than any of the previous peace movements.

In the early 1950s there were individual and small group protests. In 1952, for example, eleven people conducted a peaceful protest that obstructed the entrance to the War Office and led to them being fined. Leaflets were given out to staff at the Aldermaston Atomic Weapons Research Station, at the American airforce base at Mildenhall, and at Porton Down Microbiological Research Centre. Several Labour MPs questioned their party's commitment to the new weapons. In 1958 a gathering of several opponents of nuclear weapons led to the creation of the Campaign for Nuclear Disarmament. Labour leaders like Michael Foot were prominent in it, but it went beyond Labour ranks. The elderly Bertrand Russell joined, so too did the historian A. J. P. Taylor and the writer J. B. Priestley. At the head of the movements stood Canon John Collins.

On Easter Day 1958 CND held its first march. It was organised by a direct action committee, and 600 people set off on a lengthy walk, after a rally attended by 5000 people. In the following years these marches became major events. The second march, in 1959, started at Aldermaston, and by the time it had reached London for a rally in Trafalgar Square its numbers had totalled 15,000. The 1960 march ended with about 40,000 people. CND drew to it all sorts of different groups. Under its badge marched pacifists, members of religious groups, Labour left-wingers, and environmentalists. It attracted the backing of some trade unionists, notably Frank Cousins, leader of the Transport Workers. Its ideas were spread through magazines like *Peace News* and *Tribune*. The Labour Party felt its impact, for the CND cause provided a useful focus for those who felt that the party leader, Hugh Gaitskell, was drifting too far to the right and was too pro-NATO in his views. Having just lost an election in 1959, Gaitskell was not well placed to resist. In 1960 the Labour Party Conference voted in favour of Britain following a policy of unilateral nuclear disarmament, offering a lead it was hoped that other lands would follow.

However, Gaitskell refused to accept this decision, mobilised support in favour of a policy of multilateral disarmament, and eventually triumphed. By the end of 1961 – despite a huge rally that year – CND was showing signs of splitting up. The last great Easter march took place in 1963.

CND remains an important and active pressure group, however, and offers a model for non-violent protest that other groups have now copied.

## ESSAY

Choose one of the following titles. Plan and write an answer in essay form.

1. 'The outbreak of the First World War initiated a process of disintegration in the Liberal Party which by 1918 had reduced it to ruins.' (Trevor Wilson) Is this the main reason why the Liberal Party declined?

2. Jeremiah Wooley, leader of Preston's Weavers and the country's first Labour Mayor, declared in 1922; 'A man should have work, he should be paid for his work, he should have a decent home, he should have sufficient leisure to enjoy life, he should have clothes for to wear, he should have a little spending money in his pocket.' Was it voters' support for such aims that brought about the rise of the Labour Party?

3. 'The Labour Party has been as much a part of the historic working class as was the growth of professional football. Both saw their heyday after 1945: both declined together thereafter.' (K. O. Morgan) Why did Labour face so many problems after 1951?

# Political power in action

Post-1918 British governments faced serious social problems for which pre-war Liberal reforms provided an insufficient cure. Moreover politicians were now very aware that they were answerable to a mass electorate who increasingly seemed to expect their leaders to do something about major issues, and not to leave them to be resolved by private actions. The way in which politicians approached social questions provides evidence of their beliefs, their *ideology*; their ability to act effectively offers insights into the *authority* they were able to command; and the consequences of their actions contributed to the changing *identity* of twentieth-century Britain.

In this section two aspects of social and economic matters will be examined: the problem of mass unemployment in the inter-war years and the emergence of a 'welfare state' after 1945. The material, therefore, focuses on such issues as:

- should governments interfere in the working of the economy to try to obtain full employment?
- how is it best to care for the very needy?

# The National Government and the problem of mass unemployment in the 1930s

## TASK

Work in pairs to gather arguments for and against government policies of this period.

# The problem

From 1921 until the outbreak of the Second World War in 1939, about 14 per cent of the insured workforce were, on average, out of work. Unemployment was not, of course, a new feature of life in Britain; but its long-term persistence was one part of the problem, and the other was its depth in the early 30s. In 1932 it plunged to a figure of over 22 per cent. As a result, in these inter-war years there were always a million people out of work, and in January 1933 as many as almost three million. Moreover some unemployed workers did not register as out of work – the actual figure was certainly higher than the official one.

| 1900 | | 1910 | | 1925 | | 1935 | | 1955 | |
|---|---|---|---|---|---|---|---|---|---|
| Poor relief | 8.4 | Poor relief | 12.4 | Poor relief | 31.4 | Poor relief | 34.3 | National assistance | 11 |
| | | Old age pensions | 8.5 | Pensions | 94.8 | Pensions | 98.0 | Pensions | 94 |
| | | Housing | 0.6 | Housing | 18.1 | Housing | 42.3 | Housing | 83 |
| | | | | Unemployment | 16.9 | Unemployment | 73.9 | National insurance | 49 |
| | | | | Health insurance etc | 21.1 | Health insurance etc | 25.7 | National health service | 44 |
| | | | | | | | | Family allowances | 94 |
| Total in millions of pounds | 8.4 | | 21.5 | | 182.3 | | 274.2 | | 375 |

E. J. Hobsbawm, *Industry and Empire*, 1968.

*Main items of social security expenditure 1900–55.*

The reaction of politicians in the 1920s was to hope that the problem was short-term, and to work to restore pre-war economic conditions. Ministers did not seek to spend money to revive the economy: instead they cut expenditure, believing that finance should flow to the private sector. Between 1920 and 1925 government spending fell by a quarter in real terms. In 1925 Winston Churchill, Chancellor of the Exchequer, restored the gold standard, thus making sterling freely convertible into gold and fixing its value at the pre-war figure of £1 = 4.86 US dollars. Foreign policy was aimed at settling differences, restoring harmony, and thus reviving trade.

This still left the problem of what to do about those with no income to provide for themselves. In the 1920s ministers edged towards introducing a broader system of support that relied increasingly on Treasury rather than on local money. The Unemployment Insurance Act (1920) increased the numbers of workers able to draw unemployment insurance and cut the number of contributions required for them to become entitled to help. In the following year, as unemployment figures climbed to over two million, the government authorised the continuation of payment to people who had used up the twenty-six weeks' payment to which they were entitled. 'Uncovenanted' or 'transitional' payments were made, and these took account of family needs with a system of payments for dependants. The alternative – to continue with the old system of sending the 'out of benefit' worker to the Poor Law Guardians – was no longer possible. Guardians were already struggling to cope with those who had no insurance entitlement. Given the very intense localised nature of unemployment, with its focus in areas where old export industries (like cotton and coal) were in recession, the arrival of workers who had used up their twenty-six weeks' entitlement would have swamped the system. So the Insurance Fund took the burden, and was soon heavily in debt. It had been planned on the basis of unemployment figures that were low and short-term. Contributions from those in work no longer provided enough to sustain the unemployed; the state was drawn in.

By 1929 politicians and economists were arguing over how best to tackle the problem. The Conservative Minister of Health, Neville Chamberlain, swept away the old Poor Law and placed its duties on large-sized local authorities. Their Public Assistance Committees now dealt with those not entitled either to insurance payments or to uncovenanted benefits. In 1930 Labour shifted the burden of the latter on to the Treasury. Conservative and Labour alike relied chiefly on the revival of the economy to solve the problems; but led by Lloyd George, the Liberals began to argue that the state must intervene. Lloyd George drew on the thinking of the economist John Maynard Keynes to offer the electorate the slogan 'We can conquer unemployment'. By borrowing £300 million, he argued, the state could fund public works like roads and house-building that would provide work and improve the country. Since far too few Liberals were elected in 1929 it is impossible to know if this would have worked. It may be that Lloyd George underestimated the administrative difficulties involved.

The Labour Ministry from 1929 to 1931 tinkered with welfare provision and began a very tiny public works programme, but it spurned the ideas of one of its number, Oswald Mosley, to act more boldly by using state power to revive the economy. As a world trade depression hit Britain too, unemployment rose, confidence in sterling fell, and gold began to flood out of the country. Although they agreed that public spending cuts were needed, ministers could not agree on a 10 per cent reduction in unemployment benefit. The ministry collapsed, and was replaced by a coalition of Conservatives, Liberals and a handful of Labour politicians headed by Ramsay MacDonald himself. In front of it lay the problems of a financial crisis, of a shrinkage of exports, and of the growing numbers of unemployed.

## Economic reforms

Though no election was needed, the government began by calling one. Baldwin, especially, wanted to exploit the opportunity of establishing his grip on his party. Liberal constituency withdrawals helped about a hundred Conservatives to Westminster. Baldwin's strategy worked. Though led by MacDonald till 1935, Martin Pugh suggests that the National Government was 'in policy and tone, if not in personnel, thoroughly Conservative'. In general, according to the historians, Chris Cook and John Stevenson:

> 'the main objectives of the Government were to balance budgets and restore business confidence, a view that was shared by the great majority of economists and Treasury advisers.'
>
> (*The Slump*, 1977)

## Financial measures

The Labour Chancellor of the Exchequer, Philip Snowden, remained in office for a short while. He had long been a stern opponent of heavy government spending. Now he applied the cuts over which his former colleagues had quarrelled. Teachers and armed service personnel had their pay reduced by 15 per cent; the police suffered 5 per cent reductions; and other public pay was lopped too – including unemployment benefit. Weekly amounts to an out-of-work man fell from 17s. to 15s. 3d. The historian A. J. P. Taylor commented:

> 'The members of the National Government may be seen in a newsreel assembled for discussion, stern features, teeth clenched as they face the crisis. They would hesitate at nothing to save the country, to save the pound. The result of their courage was that the children of the unemployed had less margarine on their bread. After this resolute decision Ministers dispersed to their warm comfortable homes and ate substantial meals.'
>
> (*English History 1914–45*, 1970)

In fact not even all the cuts survived. The fleet, anchored at Invergordon, mutinied. Their pay cut had to be modified to 10 per cent. Snowden also added 6d. to income tax and 1d. duty on a pint of beer. More dramatically, Britain followed the lead of other countries by abandoning the gold standard, and began to manage its currency instead of leaving its level for the markets to determine. The value of the pound fell by the end of 1931 to $3.40. Fifteen million pounds was placed in an Exchange Equalisation Account to be used for buying and selling currency to keep the pound stable. A. J. P. Taylor noted:

> 'A few days before, a managed currency had seemed as wicked as family planning. Now, like contraception, it became commonplace.'

Deals with France and the USA in 1936 settled that the three countries would not alter their rates without consulting one another.

The National Government also reduced the bank rate. Snowden left office in 1932, and was replaced by Chamberlain (till the latter became Prime Minister in 1937, following Baldwin's leadership from 1935 to 1937). Both men were equally committed to containing government spending and the interest payments on money borrowed by the government were adjusted downwards as a result of the bank rate falling to 2 per cent. This policy alone saved £86 million a year of ministry expenditure. In addition, low interest levels encouraged private borrowing, helping firms and individuals to finance their efforts. Cheap money played a big part in the 1930s housing boom, funding both construction work and mortgages for house purchase. The crisis jolted the thinking of politicians, and it even led to Keynes joining the official Committee on Economic Information; but it did not radically alter the official view that heavy state spending to revive the economy was not desirable. Supporters of this view can be found in all three political parties. Critics were present in all three too, though their numbers in the Conservative Party were small. By 1936 the tense state of foreign affairs meant that spending on rearmament could not be avoided: even here Chamberlain's desire for a balanced budget chopped back the £97 million sought by the RAF to £59 million. The modern four-engined bomber building programme was held back, while cheaper fighters rolled off production lines.

## Trade

In 1932 Philip Snowden resigned from office; so too did half the Liberal group, led by Herbert Samuel. What drove them out was the long-term commitment of the government to taxing imports. Baldwin had long been under pressure from some in his party to introduce tariffs – indeed he had offered this policy to the electorate in the early 1920s only to see most voters plump for free trade candidates from other parties. By 1931 he had agreed to make tariffs official policy, for the circumstances of the time seemed to suit this move. British producers feared that the country would be a dumping ground for cheap foreign goods sent here by countries that taxed imports into their own lands. The campaign waged by Lord Beaverbrooke's paper, the *Daily Express*, from 1929 onwards for imperial free trade formed another aspect of a policy of tariffs. Ever since Joseph Chamberlain had produced his proposal in Edwardian times, some Conservatives had argued that a prosperous British economy could best be obtained by tying together the different parts of the Empire as an economic unit, while taxing non-imperial goods.

The 1932 Import Duties Act imposed taxes on around three quarters of imports at levels of around 20 per cent, though in the case of iron and steel it was $33\frac{1}{3}$ per cent. A conference in 1932 was held at Ottawa to discuss trade between Empire and Commonwealth lands. Britain guaranteed free entry to her markets for most dominion goods, and got minor tariff concessions in return. In fact dominion governments were determined to protect their own farmers and industrialists, so the idea of a vast imperial free trade area proved to be unrealistic. In any case the government was not wholly committed to the idea. In 1933 MacDonald held a World Economic Conference in London to try to liberalise trade and to stablise exchange rates. It failed to live up to his hopes, though tariffs did prove to be a helpful bargaining counter in doing deals with other states. Between 1933 and 1938 twenty bilateral trade agreements were signed. The enthusiasts for imperial free trade were not happy about this approach, but during this period there was certainly a drift to more trade with the Empire. By 1938 47 per cent of exports from Britain went to the Empire and Commonwealth; and 39 per cent of imports into Britain came from there. The adoption of protection was a major shift in British policy, though the historian Trevor May suggests:

'The slow process of recovery which began in the 1930s seems to have owed little to protection, for one of the features of the inter-war economy was the decline in importance of international trade and the growth of the home market.'
(*An Economic and Social History of Britain 1760–1970*, 1987)


## Reforming the British economy

Stephen Constantine has suggested that

'the timidity of ministers was not due to the absence of alternative economic theories but to a failure of political will.'
(*Unemployment in Britain between the wars*, 1980)

Not all historians agree with the critical implications of this view. Chris Cook and John Stevenson maintain:

'It is a harsh judgement which condemns the National Government for failing to alter the regional imbalance of unemployment at a time of world recession and when the problem still remains.'

(*The Slump*)

There were plenty of critics at the time. Oswald Mosley built up the British Union of Fascists, pointed to the Italian and German governments' efforts, and argued for more state controls and spending. In 1935 Lloyd George repeated his earlier proposals, modifying them in the light of US government policies, and calling them a 'new deal'. Keynes published his major work, *The General Theory of Employment Interest and Money*, in 1936, arguing that full employment would not come from the automatic operation of market forces, and that state action was needed to affect both investment and consumption. Yet no one can tell if these ideas would have worked, and most advisers urged ministers to follow traditionally cautious policies. Nor did the government control the huge bureaucracy of modern times: it is not clear that large-scale peace-time state intervention would have been either practical or politically acceptable. The National Government had a huge majority in 1931 and a very comfortable one in 1935.

Initial policies were negative. Labour's subsidies for public works were ended, for fear of channelling resources away from private ventures. Ministers grumbled at local authorities that spent on public works, complaining they were wasteful. As signs of recovery appeared and public pressures were felt, so the government edged cautiously into a number of initiatives. Ministers were aware of political upheaval in other lands and were nervous of similar events in Britain. During the 1930s there were a number of marches and protests, the most famous being the 1936 Jarrow March, of men from a town ruined by the closure of Palmer's shipyard. Over 11,000 signed a petition stating:

'Whereas for fifteen years Jarrow has endured industrial depression without parallel in the town's history, all efforts for the resuscitation of industry have failed and the future holds no prospect of work for the many thousands unemployed. Therefore the petitioners humbly pray that the necessary active assistance be given by the Government for the provision of work in the town of Jarrow . . .'

Baldwin had no time for this form of pressure. He observed:

'In the opinion of H. M. Government such marches can do no good to the causes for which they are represented to be undertaken, are liable to cause unnecessary hardship to those taking part in them and are altogether undesirable in this country governed by a Parliamentary system where every area has its representative in the House of Commons to put forward grievance and suggest remedies, processions to London cannot claim to have any constitutional influence on policy . . . Ministers cannot consent to receive any deputation of Marchers.'

(*The Times*, 15 October 1936)

What the National Government actually did may have been reluctantly undertaken, and was certainly a piecemeal strategy rather than a clearly thought out coherent one; but it showed signs of a commitment to manage the economy that bears out Stephen Constantine's view:

'In the new thinking which emerged between the wars, government was given an increasingly predominant role. For this the unemployment problem was largely responsible.'

Government backing went to railway building, and London Transport and road building (from 1935). Government loans made possible the resumption of work on the half-built luxury liner *Queen Mary* on the Clyde. When rearmament began, contracts were placed in depressed areas to help the iron and steel and the shipbuilding industries. The 1929–31 Labour Government had established government-backed agricultural marketing boards that the National Government developed. Separate boards for milk, hops, potatoes and meat, together with support for the sugar-beet industries, ate up forty million pounds a year in subsidies by 1936, and people approved. One farmer commented:

> 'The Milk Marketing Board started in 1933. My father kept bullocks, milked a few cows, and mother took butter to Exeter and sold it for about 1/10d. a pound. We probably took £5 a week. It was not a very good way of making a living. But through the formation of the Milk Board everybody was paid the same price for milk throughout the country. We were then getting the equivalent of double the price for liquid milk . . . and this stabilised Devon farming in particular because here was an ideal grass-growing area, and we could keep cows and it could be profitable.'

(Quoted in Pagnamenta and Overy, *All Our Working Lives*, 1984)

Some effort was made to overhaul and reduce the capacity of old-fashioned industries. Attempts to rationalise the coal industry came to little, though royalties paid to landowners where pits were developed were nationalised. The 1935 Finance Act offered tax relief to industries that were reorganised to shed excessive capacity. Iron and steel in particular received a high level of tariff protection in return for promises to reform. An Act of 1936 attacked the problem of surplus cotton-spinning capacity, by setting up a Spindles Board which bought up and scrapped cotton-spinning machinery using money raised by levies on existing machines. The formation of the National Shipbuilders Security Ltd, led to the closure of twenty-eight antiquated yards by 1937, and this was paid for by a 1 per cent levy on members. Government loans encouraged owners of tramp-steamers to scrap old vessels and build new ones.

By 1934 the evidence of severe long-term unemployment in certain parts of the country led to the Special Areas Act. Two commissioners were allowed to spend two million pounds a year to encourage employment in the designated districts of South Wales, southern Scotland, north-east England and western Cumberland. But the tiny amounts of money involved made it difficult to do much. The commissioners supported local amenity schemes, encouraged land settlement, and tried to draw in new businesses. In his 1936 report, the commissioner responsible for

England and Wales stated:

'It has to be admitted that no appreciable reduction of the number of those unemployed has been effected. Such increased employment as is likely to result from the operation of the many schemes initiated will prove altogether insufficient, in the absence of a spontaneous growth of new industries and expansion of existing industries, to offset the release of labour brought about by increased mechanisation and rationalisation . . .

The all-important question that arises from a study of the results obtained from its administration is whether the time is now ripe for a second experiment which, whilst continuing work already embarked upon, would make an attempt to deal more directly with the problem of unemployment... My recommendation is that by means of State-provided inducements a determined attempt should be made to attract industrialists to the Special Areas.'

(*Third Report of the Commissioner for the Special Areas*, 1936)

In 1937 the money involved was increased, and the Treasury was given power to aid companies ready to move into distressed areas. Some 121 new firms did begin business, including a new steel works at Ebbw Vale, yet the overall effect of the commissioners' work was the creation of, at most, 50,000 new jobs.

# Welfare

By 1931 governments had accepted that it was their responsibility to help the unemployed. Perhaps this in part was motivated by the desire to keep protest down to modest levels. In fact Britain in the 1930s remained mainly peaceful, helped by the absence of inflation (which so upset the middle classes in Germany by destroying their savings) and by a significant fall in the cost of living. Only about 18,000 people joined the Communist Party. The British Union of Fascists attracted about 40,000, but by 1936 ministers felt confident enough to clamp controls on its uniform-wearing and marching. The National Union of Unemployed Workers recruited 50,000 members.

Some contemporaries wondered why protests did not take place on a bigger scale. The writer George Orwell suggested:

'The post-war development of cheap luxuries has been a very fortunate thing for our rulers. It is quite likely that fish and chips, art, silk stockings, tinned salmon, cut price chocolate, the movie, the radio, strong tea and the football pools have, between them, averted revolution.'

(G. Orwell, *The Road to Wigan Pier*, 1937)

And an ordinary inhabitant of Ashton under Lyne thought:

'At that time there was that Victorian hangover and people were that cowed, they were afraid of authority.'

(N. Gray, *The Worst of Times*, 1985)

One historian has argued that voluntary efforts to aid the needy played a significant part. Charitable bodies (as well as local authorities) provided clothes, food, allotments, and centres where the unemployed were offered recreations. In the late 30s such centres had a membership of 200,000, and R. H. C Hayburn suggests that:

'In alleviating the suffering of those out of work, the state's efforts were overshadowed by those of a voluntary nature.'

(*Journal of Contemporary History*, VI, 1971).

In 1936 Seebohm Rowntree re-examined York, and found significant improvements in the lives of people, when compared with his findings in 1899. He offered an analysis of the reasons for this:

'The first is the reduction in the size of family. The second reason is the increase in real wages, probably amounting on the average to about 35 per cent. The effect of this would have been greater but for the heavy unemployment in 1936. A third cause is the remarkable growth of social services during the period under review. In 1899 the only financial aid given from public sources to persons living in their homes was Poor Relief, the acceptance of which rendered the recipients paupers; they lost their rights as citizens, for they could not vote.

Our schedules show that in 1936 no less than £5,309 was paid out weekly for the following social services:–

|  | £ | s. | d. |
|---|---|---|---|
| Unemployment benefit | 1801 | 18 | 5 |
| Health benefit | 113 | 7 | 6 |
| Old age pensions and Pensions for widows and orphans | 2624 | 10 | 3 |
| Public assistance | 753 | 5 | 9 |
| Milk and/or meals for school children | 16 | 14 | 9 |

£5,309 is equal to 6s. 6d. per working class family and to 1s. 11d. per head of the working class population. Of this total, £3,412 went to the 5088 families living below the minimum. This is an average of 13s. 5d. per family and 3s. 11¾d. per head.'

(S. Rowntree, *Poverty and Progress*)

Certainly ministers were bombarded with data and reports from all sorts of pressure groups who believed that the state should act to improve health care, housing, and diet, and to bring in family allowances. As Stephen Constantine notes:

'The origins of the post-war welfare state were to be found in the discourses and proposals which inter-war unemployment, not exclusively but substantially, generated.'

(S. Constantine, *Unemployment in Britain Between the Wars*)

The 10 per cent cut in unemployment benefit of 1931 was accompanied by a close scrutiny of the income of the household in which the unemployed person resided. It involved an examination of savings, pensions, lodgers' rents, and income from other family members: it was much resented. George Orwell claimed that it broke up families as elderly and young people left the home rather than see payments reduced or stopped to an unemployed family member. Though the 10 per cent cut was restored in 1934, the hated means test remained.

In 1934 Chamberlain introduced the Unemployment Act to rationalise support of the needy. He disliked the way Public Assistance Committees treated requests in a fashion that varied from place to place. PACs in Rotherham and County Durham were considered to be so over-generous that Ministry of Labour Commissioners replaced them. Now Chamberlain proposed to reorganise the unemployment insurance scheme, by tightening its operations, widening its scope (to include farm workers, for instance) and confining its task to those whose contributions provided genuine twenty-six-week entitlement. William Beveridge was put in charge of a Statutory Committee to run the operation. It prospered, and it was soon able to increase dependants' allowances – though Rowntree reckoned that insurance income of 35s. a week for a family of five fell well below his figure (43s. 6d.) of what such a family needed to stay out of real poverty.

The burden of supporting those who had used up their insurance entitlement, or who had never had any entitlement, was shifted from PACs to a new Treasury-funded body, the Unemployment Assistance Board, which distributed standard rates of support through local Labour Exchanges. When rates were announced, there was uproar: so many PAC rates were higher than UAB figures that the Government had to delay introducing the new rates until 1937. Till then current PAC rates, or UAB rates (whichever were higher) were paid. The reform left the PACs to deal with the elderly, sick, widowed, or very young who were in desperate need.

# ESSAY

Choose one of the following questions. Plan and write an essay to answer it.

1. Why did the harsh economic conditions of the 1930s produce such limited support for extreme political movements?

2. 'We should praise the National Government for doing as much as it did for the economy and the unemployed, not blame it for not doing more.' Do you agree?

# The Labour Government of 1945–51 and the welfare state

In the years after the Second World War the Labour Government led by Clement Attlee created what is commonly called 'the welfare state'. Was this creation the completion of a long process involving other political parties, or was it a genuinely Labour creation that no other party would have attempted? Opinions differ on the matter.

## TASK

Plan and write an answer to this statement, using material already studied as well as information in the rest of this chapter.

'The post '45 welfare state was less a Socialist achievement than the ending of a process owing much to Liberals and Conservatives.'

## *The background*

The Second World War ended the unemployment crisis and brought Labour leaders into office. The Labour Party made clear its view that:

> 'After the war, the national war effort must be turned to the building of a new Britain.
>     While planning the war, the Government must plan for peace and a new society. Instead of regarding each item of state control as a temporary infringement of the normal, the occasion should be seized to lay the foundations of an efficient economic system.'

The wartime ministry brought Keynes into the Treasury and absorbed his ideas. In 1944 a white paper *Full Employment in a Free Society* showed that all members of the coalition were committed to using the power of the state to prevent the return of the 1930s. Memories of this time may have helped Labour win power in 1945: they at least had been out of office then and could claim to be blameless. And the huge issues raised by total war had made massive government intervention in daily life inevitable: people were conscripted for the forces and for civilian work; food was rationed; and the economy managed by new ministries.

# Welfare reforms

Once more war highlighted some of the flaws in British society. The Ministry of Food planned the rationing scheme with a view to improving the nation's health. Calcium, iron, minerals and vitamins had to be added to certain foods. The Emergency Milk and Meals scheme of 1941 supplemented basic rations with extra items for expectant mothers and young children. Cheap milk and cod liver oil and orange juice went to mothers; the price of milk and school meals was kept low by government subsidies. Children unable to afford even subsidised foods, were given them free: by 1945, 1.65 million children were served with school meals daily. Churchill approved of this policy: 'There is no finer investment for any community than putting milk into babies,' he said.

Pre-war medical care still excluded over half the population, i.e. those who were not part of the 1911 insurance scheme: it was therefore particularly severe on women. Doctors charged fees to those outside the scheme, and in any case it did not cover specialist treatment, or dental and eye care. Pre-war hospitals were not part of a co-ordinated system: about 1000 were voluntary organisations depending on fund-raising, on bequests, and on contributions from patients; and about 2000 were local authority hospitals (often developed first by Poor Law Guardians) which relied partly on fees. The war shook up this confused muddle. Hospital care had to be extended to cope with the war-wounded who were given free treatment. The war-wounded could also include civilians injured by bombs. The local authority hospitals, and the hospitals set up by voluntary charities, soon had many 'emergency beds' whose occupants received treatment paid for by the state. A free immunisation programme soon produced a sizeable fall in deaths from diphtheria from nearly 3000 in 1938 to 818 in 1945.

During the war prices rose quite sharply. The government tried to keep them down by paying subsidies to food producers, but old age pensioners found it especially hard to manage. In 1940 the Unemployment Assistance Board was given power to pay supplementary amounts to needy elderly folk, a step which widened the work of the Board and made it more popular. The Board also helped bombed families who could not support themselves in the disastrous circumstances following the destruction of their homes. In 1941, as a result of pressure from Ernest Bevin, the Board abolished the household means test.

These were separate welfare reforms, which came at a time when there was a growing awareness among politicians that war would produce an overhaul of welfare. In addition, a planning group that included Conservatives produced this statement for the Ministry of Information:

'Wartime conditions have already compelled us to make sure,

not only that the rich do not consume too much, but that others get enough. The needs of war production call for new measures for improving the housing, welfare and transport of workers. The evacuation scheme should give the impetus to radical improvements in our educational system and social services. The wartime measures to protect the standard of living point the way to a planned population policy. The mobilisation of manpower should spell the end of mass unemployment. War measures for rationalising the distribution of various products should lead to a remodelling of distribution as a whole, so as to transform increased productivity into increased consumption on a higher standard.'

(Quoted in P. Addison, *The Road to 1945*)

By 1942 the Ministry of Health anticipated a new kind of post-war hospital service:

'In the last year or so the numerous organisations and authorities whose interests lie in the hospital world have been giving increasing thought to the future. All start from the accepted premise that there can be no return to the pre-war position of unrelated hospital units pursuing independent and often wastefully competitive courses.'

(Quoted in A. Marwick, *Britain in a Century of Total War*)

## *The Beveridge Report*

In 1942 an overall welfare plan was published. It was written by Sir William Beveridge. This Beveridge Report was the result of pressure from the TUC, which told the Labour minister, Arthur Greenwood:

'We are definitely of the opinion that the country cannot continue to afford the inefficient and incomplete services rendered to insured workers together with the expensive muddle and waste associated with it. We ask the Minister of Health to take the lead in an examination of the whole position with a view to plans being produced which would provide a properly balanced scheme.'

(Memorandum by the TUC in J. R. Hay, *The Development of the British Welfare State*, 1978)

Beveridge's suggestions were the response to this pressure. Greenwood gave him the task of leading a committee to study insurance, and the resulting ideas were very much Beveridge's own notions. He wanted to see the whole system made much more simple and more efficient; he believed that insurance should protect people against all the serious hardships of life, and he thought that the scheme should cover the whole population of the country. The insurance payments he planned were seen as the rightful due of all, not money to be doled out carefully in differing amounts according to a means test. But he did not think payments should be generous. Beveridge was a Liberal, a believer in the principle of people contributing to the savings organised by the state, and if people wished to make more generous provision for themselves, then he believed that they should turn to private insurance schemes.

He did not confine himself simply to looking at insurance. He argued that:

> 'the organisation of social insurance should be treated as one part only of a comprehensive policy of social progress. Social insurance may provide income security, it is an attack on Want. But Want is one only of five giants. The others are Disease, Ignorance, Squalor, and Idleness.'

To fight these giants, Beveridge stated that it would be necessary to have a proper national health service, a policy of full employment, and allowances paid to families with children. He said of his ideas:

> 'The scheme proposed here is in some ways a revolution but in more important ways it is a natural development from the past. It is a British Revolution.'

## The main points of the Beveridge Report

1. The appointment of a minister to control all the insurance schemes.
2. A standard weekly payment by people in work as a contribution to the insurance fund.
3. The right to payments for an indefinite period for people out of work.
4. Old age pensions, maternity grants, funeral grants, pensions for widows and for people injured at work.
5. Payments at a standard rate, the same for all whatever their private means, paid without a means test.
6. Family allowances to be introduced.
7. A national health service to be set up.

Beveridge was criticised by the private insurance companies, who felt that his plans would hurt their business. One of their officials declared of the report, 'The author is an economist turned spendthrift, destroying every vestige of self-reliance and self-help.' And the Prime Minister, Churchill, was worried about the cost of the proposals. The war was hurting Britain, but Churchill believed that post-war Britain needed strong defence forces to prevent another war. He wrote:

'A dangerous optimism is growing up about the conditions it
will be possible to establish after the war. Our foreign
investments have almost disappeared. The United States will be
a strong competitor. The question steals across the mind
whether we are not committing our people to tasks beyond
their capacity to bear.'
(W. S. Churchill, *Cabinet notes in the Second World War IV*, 1951)

But there was no doubt about the general reaction to the
Beveridge Report. Though it was written in dry and difficult
language, it became a bestseller. The Labour Party and the trade
unions welcomed it with enthusiasm. The Ministry of Information found it to be a major topic of conversation: its officials on
Clydeside, for instance, reported:

'Interest in the Beveridge Plan on its publication was really
tremendous. For a week or two the war news tended to take a
back seat. Practically everyone approved of the underlying
principles. Soldiers writing home spoke of their pleasure at the
Scheme.'

In Parliament, ninety-seven Labour and twenty-two Conservative and Liberal MPs voted that the report should be put into
operation as soon as possible. One of them, the Labour MP James
Griffiths, told the House:

'It is by acceptance or rejection of the plan that we shall be
judged by the nation. I suggest that the question which we
ought to ask ourselves is not whether we can afford the plan,
but whether we can afford to face the post-war period without
it.'

In contrast, the *Daily Mirror* refused to get excited:

'Too much has been made of the Beveridge Report. It is no
revolutionary document. Mainly it is a co-ordination of existing
services with certain modest additions thereto. It is a beginning,
not an end, and it must not be confused with reconstruction in
the larger sense.'
(Quoted in A. Marwick, *Britain in a Century of Total War*)

But even before the Coalition had come to an end, work had
begun on some of Beveridge's ideas.

Firstly, in 1943 a ministry to supervise insurance was set up,
and in 1945 family allowances were agreed. These allowances
were less generous than Beveridge had proposed, being 5s. a week
for every child after the first one, not 8s. for every child without
exception. The payment of these sums did not begin for another
year.

Secondly, the Coalition had also created a Ministry of Town and Country Planning (1943). One of its first reports suggested the setting up of new towns to reduce congestion in London. Temporary homes were built, at state expense, for some of Britain's homeless, and the price of building materials was controlled to stop house prices getting out of hand.

And in 1944 a Conservative, R. A. Butler, piloted through parliament a new Education Act. The act provided for free secondary education for all from the age of eleven (twelve in Scotland) up to the age of fifteen.

These were real achievements, and there were also government White Papers showing what was planned in the near future. There were statements to show that a high and stable level of employment, and the creation of a national health service, were matters to which the government was committed. If the Coalition could agree on so much, then both the Labour and the Conservative Parties felt that social welfare policies must be pursued after the war.

The veteran social reformer Seebohm Rowntree summed up the situation, saying:

'The whole of the social and economic life of the nation has been uprooted by the war as by an earthquake. When peace comes, the social and economic evils and injustices for which the community suffered before the war must not be permitted in the new world which has to be created.'

But Winston Churchill again worried that too much was being expected of post-war Britain. He did not attack Beveridge in principle, but rather concerned himself with the cost of welfare when there were other burdens to be borne after the economy had been so badly hurt by warfare.

## Labour's welfare policies from 1945 to 1951

Throughout the 1945–51 period the country was free of serious unemployment problems save those temporarily caused by the exceptionally severe winter of 1946–47. However, the government's determination to keep Britain militarily strong did mean that social welfare reforms were not the only call upon the country's limited resources. Britain at this time supported a large army, air force and navy; she kept bases across the world; and she developed atomic bombs. There were also conflicts into which Britain was drawn. To push vigorously ahead in such times required both courage and optimism; but at least British people seemed much more ready than they had been after 1918 to wait for reforms to come, and to accept the continuation of wartime controls in peacetime.

## Insurance

James Griffiths was in charge of converting Beveridge's plans for a simple comprehensive scheme of insurance into reality. Like Attlee, Griffiths saw his work as the completion of a process that had been going on for many years. A speech by the Conservative R. A. Butler showed that there were no big differences between Labour and Conservatives on this issue, for Butler welcomed the scheme, declaring:

> 'I think we should take pride that the British race has been able, shortly after the terrible period through which we have all passed together, to show the whole world that we are able to produce a social insurance scheme of this character.'
> (Quoted in S. H. Wood, *The British Welfare State*, 1982)

As Beveridge had suggested, the scheme put into place involved weekly contributions from employees, employers and the state, and it paid benefits at standard rates. The cost of old age pensions had particularly worried Beveridge. He had suggested that there might even be a twenty-year delay in bringing in pensions for men at sixty-five and for women at sixty years; but Griffiths did not delay. He brought in the measure at once. As Beveridge had suggested, a scheme was introduced to provide compensation for people who were injured at work. The Industrial Injuries Act provided payments to those temporarily hurt and long-term payments for those put permanently out of a job. For the latter group, because an injured person might have extra expenses, the rates of payment were more generous than for the unemployed.

In 1948 a National Assistance Board was set up to help people for whom the insurance scheme did not provide enough help, or the right kind of help. For some people the insurance benefits were simply not enough, and as time passed this problem became increasingly serious. The insurance benefits did not rise sufficiently often to keep up with the now steadily rising cost of living, and old people in particular had to turn to the Assistance Board for further help. This help was given only to the needy: the Board's officials had to question the applicant to make sure that they were dealing with a genuine claim. This 'needs test' was less harsh than the old means test for it did not include a check on the earnings of other members of the claimant's family. The Board's help might consist of weekly payments, but it could also give single payments to solve a particular problem (such as an urgent need for bedding or clothing).

The insurance and national assistance schemes were huge undertakings. Thousands of new staff were needed, new offices had to be built, and the files and records of information about Britain's citizens began to grow.

## Insurance reform

| 1946 | 26s. a week for a single person, 42s. for a married man, at times of old age, unemployment (up to 180 days), and illness. |
|------|------|
| 1946 | Compensation for people injured at work – 45s. a week, with a further 16s. if married. Maternity grants and allowances. Death grant of £20. Payments to widows. No means test. Standard weekly contribution for those in work. |
| 1948 | National Assistance Board set up, to help those for whom insurance did not do enough (e.g. pensioners whose pensions did not keep up with the rise in the cost of living). Old age pensions were paid to men over sixty-five and to women over sixty. The government found that old age pensions were soon eating up two thirds of all insurance spending. |

## The National Health Service

The new Minister of Health was Aneurin Bevan. By 1945 Bevan had won himself a considerable reputation as a very forthright speaker who held strong socialist views. During the war he had been Churchill's most determined and persistent critic in parliament, and Conservative politicians regarded him as a person of extreme views. His task of building a national health service meant that he had to win the co-operation of doctors. A great many of them, already worried about what a health service might do to their jobs, were even more concerned when faced by Aneurin Bevan. What doctors feared was that they would be turned into state officials, would lose independence, and would be sent to work wherever the government chose to place them.

Bevan brought in a bill in 1946 to outline the features of the health service he wished to set up, and allowed a two-year delay before the service would begin. During this time he hoped to win over the majority of doctors. In introducing his bill, Bevan pointed out that the old health insurance system:

'covered only twenty-one million, the rest of the population have to pay whenever they desire the services of a doctor; the National Health Insurance scheme does not provide for the self-employed nor the families of dependants. It gives no backing to the doctor in the form of special services. Our hospital organisation has grown up with no plan. This Bill provides a universal health service with no insurance qualifications of any sort. It is intended that there shall be no limitations on the kind of assistance given – general practitioners' service, specialists, hospitals, eye treatment, dental treatment, hearing facilities.'

The detailed arrangements for the health service were then worked out during two years of discussion. When doctors actually met the man they had thought of as a fierce Welsh socialist, they found him charming, witty, and ready to negotiate. Hospital staff were won over quite readily. Their buildings and medical equipment were so expensive and so much in need of overhaul and additions that they realised that only the government could provide what they needed. Bevan agreed that hospital doctors could continue to treat private patients as well as working for the health service, and that hospitals should have a number of beds for patients who wanted to be treated privately and could afford to pay. The hospitals were organised in groups, and each group was controlled by a Regional Board appointed by the minister. Each hospital had a management committee to watch over its affairs. Major hospitals which were centres for the training of new doctors had their own separate governors whom the minister himself appointed.

Winning over GPs was not so easy. In 1946 a poll amongst them showed that 64 per cent were opposed to Bevan's plans. The British Medical Association organised and led a campaign that argued that what was proposed would destroy doctors' freedom to treat patients as they thought right. But the doctors became increasingly isolated, for popular opinion ran very strongly in favour of the health service. Lord Moran, President of the Royal College of Physicians, helped Bevan gradually to calm doctors' fears, although at times the discussion between the two sides became quite angry. (Bevan once called the BMA 'a small body of politically poisoned people'!) By 1948 the detailed arrangements the minister was ready to make had persuaded a quarter of the doctors in England and a third of those in Wales and Scotland to sign on for the new service. Early in 1948 organised opposition collapsed, and the health service was able to come into operation on 5 July 1948.

Its impact was enormous, as illustrated by this example. In 1948 Alice Law lived in Manchester. When the NHS began, her mother:

'went to the optician's, obviously she'd got the prescription from the doctor, she went and she got tested for new glasses, then she went further down the road . . . for the chiropodist, she had her feet done, then she went back to the doctor's because she'd been having trouble with her ears and the doctor said . . . he would fix her up with a hearing aid, and I remember, me mother was a very funny woman, I remember her saying to the doctor on the way out, "Well the undertaker's is on the way home, everything's going on, I might as well call in there on the way home!"'

(Quoted in P. Addison, *Now the War is Over*)

The service that emerged was paid for, very largely, by taxes. The weekly insurance stamp did include a little for health insurance, but enough to pay only 9 per cent of its cost in 1949, and 10 per cent by 1954. Bevan calmed the doctors' worries about becoming state officials by agreeing not to pay them by direct salary. New doctors received some direct salary from the government, but in general the pay that doctors received depended on the number of patients on their lists. When medical practices had been private, doctors had bought and sold them. Bevan insisted that this must stop, arguing that patients were being treated like cattle. But he did set aside £66 million for doctors to draw upon when they retired, to compensate them for no longer being able to sell practices they had spent lifetimes building up. The work of GPs was henceforth watched over by executive councils set up in each county and borough, and these were made up of equal numbers of medical and lay people.

Some aspects of health care were kept by local authorities. Their Medical Officers supervised services such as vaccination, immunisation, health visiting, child care, and provision for the destitute (especially the elderly).

When the health service started, it brought such a flood of people seeking treatment that Bevan himself declared, 'I shudder to think of the ceaseless cascade of medicines which is pouring down British throats at the present time.' Prescriptions had cost about £7 million a month before the health service was created; within three months they cost twice that figure, and they continued to rise. Dentists had expected about four million patients a year, yet twice that number sought treatment. The National Health Service became an increasingly heavy burden on British finances and, much as Bevan and some of his colleagues resented it, charges for some of its services had to be introduced by 1951.

## Housing

Post-war Britain faced a huge shortage of housing. The war had damaged and destroyed thousands of homes and had prevented normal house-building work from going ahead. Moreover the slum-clearing programme of the 1930s had barely begun to touch the problem of sub-standard housing. The burden of tackling the problem fell upon Bevan's Ministry of Health, but the ministry had already more than enough to do in attempting to set up the National Health Service.

The ministry's first task was to house the homeless, and to this end it continued the Coalition policy of putting up temporary factory-made 'pre-fabricated' homes. This provided 157,000 dwellings – far too few to satisfy the country's needs. The fact that building supplies and skilled labour were not plentiful compelled Bevan to choose where to concentrate conventional house-building. He put the emphasis on the building of council houses for rent, placing severe restrictions on private building. People in homes that needed considerable spending to raise them to a decent level received help from the Treasury, but the fact remained that by 1951 there was still a very serious shortage of housing in Britain.

The government's housing policy did show concern for the future, as well as efforts to meet an immediate need. Bevan insisted that the council houses must satisfy quite a high standard. In 1946 the New Towns Act set out plans for dealing with overcrowding in older cities. New communities were to be carefully designed and built, with government help; twelve were planned by 1950. In 1947 the Town and Country Planning Act gave counties and county boroughs much more power to plan their communities, and to buy up properties in areas that they wanted to redevelop.

The government's life ended before really massive signs of what it proposed were visible, but in the following years the rebuilding of old communities and the creation of new ones went ahead on the basis of these post-war plans.

## Child welfare

By 1947 the Education Act of 1944 was in operation. The government raised the age at which children could leave school to fifteen, at a time when the country was short of workers. It also had to spend more of its precious resources on school-building and on an emergency programme to train enough teachers to staff the schools. Schools were organised so that at age eleven (twelve in Scotland) children were examined and divided up between grammar schools for the most able and secondary modern schools for the majority. The Education Act proposed a third kind of school – technical schools – but not many of these were provided.

The idea of sorting children into different schools on the basis of an examination did arouse a little criticism at the time: by 1947 the London County Council in particular had become unhappy about the system and planned comprehensive schools instead. London's first comprehensive, Kidbrooke School, opened in 1954.

The government also planned a big increase in opportunities in higher education. Universities and colleges were to be expanded and there was to be a system of grants from the state or the local authority so that students able to win higher education places could accept them even if their parents had little money.

In 1948 the Children's Act tried to provide a better service for children who needed special care and protection. Local authorities were now required to appoint Children's Officers, whose job it would be to see that children taken into care by the local authorities were decently housed and properly cared for.

The range of reforms carried through by 1950 adds up to a system that is generally called 'the welfare state'. The closing stages of this work were supervised by Labour Party ministers, but they knew very well that what they were doing was building on foundations laid by the Liberals and the Conservatives. The care of people in need and the improvement of people's health, housing and education were policies that statesmen of all three parties had at times thought necessary. When a Conservative government replaced Labour in 1951, it did not at once start attacking the social reforms of the previous five years, but accepted these reforms and even added further improvements.

Certainly the health, housing and education of the British people have been much improved during the twentieth century. In 1950 Seebohm Rowntree carried out a third study of York, and found far less overcrowding and poverty. Whereas those on poor pay and those who were unemployed had once been the main victims of poverty, but 1950 it was the elderly who formed the main group of the poor. But even for them life was far more comfortable than it had been fifty years earlier. A great deal of money had been spent, and large numbers of officials had been appointed to make the system work. Far more people paid taxes; and taxes were fixed at higher rates. Controls over people's lives were more detailed and numerous, and the power of the government was increased. But everyday life, for the majority of people, was vastly improved.

## *Historians' views*

David Dutton has written:

> 'The major achievement of the Labour Party after 1945 was to complete and consolidate the work of the war-time coalition.'
> (*British Politics since 1945*, 1990)

Kathleen Woodroofe notes how state action created a system, in which welfare support was believed to be a right, free of the shame of the old Poor Law.

> 'By government policy and a network of social services she [i.e. Britain] hoped to provide employment for those who were unemployed, to insure her citizens against the major hazards of life and eventually to give them a national minimum of health, wealth and well-being. These were not favours to be dispensed by the bountiful... They were social rights... to accept assistance no longer meant loss of personal liberty or disenfranchisement.'
> (*Twentieth Century Britain – National Power and Social Welfare*, 1976)

Several historians have commented on the Conservatives' ready acceptance of Labour's programme, with the exception of aspects of the NHS. Nevertheless, Arthur Marwick believes Labour's achievements:

> 'were not simply the inevitable response that any government would have made to the particular historical circumstances of 1945. They were the endeavours of a political party that, over a long period of time, had thought hard, if unevenly, about the issues of welfare policy.'
>
> (*Modern History Review*, Vol 2 No 1, 1990)

To support his case, he points to Labour policy proposals in the early twentieth century; to some of its activities when briefly in office; and particularly to the boldness of Bevan's plans for health and housing.

Kenneth Morgan's work, *The People's Peace* (1990), includes observations on Churchill's very suspicious view of the cost of Beveridge, and of aspects of health service ideas: for Churchill's interests lay in visions of world affairs that might well have severely constrained welfare reforms had he led the post-war government. Certainly at the time Bevan believed this to be the case.

# ESSAY

How do you account for the twentieth-century development of governmental policies that treated welfare as being every citizen's right?

# A United Kingdom?

During the later nineteenth century the pressure for home rule for Ireland and for Scotland failed to achieve success. During the twentieth century this pressure exploded into open warfare in Ireland – a conflict that produced a huge dent in the notion that the United Kingdom ought to be a single political entity. In Scotland and in Wales political movements developed, demanding special consideration for these areas. Thus the view that Westminster's *authority* ought to control the whole United Kingdom has been challenged on the grounds that the country contains great differences and does not have a single political *identity*. The *ideology* of the parties pursuing the Welsh, Scottish or Irish causes is less easy to establish in any positive fashion, although opposition to rule from London and hostility to domination by English interests has been their main binding force. The material in this section focuses primarily on Scotland and is concerned with the issue of Scottish political identity.

## TASK

Consider this issue:

In what ways and for what reasons were efforts made to recognise a Scottish political identity?

Work through this chapter, gathering material to make possible a discussion of the issue. Then each member of the class should in turn offer one example of change, together with supporting evidence. Finally, discuss whether reasons for change can be ranked in order of importance.

# The wider context

People eager to see home rule – or even independence – for Scotland were bound to be influenced by what was happening elsewhere in the United Kingdom.

Welsh pressure for reform focused particularly on the issues of the Church and the Welsh language. In 1914 the Anglican Church's position as the official, established Church in Wales was ended. In the years since 1945 increasing emphasis has been placed on the importance of Welsh in schools, in the media, in official documents, and even in the labelling of streets and communities. But when, in 1979, the people of Wales voted on whether they favoured an assembly for Wales, their response was over-whelmingly (4 to 1) hostile.

Events in Ireland took quite a different turn. The outbreak of the Great War in 1914 prevented the implementation of home rule, even though the necessary legislation had been passed. By 1918 the political situation had been transformed. The supporters of home rule had rallied to their leaders' backing of the war effort. They joined the armed forces in thousands and served abroad. This left the way clear in Ireland for those who sought independence and viewed the Great War as an opportunity to obtain it. An uprising in 1916 failed, yet it gave those who risked all in this event the image of martyrs. The brutal behaviour of the British government did not help the cause of those opposing the Sinn Fein Independence party. In the 1918 election Sinn Fein won seventy-three seats. The new members refused to come to Westminster, and one of their leaders, Michael Collins, developed the Irish Republican Army to resist any attempt to crush the independence movement.

The British government's use of force failed to end Irish resist-ance. But the question of Irish political identity was confused by the presence – especially in Ulster – of a sizeable Protestant group fearful for their future in an independent Ireland and determined to remain in the United Kingdom. In 1920 the Government of Ireland Act offered Ireland two parliaments – one for the north and the other for the south. Ulster accepted this, and in 1921 its parliament met. This was the start of a period of home rule there, but it ended in 1973 when Westminster took direct control as part of an attempt to ease the fears of Ulster Catholics. In December 1921 a treaty for the rest of Ireland was signed, making it an independent state within the British Commonwealth. Irish identity, the relationship between the different groups in Ireland, and Ireland's relationship with mainland Britain have remained issues which have yet to be solved in a way that will suit all concerned.

# Developing a Scottish administration

Prior to 1914 Scottish affairs were overseen by a Scottish Secretary supported by a tiny London-based administration. The following years saw the growth of the power and scope of this administration and its shift to Edinburgh.

The Scottish Secretary began the period as a very junior cabinet member who was in the uneasy position of answering for Scottish affairs that were administered either by United Kingdom government departments or by nominated boards which were not strictly answerable to him. In 1926 his position was up-graded to that of a full Secretary of State, and in 1928 work began on converting the various boards (such as the one for agriculture) into properly staffed departments equipped with the necessary expertise. In 1929 Scottish local government was radically overhauled: parishes were left as little more than religious and registration units; four cities, twenty large burghs (with populations of over 20,000), and county councils exercised most power.

In 1937 the Gilmour Report proposed a rationalisation of the administration that was implemented in the Reorganisation of Offices Act of 1939. The whole focus of the government of Scotland was shifted to Edinburgh, and located in the newly built St Andrews House. The Scottish Secretary was clearly vested with authority over the various departments, namely Agriculture, Education, Health, and Home Affairs. Each department had its own administrative head directly answerable to the Secretary, but was also able to meet with other department heads under the chairmanship of a Permanent Under-Secretary with responsibility for overseeing Scottish Office affairs. Developments in subsequent years have all boosted the size and authority of the Scottish Office, but have still left it in an uneasy relationship with those United Kingdom departments whose actions obviously affect Scotland directly, such as the Treasury. The political team overseeing affairs was expanded to five, with a full Minister of State as well as the Secretary, and three parliamentary Under-Secretaries. By 1954 the Scottish Office was in charge not only of the North of Scotland Hydro Board (founded in 1943) but also of Southern Scotland Electricity.

The report of the Balfour Commission, set up by the Churchill Government of 1951–55, recommended that Scottish needs and points of view should be known and taken into account. It suggested increasing the authority of the Scottish Office, and from now on it therefore had control over JPs, responsibility for trunk roads, and authority to deal with animal diseases. The 1961 Toorhill Report considered Scottish economic troubles, and led to the creation of the Scottish Development Department (1962), with responsibility for industry, electricity, roads, local government housing, town and country planning, and the environment. The Department of Agriculture had already added the management of fisheries to its duties; the Home and Health Department supervised law and order, welfare and health service matters.

In 1973 a new department was established to manage economic planning and support for the oil industry, electricity and transport. It was named the Scottish Economic Planning Department. The Scottish Education Department (in Edinburgh from 1939) remained intact, but grew in size. Special initiatives aimed at encouraging the Scottish economy were represented by the creation of the Highlands and Islands Development Board in 1965 and the Scottish Development Agency in 1975. By 1977 there were 65,000 civil servants in Scotland.

These developments represent an increasing shift of authority for administration from UK departments to Scottish departments. Yet the UK departments remain, and the Treasury, above all, has a crucial control over Scottish affairs. In addition, a devolved administration may leave political control of its machinery in the hands of a party that has a majority in parliament, but represents only a minority of Scottish voters.

# Political issues

Pressure for Scottish home rule was a feature of politics for many years before 1914, and the Liberal Party in particular advocated such a reform. An act to implement the change was passed in 1913, but it failed to come into effect because of the Great War. The issue has reappeared repeatedly since then – indeed it has widened into a discussion that reaches beyond home rule and now considers the independence of Scotland.

Increased political freedom for Scotland is an issue that has attracted fluctuating support, and some commentators have suggested that this is chiefly determined by economic affairs. The demand for increased freedom emerged in the 1920s as the Scottish economy suffered a period of serious recession. It re-emerged in the 1960s at a new time of troubles once the hopeful period of growth and full employment in the 1950s was over.

The discovery and exploitation of oil has added the argument that 'It's Scotland's oil', and that the mineral makes an independent Scotland a realistic economic possibility. One historian has argued that a whole range of factors have brought about a change in Scottish political attitudes so that by the 1970s:

'the Scottish electorate . . . began to perceive themselves as Scots in terms of their political interests rather than as, for example, members of the working class.'

(J. Brand, *The National Movement in Scotland*, 1978)

Both through support for Scottish sports teams and through viewing programmes offered by Scottish-based television companies, Scots have been encouraged to consider their separate identity. Jack Brand points to signs such as the unpopularity of the national anthem at sporting occasions as clues to this shift in mood. Scottish law and the Scottish Church remain as distinctive as ever, while the special shape of Scottish education has assumed great importance in a century that has put so much more stress on schooling. And although Gaelic does not have the status in Scotland that the Welsh language has in Wales, nevertheless vigorous efforts are being made to revive it.

By 1979 attempts at home rule had come to nothing. The Scottish National Party, which is specifically devoted to the Scottish cause, briefly managed to secure eleven MPs, but has more commonly fared badly. The rapid decline of the Liberal Party wrecked the power of the group that had been most openly committed to home rule. Conservative attitudes tended to be unsympathetic: the Conservative Party did not include the word 'Unionist' in its title as a result of its hostility to Irish home rule, only to abandon it when faced with Scottish pressure. For a time in the late 1960s Edward Heath seemed to be pushing his party towards acceptance of devolution, but the election of Margaret Thatcher to the Tory leadership soon shifted policy back towards its more traditional dislike of Scottish home rule.

The Labour Party developed a position in Scotland that became formidable. Some of its early leaders – notably Keir Hardie – spoke in favour of a separate Scottish parliament. Ramsay MacDonald, too, seemed supportive. But others in the Labour Party were hostile to devolution: they saw policies in terms of the needs of working people throughout the United Kingdom, and regarded nationalism as a regrettable and reactionary force that clashed with socialism. The historian William Ferguson observes: 'For most Scottish socialists, the more left they were, the less nationalist in outlook' (*Scotland 1689 to the Present*). When in office, Labour seemed inclined to do little. Tom Johnston, the able Labour politician who had spoken strongly for home rule in the 1930s and encouraged London Scots to back devolution, seemed to lose his enthusiasm for it once he was in office in 1940 as Scottish Secretary. He increasingly preferred to concentrate on the economic revival of Scotland and especially on his favourite project, the setting up of the North of Scotland Hydroelectric Scheme. He did secure the creation of a Council of State to be made up of former Scottish Secretaries, whose task it was was to vet legislation. The post-war Attlee Ministry was preoccupied with its huge programme of reforms, and created a range of bodies that operated throughout the United Kingdom, thus increasing the authority of the central government. Walter Elliot shrewdly noted 'for Scotland nationalisation means denationalisation'.

Liberal decline and the failure of Labour to try to act in 1924 may well have contributed to the emergence of movements which sought some sort of special political status for Scotland. Also in the 1920s there developed the cultural movement of the 'Scottish Renaissance', which included the poet C. M. Grieve (better known by his pen name, Hugh MacDiarmid) who was eager to see the growth of a distinctive Scottish literature. It was a mixture of intellectuals and frustrated ILP members who formed the National Party of Scotland in 1928. The party was established by the fusion of the Scottish National Movement, the Scots National League, the Scottish Home Rule Association, and the Glasgow University Scottish National Association. Key figures in it included Roland Muirhead and an ex-ILP man, the twenty-four-year old Glasgow solicitor John MacCormick. In 1930 the latter was one of a group who met at Stirling to celebrate Bannockburn and to agree on a National Covenant stating 'the urgent necessity of self-government for Scotland'. The NPS grew to 5000 by 1929, a size comparable with that of the ILP in Scotland. It met with no electoral success, though one of its supporters, the writer Compton Mackenzie, was elected Lord Rector of Glasgow University in 1931.

In 1934 the NPS merged with another, more cautious, nationalist group, the Scottish Party, to form the Scottish National Party. But electoral success still eluded it. Power lay with the unionist-dominated National Government. The key figure here was Walter Elliot, the able Scottish Secretary, who oversaw the Gilmour Report and its implementation. Elliot was ready to spend on housing and education, and to support special economic reforms for Scotland, as well as an overhaul of the administration, but he was not willing to support political reform. The depressed Scottish economy was allocated its own Commissioner to help its revival: between 1935 and 1938 this official spent fourteen million pounds in Scotland.

During the war the SNP achieved a brief but remarkable breakthrough with a by-election success at Motherwell in April 1945. This was perhaps due in part to votes from those who did not want any delays in social reforms. But it lost the seat at the general election three months later. During the late 1940s and the 1950s the SNP was divided and weakened. Publicity went instead to John MacCormick's efforts to establish an annual gathering of all those who wanted to work for a separate Scottish parliament. (By now MacCormick had taken his pro-Liberal views so far that he left the SNP in 1945 and stood in the general election as a Liberal.) The first of these conventions was held in 1947, and delegates came from churches and local government as well as from political groups. The 1200 delegates at the 1949 convention signed a Scottish Covenant asking for home rule. Nearly two million more signatures were gathered in the following years. In

1950 a group of Covenant supporters won major media attention by snatching the Stone of Destiny (on which Scottish kings had been crowned) from its resting place in Westminster Abbey. But after this episode the Covenant movement faded in importance. The Conservative Government of 1952 dealt with pressure from Scotland by setting up the Balfour Commission (1952–54) on Scottish affairs. Minor administrative changes followed its report.

The fortunes of the SNP began to improve in the late 1950s, and by-elections in 1961 at Glasgow Bridgeton and in 1962 in West Lothian produced encouraging votes for the SNP candidates. The Bridgeton candidate, Ian Macdonald, was so encouraged that he played a big part in building up the party's organisation. A whole network of local branches were set up, supervised by a well-run central office. Money was raised and used to spread SNP views. The West Lothian candidate, the businessman William Wolfe, became Party Chairman. By 1964 the party was able to contest fifteen seats, and in West Lothian Wolfe came second with a much increased vote.

This improved performance may have been partly due to the SNP's ability to exploit Britain's economic difficulties. Old-fashioned Scottish industries were struggling to survive, and there were not enough new industries to offset growing unemployment. The feeling that Scotland was suffering more than England was used in order to argue that Scots should control their own affairs.

The SNP grew. In 1967 the party captured Hamilton from Labour in a by-election. In the municipal elections of 1968, 30 per cent of voters chose the SNP candidates, giving the party a gain of 100 seats. The number of party members, which had been 2000 in 1962, climbed to 120,000 in 1968. And although Hamilton was lost at the next general election in 1970, success in the Western Isles helped to offset this setback.

In the early 1970s the party enjoyed a real surge in its fortunes. It did well in three by-elections without actually winning, then in 1973 it took the Labour seat of Govan with a majority of 571. By the time of the February 1974 general elections, the SNP was ready to provide candidates in all the Scottish constituencies except Orkney and Shetland. It was able to offer to voters the promise that an independent Scotland would prosper by claiming control of North Sea oil and by using its revenues for the benefit of Scotland. In that election Govan was lost, but the Western Isles seat was held with an increased majority, and six other seats were won: four were captured from the Conservatives, and two from Labour. SNP MPs now sat for the Western Isles; Aberdeenshire East; Argyll; Banff; Dundee East; Moray and Nairn; and Clackmannan and East Stirling. In October 1974 four more seats – all formerly Conservative – fell to the SNP. This raised its representation at Westminster to eleven. 30.4 per cent of Scottish voters had chosen the SNP, and it came second in forty-two other seats; it could genuinely claim to have become second only to Labour.

The Labour Party moved slowly to respond to this mood, so slowly that a frustrated group led by Jim Sillars and John Robertson broke away in 1976 and formed the Scottish Labour Party. The Labour Government of the late 1970s had a very slender majority and the goodwill of the SNP, Plaid Cymru (with three MPs) and Liberal MPs mattered a great deal. The result was a scheme for home rule (1978) that would be implemented provided a referendum produced a favourable vote from at least 40 per cent of the electorate. These proposals may well have helped Labour hold on to seats at by-elections at Garscadden and Hamilton – seats which the SNP had been expected to win. The planned Scottish Assembly was to be funded by a block grant agreed by an independent board: it lacked power to raise revenue itself or seriously to shape economic policy. In fact, in the devolution referendum in March 1979, only a little over 63 per cent of the electorate voted, and though a majority of those who turned out favoured devolution, their numbers fell short of the required 40 per cent by over 7 per cent.

The 1979 election cut back SNP representation in parliament to two MPs, and the new Conservative ministry set its face against devolution. Scottish affairs had to make do with the debates of the Scottish Grand Committee: this was where Scottish MPs gathered, together with up to fifteen other MPs who attended in order to make the party balance approximate to the overall balance at Westminster. Since 1894 this body has dealt with the committee stage of non-controversial bills. After 1948 it began to consider bills at second reading stage and to debate Scottish estimates. The Grand Committee represents one of the dilemmas of devolution. It originally emerged as a device to head off the pro-home-rule views of most Scottish Liberals: their party leaders had needed their Scottish MPs at Westminster if they were to stay in power. The same dilemma has faced the Labour Party in more recent times. Since 1957 the Grand Committee has confined its activities to second reading debates, to Scottish estimates, and to a session on Scottish affairs. The committee stage of bills is dealt with by the Scottish Standing Committee made up of sixteen Scottish MPs and up to thirty-four others. The powers of these bodies are so very limited and so easily overruled as to be no sort of substitute to satisfy supporters of devolution.

The different political parties hold Scottish conferences and have Scottish organisations: the Scottish TUC meets quite separately from its UK counterpart. None of this satisfies those seeking devolution.

Perhaps British membership of the European Community will alter the whole context of the issue.

## ESSAY

Choose one of these titles. Plan and write an answer in essay form.

1. 'It is not the emergence of the SNP, but its lack of success that is surprising.' Do you agree?

2. In what ways, and with what success, did politicians unsympathetic to home rule nevertheless try to take account of a distinctive Scottish dimension?

# Essays on Part 2

1. 'Social reform after 1914 owed little to which party was in power and more to the pressure of circumstances.' Do you agree?
2. 'Warfare stimulates welfare.' Does your study of the period suggest that this is true?
3. How has the coming of universal suffrage affected the behaviour of political parties?
4. 'British voters prefer cautious politicians to radical reformers.' Do events since 1914 indicate that this is an accurate analysis?

# General essays

1. In the light of your studies of this period, discuss Disraeli's comment, 'I believe that without Party, Parliamentary Government is impossible.'
2. Do you agree with Sir David Steel's view that Britain suffers from a system in which 'small changes in public opinion have led to violent switches in public policy'?
3. What factors account for the emergence and establishment of the Labour Party?
4. Why did women win the vote?
5. Why has over a century of pressure for Scottish home rule failed to obtain it?
6. Account for the varying fortunes of the Liberal Party since 1850.

# Extended essays

The extended essay is intended to provide evidence of investigatory skill such as

● the ability to identify an issue and place it in context

- the ability to select and organise information from a variety of sources
- the ability to present the findings in a form that shows some attempt at analysis.

The period of British history surveyed in this book provides ample opportunities for this work. Issues already identified and essay titles already suggested may provide suitable topics. Since it makes sense to select an issue from an area that is adequately resourced, the following bibliography offers a guide to some possibilities.

Extended essays explore issues that are often best expressed in question form. They tend to fall into a number of categories, such as:

1. A consideration of the importance of an *individual* in contributing to a change or circumstance. (e.g. How far was Liberal decline due to the activities of Lloyd George?)
2. An evaluation of the reasons for particular *events*. (e.g. Why did votes for women have to wait till 1918?)
3. A discussion of the *relationships* between political events and the context provided by social, economic, military, or world affairs. (e.g. Did the Great War transform the political scene in Britain?)
4. An evaluation of the reasons for the nature of and effectiveness of *particular polices*. (e.g. What social problems were Liberal reforms between 1905 and 1914 intended to solve, and how effectively did they solve them?)

# Bibliography

## General books

Adelman P 1987 *British Politics in the 30s and 40s*
Bentley M *Politics without Democracy*
Dutton D 1991 *British Politics Since 1945*
Evans E *The Forging of the Modern State – Early Modern Britain 1783–1870*
Lloyd T 1970 *Empire to Welfare State*
Marwick A 1982 *British Society since 1945*
May T 1987 *An Economic and Social History of Britain*
Morgan K O 1990 *The People's Peace*
Pugh M 1982 *The Making of Modern British Politics*
Robbins K *The Eclipse of a Great Power, Britain 1870–1975*
Stevenson J 1984 *British Society 1914–45*
Taylor A J P *English History 1914–45*
Williams G and Ramsden J 1990 *Rule Britannia*

# Party politics and beliefs

## Conservatism

Blake R 1985 *The Conservative Party from Peel to Thatcher*
Coleman B 1988 *Conservatism and the Conservative Party in Nineteenth-Century Britain*
Lindsay T F and Harrington M 1974 *The Conservative Party*
O'Gorman F 1986 *British Conservatism*
Ramsden J 1978 *The Age of Balfour and Baldwin*

## Liberalism

Adelman P 1981 *The Decline of the Liberal Party*
Bentley M 1987 *The Climax of Liberal Politics*
Cook C 1976 *A Short History of the Liberal Party*
Morgan K O 1979 *Consensus and Disunity*
Vincent J R 1966 *The Formation of the British Liberal Party 1857–68*
Wilson T 1968 *The Downfall of the Liberal Party*

## Labour

Addison P 1975 *The Road to 1945*
Adelman P 1972 *The Rise of the Labour Party*
Brand C 1965 *The British Labour Party*
Campbell J *Nye Bevan and the Mirage of British Socialism*
Laybourn K 1988 *The Rise of Labour*
McKibbin R 1977 *The Evolution of the Labour Party*
Miliband R 1961 *Parliamentary Socialism*
Morgan K O 1984 *Labour in Power*
Pelling H 1962 *A Short History of the Labour Party*

Pimlott B 1977 *Labour and The Left in the 1930s*
Ponting C *Breach of Promise, Labour in Power 1964–70*
Skidelsky R 1967 *Politicians and the Slump*

## General

Ball A R 1981 *British Political Parties*
Belchem J 1990 *Class, Party and the Political System in Britain 1867–1914*
Evans E J 1985 *Political Parties 1787–1867*
Finer S E 1980 *The Changing British Party System 1945–79*

# Electoral change

Braybon G *Women Workers and the First World War*
Garner L *Stepping Stones to Women's Liberty, Feminist Ideas in the Women's Suffrage Movement*
Holton S *Feminism and Democracy, Women's Suffrage and Party Politics in Britain 1866–1914*
Jalland P *Women, Marriage and Politics 1860–1914*
Liddington J and Norris J *One Hand Tied Behind Us*
Pugh M 1978 *Electoral Reform in War and Peace*
Pugh M 1989 *The Development of the British Electoral System 1832–1987*
Pugh M 1986 *Women's Suffrage in Britain*
Walton J K 1987 *The Second Reform Act*
Wright D G 1970 *Democracy and Reform*

# Class, culture, trade unionism

Barnett C 1986 *The Audit of War*
Barnett C 1972 *The Collapse of British Power*
Belchem J *Class, Politics, and the Political System in Britain 1867–1914*
Hindess B *The Decline of Working Class Politics*
Hinton J 1983 *Labour and Socialism 1867–1914*
Houghton W E *The Victorian Frame of Mind*
Howell D 1983 *British Workers and the ILP*
Joyce P *War, Society and Politics*
Marsden G (Ed) 1990 *Victorian Values*
Martin D 1979 *Ideology and the Labour Movement*
McKibbin R *The Ideologies of Class 1880–1950*
Meacham S 1977 *A Life Apart*
Moorehead C 1987 *Troublesome People: Enemies of War 1916–86*
Neale R S 1973 *Class and Ideology in the 19th century*
Pelling H *A History of British Trade Unionism*
Pimlott B *Trade Unions in British Politics*
Sigsworth E M *In Search of Victorian Values*
Sked A 1987 *Britain's Decline*
Wald K D *Crosses on the Ballot*

# Scotland

Brand J 1978 *The National Movement in Scotland*
Checkland S 1984 *Industry and Ethos, Scotland 1832–1914*
Hanham H J 1969 *Scottish Nationalism*
Harvie C 1981 *No Gods and Precious Few Heroes, 1914–80*
Harvie C 1977 *Scotland and Nationalism*
Hutchinson I *A Political History of Scotland 1832–1924*
Kellas J 1980 *Modern Scotland – the Nation since 1870*
Kellas J 1988 *The Scottish Political System*
Robbins K 1988 *Nineteenth-Century Britain: Integration and diversity*
Smout T C 1987 *A Century of the Scottish People*
Webb K *The Growth of Nationalism in Scotland*

# The welfare issue

Birch R C 1974 *The Shaping of the Welfare State*
Bruce M 1961 *The Coming of the Welfare State*
Constantine S 1980 *Unemployment in Britain between the Wars*
Cook C and Stevenson J 1977 *The Slump*
Fraser D 1973 *The Evolution of the Welfare State*
Hay J R 1978 *The Development of the Welfare State*
Hay J R 1975 *The Origins of the Welfare State*

# Politicians

Adelman P 1989 *Gladstone, Disraeli and Later Victorian Politics*
Feuchtwanger E J 1968 *Disraeli, Democracy, and the Tory Party*
Feuchtwanger E J 1975 *Gladstone*
James R R 1973 *Churchill, A Study in Failure*
Marquand D 1977 *Ramsay MacDonald*
Middlemass K and Barnes J 1969 *Baldwin*
Montgomery Hyde H 1973 *Baldwin*
Montgomery Hyde H 1976 *Neville Chamberlain*
Morgan K 1974 *Lloyd George*
Morgan K 1971 *The Age of Lloyd George*
Pelling H 1974 *W. S. Churchill*
Willis M 1989 *Gladstone and Disraeli, Principles and Policies*
Young K 1976 *Baldwin*

# Index